A Real Living Contact with the Things Themselves
Essays on Architecture

A Real Living Contact with the Things Themselves
Essays on Architecture
Irénée Scalbert

PARK BOOKS

For Peter St John

The Nature of Gothic 10

Building in Japan 62

A Real Living Contact with the Things Themselves 94

Mind into Matter 136

The Rococo Revolution 162

Architecture is not Made with the Brain 190

The Seed 226

The New Art Gallery and its Geography 248

London After the Green Belt 280

The Nature of Gothic

You don't have to understand, you just have to believe.
Jean Cocteau, *Orpheus*, 1950

Within a radius of 150km from Paris can be found the cathedrals of Amiens, Beauvais, Rouen, Chartres, Troyes, Reims and Laon. In Paris itself there are Notre Dame and the abbey of Saint Denis. To these great churches can be added the less familiar names of Evreux, Le Mans, Sens, Senlis, Soissons, Noyon and Saint Quentin. With the exception of Normandy, the concentration of gothic diminishes beyond this radius. Still, imagine having within the same distance from Athens the temples of Aegina, Sounion, Bassae, Ephesus, Cyrene, Agrigento, Selinunte, Segesta and Paestum. The geographical range of gothic reaches from Gloucester in the west to Gdansk in the east, from Linköping in the north to Seville and Lisbon in the south, but only the region of Île-de-France prides itself with not one or two but a dozen gothic Parthenons. Nowhere else in Europe, perhaps nowhere else in the world, is there a comparable density of great buildings.

And yet, in spite of this concentration, modern architects paid little attention to gothic architecture, beyond the occasional allusion to its structural prowess. Mies van der Rohe praised, not Erwin von Steinbach, the architect of Strasbourg cathedral, but the neo-classicist Karl Friedrich Schinkel. Le Corbusier was moved less by cathedrals (in spite of his revulsion over the shelling of Reims during the First World War) than he was by the Parthenon. Bar one or two eccentrics such as Gaudí, gothic has had little or no impact on the architecture of the last century.

What did impress modernists was the size of gothic constructions. Indeed, size is almost the only characteristic which makes a cathedral seem familiar and allows comparison to a dam, a bridge or an ocean liner. Almost everything else about the gothic seemed contrary to the modernist sensibility: the extreme verticality, the superabundance of ornament, the imperfections, the frequent presence of decay, the piety, the irrationality. There is in the gothic cathedral something venerable and old which is fundamentally alien to the modern craving for newness, cleanliness and simplicity. The admiration of John Ruskin, William Morris and Eugène Viollet-le-Duc for gothic has been cited as evidence of a medieval lineage in modernism, but these claims attach not to gothic but to Ruskin, Morris and Viollet-le-Duc. Gothic was the greatest architectural rediscovery of the nineteenth century. But the incompatibility between gothic and modernism was insuperable.

In the nineteenth century an account of gothic architecture invited descriptions accompanied by a profusion of details. In the twentieth it seldom entailed more than the facade of Notre Dame and a typical section showing the structural principle of the flying buttress – the moderns saw gothic no better than they understood it. To this day, in approaching a gothic building, one senses not its familiarity but its strangeness.

Consider, for instance, the Sainte Chapelle of Saint-Germer-de-Fly, in many ways a cathedral in miniature. The chapel appears as the quintessence of French gothic, as one of the most accomplished examples of the *style rayonnant*. Situated to the west of Beauvais in a little-visited part of France, it was built to receive the relics of Saint Germer and forms a disproportionately large appendage to an earlier abbey church. A vestibule connects the two like a train coupler connects two carriages, but it is a building in its own right, commissioned by an abbot who planned to be buried in it rather than in the chapel dedicated to the Virgin Mary.

The detailing of the vestibule is exceptionally fine. Inside, piers are faced with clusters of no fewer than nine colonnettes, each not much wider than a hand, with a further two colonnettes, set back, which belong to the tracery windows on either side. The effect is so delicate, and so taut, that it seems perverse to have realised the piers in stone rather than in timber. Inside the chapel proper the vault is broad and the inflection

Previous
West front,
Bourges Cathedral
© The Courtauld
Institute of Art,
London

Vestibule looking east, Sainte Chapelle of Saint-Germer-de-Fly, Oise, Picardy © Bildarchiv Foto Marburg

point in the arch is barely discernible, contributing a subtle and graceful quality to the space. The light is bright and even. With the exception of the apse, the twelfth-century stained glass has been lost, confounding expectations raised by visits to Paris's Sainte Chapelle.

The structure of the nave reprises that of the vestibule as if in a major key. Again, the bays are divided by piers faced with nine colonnettes, but now scaled up to match the larger space. Springing at different heights depending on whether they belong to the vault or to the clerestory windows, the capitals provide barely a break in the cluster of lines that form the pier, and it is clear that their role is not to provide support. Deprived of their architectonic role, they seem to effloresce freely between the ribs of the vault. Gothic may be full of details – in the stone carvings of capitals and bosses, in the stained glass of clerestories, in the timber carvings of stalls – but these are too numerous, too distant and too small relative to the whole to hold our attention for long. Instead, the eye is presented with an orderly succession of vertical lines.

These lines are also too numerous to be observed individually. As one stands in a gothic nave, the eye feels no urge to follow them from pier to vault and down again. (Only a historian would make the effort to observe whether the bays are barlong or sexpartite; whether there is, in addition to the triforium, a tribune; whether the clerestories are divided into three, four, five or six lancets.) Instead, the eye looks straight ahead. It is this stillness that expands the sense of time. Anyone who has attended a service in a gothic building will be familiar with the ennui. Like music, the impact of the architecture is soothing and relentless and presents few moments of heightened interest. We sometimes hear gothic structures being described as a cage. But it is not the structure that is confining; rather, the eye, having no specific place to rest, dilates, fills the space and becomes one with it.

The strangeness of gothic becomes even more apparent when we examine the arcade wall that extends along the lower section of the chapel. Here, the sole ornament is the highly stylised foliage on the capital of each engaged colonnette. Above it the mouldings of the arcade spring in a manner that is almost repellent to a modern sensibility. They express nothing: not the stone of which they are made, not the structure (to which they do not contribute), not the assembly of ribs which intersect and overlap with no articulation. The ribs on the arcade wall of Sainte Chapelle in Paris are almost identical, only slightly more elaborate in form and painted gold. Viollet-le-Duc referred to such ribs as *boudin*, a word which in French also means black pudding. They are circular in section, like the steel tubes commonly used in high-tech structures, but they do not suggest structural calculations and the graceful transfer of load to the ground. Yet these *boudins* are the essence of gothic design: lines coursing with blood, capillaries in a proliferating network.

If we turn around to face the entrance of the Sainte Chapelle of Saint-Germer, a large rose window magically comes into view, a window which is in a clear line of filiation with the best French examples – in the south transept of Notre Dame or the north transept, known as the *Portail des Librairies*, of the cathedral of Rouen. The motif of the rose, so common in cathedrals, confounds interpretations of gothic as structure which have been dominant for at least a century. The arches at the end of its petals are as often upright as they are upside-down and, at Saint-Germer-de-Fly further mullions in the outer ring of the rose spring from the structurally weak midpoint of ogives. Clearly the structural model for the rose was not that of the vault in which it is inscribed but, strangely, that of the wheel. Saint Catherine is the patron saint of masons and her attribute is the wheel, the instrument of her martyrdom. But this detail alone at best partly explains what is so compelling about this motif.

Interior looking west, Sainte Chapelle of Saint-Germer-de-Fly, Oise, Picardy
©The Courtauld Institute of Art, London

North facade, Sainte Chapelle of Saint-Germer-de-Fly, Oise, Picardy Photograph Henri Deneux © Médiathèque du Patrimonie / RMN-Grand Palais

Moreover, the perimeter of the rose is not fitted within the arch of the vault. It is not even tangential with its curvature; rather, it seems roughly inserted behind it, like an old-fashioned film slide inserted within the guides of a projector. The same approximate positioning can be found in other chapels, for instance in the Chapelle Royale at Saint-Germain-en-Laye. The motif of the rose, like the detailing of the arcade at Sainte Chapelle, demonstrates that the distinction between structure and ornament does not apply to gothic: nothing that is structural is not also ornamental, while much that is ornamental is also structural.

The strangeness of gothic is even plainer on the exterior. For a start, the arches of the windows collide with the buttresses on either side, penetrate them and then disappear, refuting, in the process, the notion that there exists in gothic a sense of order in which every part is clearly individuated and articulated. More striking still is the manner in which the fine vestibule meets the church and the chapel on either side. Again, the end bay to the east vanishes behind a buttress of the chapel, like a concertina in a train carriage. Even as we lean forward into the narrow crack between vestibule and chapel, we search in vain for the remainder of the bay arcature. To the west, the effect of the collision of the vestibule with the apse of the church is barely alleviated by the superposition of an entrance porch, a half-size reduction of the window behind it. The effect is abrupt, expedient and ultimately satisfying, like the medley of flying buttresses which somehow cohere in the corner between transept and choir in most cathedrals.

The strangeness of gothic – its sometimes fastidious, sometimes lax sense of consistency, its combination of prolix care and unstudied expediency – evokes a freedom that seems unattainable today. The means by which architectural design is commonly circumscribed and fixed in time, the recourse to drawing which obsessed the nineteenth century and was reinforced in the twentieth, the programmes, the plans, the

elevations which freeze architecture in a slice of time and seem to us so necessary, were seldom if ever used in gothic. Its accordance with religious faith and ritual notwithstanding, gothic impresses with its fluidity, with a plasticity that embraced design adjustments in real time, in a pre-modern anticipation of digital procedures.

Plan

It has become customary in modern times to display the plan of a cathedral near its entrance. At Troyes this plan shows a layout which to the uninitiated, and to most architects, must seem absolutely standard: a regular succession of piers, disrupted halfway by the transepts, ending at the top of the sheet in a flourish of chapels. Different colours indicate a succession of building campaigns and, by implication, a succession of styles. The plan also gives a few dates: construction began in 1208; the cathedral was consecrated two centuries later, in 1430; and a further 200 years were required before it was completed, in 1638. I doubt whether anyone takes much notice of the drawing.

Twentieth-century plans of cathedrals are exceptionally uninformative. They do not indicate entrances, let alone doorways. They ignore screens, stalls, altars, monuments, seats, relics, pulpits and organs, not to mention ticket offices, bookshops and washrooms. They rarely show the paving or the profiles of the piers. They merely indicate, in thin black lines reaching from pier to pier, the position of the ribs on the vaults above. In doing so, they confirm the continuing dominance of structure in the interpretation of gothic, and the legacy of Viollet-le-Duc's theory according to which gothic architecture was conceived from the vault downwards: '*C'est la chose portée qui commande à la chose qui porte*' ('It is the thing which is carried that dictates the form of the thing which carries').[1]

One cathedral plan appears much the same as any other; collectively, they seem to assert the existence of a single model.

Few architectural writers have resisted the temptation to identify the ideal cathedral form. For Ruskin, it was perhaps Amiens, the subject of his text 'The Bible of Amiens'. For Victor Hugo, it was Notre Dame. For Viollet-le-Duc, Chartres was the quintessential cathedral, even though the illustration to the entry 'Cathédrale' in his *Dictionnaire* shows a combination of the nave of Reims, the porches of Amiens and the towers of Chartres. For Jules Michelet, Cologne best represented the spirit of gothic. Yet these are not really types, but the sum of singularities assembled from several cathedrals or, when they are taken from a single building, the sum of singularities accumulated over time. The notion of a gothic type is an illusion.

In a remarkable article on the cathedral of Milan, James Ackerman describes how, nine years after the start of construction, when the piers had already reached a height of some two metres, its college of clerics was still deliberating on how best to complete the design, in consultation with experts from France, Germany and Italy. From this Ackerman deduced that there could be no connection between plan and elevation, and made the extraordinary assertion that it was 'standard procedure at Milan to permit the cathedral to grow haphazardly, without ultimate aim'.[2] Clearly Milan cathedral did not have a plan in the modern sense of the word. There is no evidence of an actual drawing or a model. Generally, in medieval times there was no setting-out drawing to which all subsequent design decisions would conform.[3] At most, drawings of parts of the building – for instance a sketch of the choir to indicate the relationship between piers and vaulting – would have been made on parchment. Or full-scale tracings might have been chiselled directly into a stone floor, for instance on the roof of the tribune in the cathedral of Clermont-Ferrand. Most decisions were made on site. Thus it is possible to imagine the masons in Milan using stakes and cords to set out the position of the piers on the ground itself.

Indented image (and overleaf) From John Ruskin, The Nature of Gothic, 1853 ©Timothy O'Hare

In the absence of plans it has been claimed that designs must have been conceived in the mind: *opus in mente conceptum*.[4] But what exists in the mind is merely an intuition; a design acquires a form only when it is externalised. The example of Milan powerfully suggests a design elaborated on site and in real time, in a continuous confrontation between mind and matter.

Gothic cathedrals, among the largest and most daring constructions ever conceived, were born of a mighty clash between a plan (in the sense of a project) which is consistent and abstract, and time, the effects of which are inconsistent and tangible – between the idea of God's will, of the Church as an eternal institution on the one hand, and the vagaries of human destiny on the other. Usually a cathedral is conceived of as the fulfilment of a plan, its every feature being rooted in Christian dogma. Of this divine plan, the plan of the building, in the form of a cross, is a kind of prefiguration, absorbing the irregularities of a cathedral in the way that eternity absorbs the span of human life. Understood thus, the physiognomy of the cathedral is indivisible. It strains towards the perfection of a type, towards the advent of a New Jerusalem. This timeless conception corresponds in the main to the view held in the nineteenth century, a view that was underpinned by Christian faith and overlaid by classical aesthetics (nothing should be added or taken away).

Less often, a cathedral is conceived of as a product of time. For scholars of this persuasion, discontinuities in the fabric can be traced to specific events and decisions during the long period of construction. For them the plan (in the sense of a project) is merely a convenient abstraction that facilitates the comprehension of the whole. Bar a few notable exceptions such as the cathedral of Cologne or the Sagrada Familia, the plan is always defeated by time. The fabric of a cathedral makes manifest the frailty of human ambitions and is by its very nature imperfect – a monumental work of *bricolage*.

In this sense the very existence of gothic architecture is a fluke. According to Jean Bony it was born of an extraordinary combination of circumstances. Like the Wright brothers' invention of the airplane, it was a gamble on the part of a small group of men who sought, most unreasonably, to combine thin walls with stone vaulting. The process of invention – one that met seemingly impossible challenges with sharp imaginative responses – gave gothic its initial direction. Its originality was obscured by the adoption of earlier Romanesque elements from different sources in ways that seem – though only in retrospect – strictly logical and necessary.[5]

The plan of a gothic cathedral is therefore a kind of MacGuffin: a prompt or a trigger after the fact; in itself it has no architectural significance. Contrary to Viollet-le-Duc's assertion it is quite clearly *not* the expression on the ground of a logical order imposed by the rib vaults above. The arrangement of the piers in Milan cathedral describes not a plan but, in effect, a horizontal section cut *a posteriori* through the building at a particular moment. Moreover, in the chronology of any cathedral we can find numerous interruptions caused by fire, collapse, storm, penury, war, plague and other disasters, often leading to radical changes in the design. This makes the existence of a plan still more problematic. Yet there must necessarily have been, if not a plan, then a motivating idea – an Ariadne's thread which guaranteed the completion of these vast construction projects.

This motivating idea was faith and the feelings it inspired. In 1833 Jules Michelet wrote a brilliant essay that deserves to be better known, 'The Passion as Artistic Principle in the Middle Ages', in which he describes how medieval thought was wholly contained within Christianity – and specifically within the Passion of Christ.[6] From this moment of darkness sprang an inexhaustible well of tears which crystallised as cathedrals. Michelet writes poetically about gothic architecture as 'a passionate vegetation of the mind', growing according to the rules of geometry and art. Gothic architecture, he claims, was superhuman, born in the belief in the miraculous, in the absurd. He quotes Tertullian's phrase (which he misattributes to Saint Augustine): *Credo quia absurdum* ('I believe because it is absurd').

The beliefs that gave rise to gothic recall the 'abstract machine' of Deleuze and Guattari's *A Thousand Plateaus*: 'a pure Matter-Function', a diagram which has neither form nor substance, neither expression nor content.[7] This abstract machine is neither plan nor drawing, in that it does not seek to represent; rather, it constructs a new type of reality. Whereas expression and content presume distinct forms, function merely manifests itself in '*traits*' and '*pointes*', in tracings and pricks which connect expression and content. 'There is a diagram', Deleuze and Guattari write, 'whenever a singular abstract machine functions directly in a matter.'[8]

In gothic architecture, this 'abstract machine' is faith. Without drawing or formal representation, it 'functions directly in a matter' to construct a reality that is yet to come, a New Jerusalem, a new type of reality in the form of a cathedral. Deleuze and Guattari describe a double movement. The abstract machine functions between strata – in gothic, between the succession of plans or, better, successive building campaigns. At the same time it prolongs the 'lines of flight' across these strata, to 'connect the dots' and define a 'plane of consistency'. For his part Ackerman refers, in the context of Milan cathedral, to a 'theory of consistent relationships'. He claims further that the specific problems of form and structure (or, in the terms of *A Thousand Plateaus*, form and substance) do not come into play. 'The overall character of the gothic cathedral', he writes, 'is determined on the basis of geometrical grids of lines and dots', namely, the basic diagrammatic sections made by the experts called in to advise the clerics in Milan.[9] Deleuze and Guattari's pragmatics resonate with the pragmatism of the medieval builder.

 Given the immense complexity of cathedrals, it is surprising that so little is known about the processes of their design. Today, an endeavour of a comparable scope would necessitate plant on a vast scale, materials and products from multiple countries, and experts in architecture, engineering, management, finance and law. Yet the sole equipment of a medieval architect comprised a straight edge, a square, a compass, a divider and a plumb line. The building was laid out with pegs and cord. As Ackerman demonstrated in the case of Milan cathedral, there was between the plan and the elevation (both of them understood as an action rather than an orthogonal projection or a drawing) no necessary connection.

Drawing

A few treatises have survived but they are of a practical nature, giving instructions in the form of procedures – algorithms – to be followed in the design of specific parts of a building: tower, spire, vault rib, window mullion, etc. For instance, Mathes Roriczer's treatise of 1487, which bears the evocative title 'The Little Book on the Rectitude of Pinnacles', outlines 234 steps supported by 17 diagrams describing how the elevation of a pinnacle can be obtained from its plan. Such knowledge was no comprehensive method by means of which a part, for instance a vault, could be related to the edifice as a whole. In this they were fundamentally different from Viollet-le-Duc's *Dictionnaire* and from most nineteenth-century writing on gothic – a difference that helps to explain the stilted character of much of the restoration and gothic revival design of the period. The medieval architect inherited his knowledge piecemeal. It consisted in design precepts that had lost their ancient connection with theoretical geometry, the laws of which masons were only dimly aware.

One such precept was progressive squaring, a method by which the juxtaposition of squares (one next to the other) and their rotation (one within the other) helped to produce the forms associated with gothic architecture. With these simple

procedures the design of most parts of a building, for instance the section of a compound pier or tracery mullions, could be obtained without taking measurements. Though often mentioned in modern times in the context of the cathedrals, the golden section and the number sequence associated with it were not known to medieval architects and played no role in building practice.

Today design problems are solved by means of drawings. The more complex the design, the more drawings are needed. In medieval times the use of drawings became common practice only in the latter part of the thirteenth century, after several cathedrals (Laon, Chartres, Paris, Amiens) had already been completed, and even then, their use was limited to sketches, tentative plans, working drawings and, occasionally, presentation drawings (Cologne). Such drawings represented parts of the building, both large and small, but never the totality. The practice of making drawings for a building, itself a novelty, probably evolved from the use of full-scale templates for the construction of the various parts of the building.

Sheets of parchment, being expensive, were washed and reused several times. On one such sheet, part of a set now known as the Reims palimpsest, were discovered faint drawings that seem to be associated with the construction of the cathedral. They represent, notably, part of a facade, the elevation of a clerestory and the outlines of an unidentified structure. Each drawing was painstakingly constructed, following a procedure reminiscent of setting-out.[10] The position of each line was established with pin pricks still visible on the sheets of parchment, like pegs on a building site. The drawing progressed slowly, one line at a time, using in addition to dry points and a pen – the same tools that were used by the mason – a straight edge and a compass.

Not until the fifteenth century did such drawings reach a level of sophistication corresponding to that of the buildings themselves. Even then, the rules of progressive squaring,

Palimpsest of Reims, mid thirteenth century
© Timothy O'Hare

West front, Reims Cathedral © Gado Images / Alamy

assisted by the same basic tools, continued to apply. Lines and points defined simple polygonal frameworks in which mathematics played no part. Instead, the process of design involved, in the words of the historian Lon Shelby, 'physical manipulations of geometric forms'.[11] Again one is struck by the close affinities between the methods of design and those of construction. Both employed the same tools and the same geometrical principles, and employed them 'physically'. Moreover, both conceived of the building in terms of its parts. The idea of the whole evolved as the building progressed, becoming definitive only it neared completion. The gothic cathedral recalls the seamless continuity between drawing and fabrication to which CAD-CAM and 3D printing aspire and, the difference in speed notwithstanding, it prefigures the ultimate digital panacea: a vision of design being realised in real time.

No element of a gothic building is autonomous; each is intimately related to every other proximate element. Whether what Ackerman called 'a theory of consistent relationships' is indeed a theory, and how consistent it is, is a matter of judgement; however, gothic did aspire to a consistent order. In his treatise Roriczer advocated the 'right measure', meaning the measure that resulted from a series of consistent geometric operations.[12] Such measure should not be confused with ancient proportional systems. Unlike, say, the heights of base, column and capital in a Greek temple, no rule existed to coordinate those of a gothic pier.

In the piers of the crossing at Chartres, the bundle of colonnettes rises to the vault, without a break, from a base that is not even waist-high. Each base consists of closely packed polygonal blocks which are chamfered at mid-height to meet the narrow shafts above. Between base and shafts, the masons introduced a transition in the form of a torus, or cushion, the shape of which resembles an upside-down Doric capital. The toruses are contiguous and, together with the crystalline assembly of polygonal blocks below, they form a wonderful

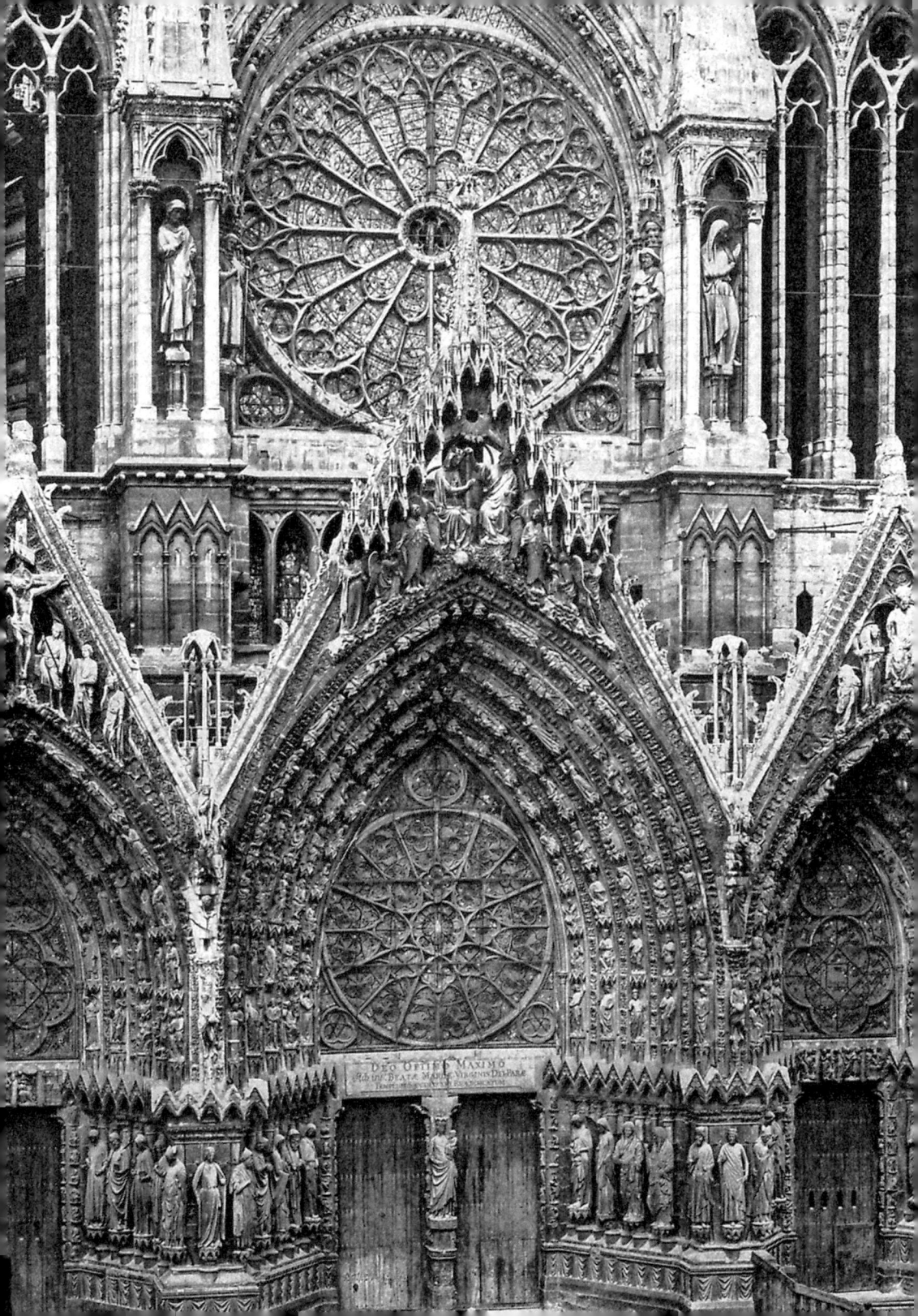

Previous
Amiens Cathedral, from Georges Durand, *Monographie de l'église Notre-Dame, cathédrale d'Amiens*, 1903
Courtesy Société des Antiquaires de Picardie

sculptural composition. Above this base, the colonnettes rise in compact formation, suggesting, not fluting, as in Doric, but piping. They seem not so much carved as blown. 'Cathedrals', Viollet-le-Duc observed, 'are like glasswork, plastic in their conception and immensely fragile in reality.'[13]

The arrangement adopted in the vestibule of Saint-Germer-de-Fly is almost identical: polygonal base, toruses and colonnettes closely packed in a bundle. But, unlike the giant pipes of Chartres, these elements appear to be as small as stone-carving would allow. More strikingly still, the polygonal blocks of the base have been elongated to an extent that makes them appear as slender and as brittle at Saint-Germer-de-Fly as they are squat and robust at Chartres. No necessary relationship exists in gothic between the dimensions of the plan and those of the elevation, which could be stretched at will.

The historian Jean Bony described gothic as a linear architecture in which space is enclosed less by surfaces than by networks.[14] The resulting 'styles of linearity' became progressively thinner and sharper, more delicate and intricate. Gothic developed into an 'art of tracing', increasingly dominated by a sense of pattern and open to complex imaginative designs.[15] Given this tendency, it is all the more surprising that drawing – the art of tracing *par excellence* – never played more than a subsidiary role.

Elevation

The history of gothic architecture extends over more than four hundred years, although some cathedrals, for instance Cologne, were completed long after the gothic moment had passed. Unlike classical architecture, gothic was never codified. There exist no canonical works which are equivalent to, say, the Parthenon or Vitruvius's *Ten Books on Architecture*. This hasn't stopped writers from attempting to summarise the characteristics of gothic. Ruskin identified six traits, including savageness, changefulness and naturalism. Erwin Panofsky ascribed to it three principles: totality, organisation and the distinction of parts; Paul Frankl, four: division, diagonality, texture and partiality. Jean Bony identified its main features as the rib vault, the pointed arch, height and openness.

One idea has been endorsed by all writers on gothic, though under a variety of names. For Ruskin the 'final definition' of gothic is the character of foliation, without which, he claims, it would remain imperfect.[16] Applicable equally to a simple arch or to tracery, foliation describes the process by which forms can be divided in patterns of three or more leaves. Whereas Ruskin argued that foliation possessed both an aesthetic and a moral dimension, being ultimately a homage to nature, Viollet-le-Duc justified the same process, which he referred to as crystallisation, on practical grounds.[17] The multiplication of mullions in tracery, he argued, made it possible to reduce to a minimum the iron framework holding the panels of stained glass in place.

Panofsky chose to proceed by analogy. Seeking to understand the essential tendencies of the medieval mind, he likened gothic architecture to the *Summa Theologica* of Thomas Aquinas. Both were said to participate in an 'orgy of logical thought', the scholastic *Summa Theologica*, in which the elements of Christian doctrine were enumerated, organised in parts and sub-parts, and interrelated, seeming to correspond perfectly to the order of gothic, with its emphasis on a hierarchy of parts and on repetition. For his part, Bony referred to a 'new system of progressive subdivision into subordinated series'. System, progression, subdivision, subordination, series: the terms used by these authors (the most learned and insightful writers, and arguably the four fathers of gothic scholarship) suggest an attempt to analyse and eventually to crack the gothic 'code', as if to expose the mechanisms which govern the design of its architecture.

It is in Amiens cathedral, allegedly, that the process of foliation or crystallisation became common practice. In Reims cathedral the high windows followed the motif, invented at Chartres, of two lancets surmounted by a rose. In Amiens, the same motif was replicated, at a smaller scale, within each of the lancet windows. Subsequently this process – which today might be called self-similar or fractal – was repeated in the clerestory windows of the transept, which have four, six and eight lancets, while in the choir they have four lancets instead of the two in Reims.

This proliferation of scaling motifs is said to have begun with the design of the rose. At Chartres the west rose consists of many smaller roses punched into the masonry of the facade. In the centre, the rim of a larger rose serves as a base from which twelve columns radiate outwards to form as many petals. Compare this with the considerably larger rose (13m wide) in the south transept of Notre Dame. Whole areas of masonry have disappeared. As in Chartres, twelve petals radiate from the centre, but now they are filled from the centre outwards by one lancet, then two, which are crowned by a quatrefoil. The entire rose is supported by the gallery below. The construction of this gallery, which is made of columns alternating in section between 36×20cm and 20×10cm, appears even lighter than that of the rose. Viollet-le-Duc mentions that when its columns are struck (no doubt he had a go) they resonate as if they were made of metal.

The audacity of this design continues to astonish. The structure of the rose is fundamentally alien to the rationale of modern engineering. Indeed, at first no member was either vertical or horizontal, the rose being offset by fifteen degrees. This must have been intentional. The structure had fallen into a state of disrepair when Viollet-le-Duc rebuilt it – and corrected what must have appeared to him as an anomaly. Thus the clock was reset, as it were, to precisely on the hour.

The foliation which gradually proliferated in most aspects of gothic design was accompanied by another tendency. Previously, building elements, including piers, colonnettes and mullions, had been carefully graded in a hierarchy of sizes; they now became increasingly uniform. Already the members of the huge rose in Paris included no more than three sectional sizes. In the basilica of Saint Urbain at Troyes (another milestone in the design of tracery) the members became thinner and more uniform. Appearing so slim and almost brittle like straw, they hardly suggest the channelling of forces to the ground. Gone is the tension between the ambitions of design and the necessities of building. The art of tracing and the art of tracery – Deleuze and Guattari's 'lines of flight' coursing through the material – have become aligned and are, by and large, indistinguishable.

Having lost its already ambiguous corporeality, gothic increasingly registered upon the eye as a network of lines. This phenomenon has been noted by many authors. Auguste Choisy wrote about 'a mode of construction in which matter becomes so to speak obliterated, in which everything is combination'.[18] In his view this development was a sign of decadence, design appearing to undermine, even to contradict the laws of structure. Wilhelm Worringer argued that, unlike Greek architecture, gothic architecture was made 'in spite of the stone'.[19] Whereas the Greeks had aspired to sensuousness, gothic was an abstract system of construction.

By the end of the thirteenth century the translation of motifs across scales and materials had become commonplace. Architectural fantasies proliferated. Tracery impressed because of its complex geometry more than its structural lightness. Articulations which had been associated with construction gradually disappeared. For instance, capitals were reduced to ornamented collars and, when it became obvious that they served no practical purpose, they too were eliminated. On rare occasions, most strikingly on the northwestern-most pier of Troyes cathedral, foliage survived in the form of small clumps of vegetation sprouting between the mouldings like weeds. Structurally, formally or even as decoration, such

West front, Rouen Cathedral
Photograph F R P Sumner
© The Courtauld Institute of Art, London

'leftovers' may seem absurd, but this is to overlook the long and fertile association between foliation and foliage.[20]

When ribs did not vault across the space without a break, the lines of mouldings, like plant stems, required a termination. For a time, they found it in wonderful buds that seemed about to burst beneath the abacuses of the capitals. Beneath these 'crockets', the leaves stood proud of the surface of the capitals, making them clearly visible even from a great distance. Nowhere are such flora more beautiful and abundant than on the capitals of the choirs at Reims and at Auxerre. The leaves of common species can still be recognised, among them plantain, arum, ranunculus, fern, clover, parsley, strawberries, ivy and oak. But these are no ordinary specimen, contradicting Ruskin's assertion that one of the six characteristics of gothic is naturalism. Gothic flora has its own laws and it is not uncommon for leaves to imitate the convexity of vaults and for veins to suggest the arcature of ribs.

The forms of gothic vegetation recall those of architecture while gothic architecture, conversely, longs for the freedom of vegetation. In the stalls of Amiens cathedral, which Ruskin admired almost as much as he did the west portals, 'there is', he wrote, 'nothing else so beautiful cut out of the goodly trees of the world… Under the carver's hand it seems to cut like clay, to fold like silk, to grow like living branches, to leap like living flame. Canopy crowning canopy, pinnacle piercing pinnacle – it shoots and wreathes itself into an enchanted glade, inextricable, imperishable, fuller of leafage than any forest, and fuller of story than any book.'[21] In this phenomenal gothic undergrowth of Amiens's choir, in the brushwood that shoots, pierces and wreathes, only the figures retained their autonomy (and some 4,700 of those have been counted).

Latent in gothic from the outset, foliation became a universal principle. In defining ornament and structure alike, and combining them in a single form, it confused both, visually as well as intellectually. The west front of Rouen cathedral

offers a compelling example. Hardly any part of this marvellous facade has not been foliated, then foliated again, and in the upper parts progressively squared, then squared again into finials and pinnacles. In 1200, after the construction on the north side of the Tour Saint Romain (which seems all the more massive for its stonework being partly undressed), two squat portals were added on either side of the main entrance. Almost two hundred years later, a new screen composed of tracery and statuary was erected above these portals. During the next fifty years, as the screen was extended outwards to fill the remaining space between the cathedral's two towers, it became even more intricate. Foliation was to gothic what pixellation is to the modern age, and it is perhaps not a coincidence that Monet chose the same facade at Rouen to demonstrate the effect of light upon the eye.

By then – in the evocative terminology coined in the nineteenth century – the 'Style Rayonnant' of the earlier tracery had morphed into the 'Style Flamboyant'. Lancet forms were deformed at will to fit within the frame of an arch or a gable. Once invariably vertical (except in the rose), they were now bent to point sideways or even downwards. Single curves were bent into double ones, lancets were twisted into *mouchettes* and *soufflets*, and oculi were pressed into lozenges.

The effect has been compared to that of lace and the comparison is apt. Individual elements became increasingly small and patterns took the appearance of finery. Moreover, as with lace, the convergence between virtuoso technique and decorative form seems to have been intentional, and even to have been relished. Like lace, tracery is a two-dimensional art (though one that requires three-dimensional skills). For this reason it was not able to embrace the depth of the wall and to achieve a correspondence between interior and exterior. Instead, it evolved into a series of loosely connected, overlapping screens, of which the multiple planes of Rouen's facade offer a good example.

Then came the completion of the upper storeys of the Tour Saint Romain, the building of the new Tour de Beurre on the south side, and the addition of pinnacle turrets which give such a distinctive silhouette to the tracery screen between the two towers. The central porch was rebuilt and crowned with a gable. The new rose window (partly occluded by the gable) was topped with a gallery and, above it, a cluster of gables, tracery and finials so dense and extravagant as to seem almost primeval.

Foliation gradually reaches across the entire facade. Evolving from the early simple portals to the extremely elaborate central gable, it migrated forward to stand proud of the main facade, sideways from the rose to the towers, upward to the tower's upper tiers, and down over the central porch. In its forms, chronology and spatial organisation, it is so dense and complex as to defy comprehension.

This facade was not built according to a conventional plan. Instead, circumstances and inventiveness were united in a process of mutual adaptation over several centuries. In a different context I have called this process 'unitary functionalism': a process, assisted today by digital technology, by which every action, whether related to programme, structure or ornament, is coordinated with every aspect of a particular situation.[22]

The general public (including most architects) are rarely able to distinguish one cathedral interior from another. They will remember the extreme darkness of Chartres before the recent restoration, the stark brightness of Laon, and the eddying crowds at Notre Dame. They might also remember a sensation of great height at Beauvais and the splendour of the stained-glass windows in the choir of Bourges, or the black-and-white paving at Amiens (a close approximation of its medieval state). For most, however, such memories will be indistinct. Sketching at Saint-Germer-de-Fly, an architect friend told me: 'I can't draw: there are too many lines.'

Loose Ends

By and large, gothic interiors seem to be nothing but lines. No single object is strong enough to hold one's attention, and details fade into the vast space.

Gothic interiors resemble one another in real life even more than they do in photographs, in which the vault is invariably prominent and comparisons can be made between the articulation of the parts: between column and capital, pier and colonnettes, tribune and triforium, nave and transept. In reality, however, interiors present themselves as crowds of vertical lines, intermittently separated by the rose of a transept or the fanning of clerestories and chapels in the curve of a choir. They recall the stripe paintings of Bridget Riley or the colour grids of Gerhard Richter (who designed the stained glass in the window of the south transept in Cologne), though softened by the filtered light, which enhances the circular forms of the piers, colonnettes and mullions.

Given the insistent, even obsessive, linearity of the interior, it is surprising that this was not usually continued on the exterior. Two memorable exceptions are the west fronts of the late gothic cathedrals of Rouen and Strasbourg, where the linearity is so powerful that it overwhelms the figurative sculpture. An earlier example is the facade of the south transept at Chartres, where a screen of exceptionally elongated colonnettes is superimposed on the massive structure of towers that were never completed. But the result is monotonous.

This mismatch between interior and exterior is characteristic of gothic architecture. Jean Bony claimed that it was first successfully resolved at Reims cathedral, a building he described as presenting an image of perfect clarity and harmony.[23] While it is true that there is a concordance between the levels of the various storeys, the huge pinnacle on top of the buttresses appears to derive from a different genre of forms from the linear scheme inside. The disjuncture between exterior and interior can be seen at its most elemental, however, in a pier at Saint-Germer-de-Fly, which forms on the outside the blunt mass of a buttress and on the inside a highly articulated sheaf of colonnettes.

Far from being a manifestation of structural rationality, cathedral exteriors display many idiosyncrasies. Even Viollet-le-Duc, who wanted to recognise in the construction of gothic cathedrals the unfolding of a logical process, believed that the use of the flying buttress stood like a reproach against the general system adopted in the construction of cathedrals.[24] Why should such props be necessary? Thus, builders did their best to conceal them with pinnacles, as at Reims, or simplify them as much as possible, as at Saint-Germer-de-Fly. For Choisy, too, the flying buttress belonged to the category of guileful expedients necessitated by limited material resources. Even Bony recognised in the desire to combine thin walls with rib vaulting a fundamental contradiction which prompted, notably, the contrivance of the flying buttress.

The makeshift nature of the interior was mirrored in the design of the exterior. In the upper part of the choir at Amiens, buttresses describe 'a sort of forest in which general directions are difficult to discern'. They are topped by a multitude of pinnacles which are as diminutive here as they are monumental at Reims. 'Everything seems to be in the process of breaking up and multiplying', giving the choir 'a bushy, spiky aspect'.[25] Compare this with Notre Dame, where the strong horizontal line of the cornice emphasises the bold geometric volume of the choir, and the decisive arc of the buttresses reaches the perimeter of the church in a single flight.

At Le Mans, by contrast, flying buttresses are multiplied to such an extent that from a distance they appear integral to the volume of the choir. Most ingeniously they divide above the outer perimeter of the choir into split ends, resulting in an appearance which is as tousled as Notre Dame's is orderly. Perhaps the most eloquent arrangement (if not the most elegant structurally) is found at Beauvais, where the extreme height of the choir is matched by the extreme height of the buttresses.

Apse, Beauvais Cathedral © Bildarchiv Monheim GmbH / Alamy

Here, the upright volume of the choir is held delicately, as if it were a precious stone, high above the ambulatory and deep inside the battery of closely spaced abutments.

Clearly, gothic exteriors show little consistency from one period to the next or from one region to another. They follow no evolutionary path which could in turn advance the development of a style. No one articulated the curious mismatch between the interior and the exterior more succinctly than Ruskin: 'The outside of a French cathedrals, except for its sculpture, is always to be thought of as the wrong side of the stuff, in which you find how the threads go that produce the inside or right-side pattern', he wrote in *The Bible of Amiens*.[26] The outside – the 'wrong' side – reveals the threads that create the pattern inside. Michelet used a related simile, describing how buttresses help to keep the church upright, as if it were Christ on the cross. Whereas the exterior of a cathedral seems to be all matter, the interior is immaterial and ethereal.

Between the unpredictable character of the exterior and the aspiration towards a flawless order inside – between the exterior, which is of necessity about materials and craftsmanship, and the interior, which is above all a construction of the mind – there is an irreconcilable contradiction, reflecting the mystery that separates the ephemerality of human life and the timelessness of religion. Unlike commentators of the twentieth century, Ruskin acknowledged this contradiction and welcomed imperfection. Like the labourers who built the churches, gothic was savage, rude, disturbed, obstinate, redundant – an admission of the fallen nature of Man. Yet, from fragments that were full of imperfections, masons succeeded in raising what Ruskin called an 'unaccusable whole'.[27]

The expression prefigures Robert Venturi's later recognition of contradiction and of a sense of 'obligation towards the difficult whole', although Venturi's emphasis is more on the formal than it is on the moral. He, like Ruskin, embraces

imperfection. 'The difficult whole', he writes, 'includes multiplicity and diversity of elements in relationships that are inconsistent.'[28] Instead of the orgy of logical thought laid bare by Panofsky, he praises 'an orgy of contrasting dualities of form', of inflections and discontinuities, of clashes and contrasts resulting from the accommodation of conflicting functions. Yet Venturi had little to say about gothic in *Complexity and Contradiction in Architecture,* beyond a few lines on the truncated choir of Beauvais cathedral, the porch of Saint Urbain at Troyes, and the bizarre sets of responds in the aisles of Rouen cathedral, which push away from the wall like the candelabras in Jean Cocteau's film *Beauty and the Beast.*

Gothic embodies a different kind of aesthetic. It calls for an idea of the whole which is not only 'difficult' but above all inexhaustible. A gothic cathedral embraces the conflicting notions of plan and event, of anticipation and adventure. It combines order and randomness, coherence and incongruity. 'Whenever it finds occasion for change in its form or purpose,' Ruskin writes, 'it submits to it without the slightest sense of loss either to its unity or majesty'.[29] In every other style of architecture discontinuities are shocking, and rarely welcome. But in gothic they are not only tolerated but are integral to its conception. No one complains about the very different age and design of the towers on the west front of Chartres cathedral, one being as solid as the other is all finery and fretwork, or about the mismatch between the end walls of the transepts in most cathedrals. No cathedral has been completed fully in compliance with an original plan.

It is therefore not surprising that the role of individual builders is rarely acknowledged. Not even the familiar names of Robert de Luzarches (the nave at Amiens), Hughes Libergier (Saint-Nicaise at Reims), and Pierre de Montreuil (the nave of Saint-Denis and the south transept of Notre Dame) evoke a particular personality. Nor do their works reflect the development of a personal style.[30] Instead, they are part of a protracted sequence of events in which individual contributions fade into the *longue durée*. In this sense gothic could hardly be more at odds with the identification between author and project that exists in the architecture of today, and with the sometimes grotesque characterisations this gives rise to. Think, for instance, of the Unité d'Habitation in Marseille, dubbed 'la maison du fada' ('the nutter's house'), or the project for a médiathèque at Pau in France, nicknamed 'le caleçon de Zaha' ('Zaha's panties').

The chronologies of cathedrals reads like a litany of major disruptions. At Reims, the construction of the main facade was delayed by the presence of houses on the site. At Amiens, the depth of the towers was reduced for lack of space. Most bizarrely, at Lausanne the nave had to accommodate a public road cutting across it. But this is as nothing compared with the west fronts of cathedrals. Viollet-le-Duc (who was temperamentally inclined to overlook idiosyncrasies) describes them as '*des amas de constructions sans ensemble, élevées successivement sans projet arrêté*' ('constructions without unity, one thing piled on to the next without a fixed project').[31]

These west fronts bear witness to a the gradual disintegration of a sense of order. Chronology aside, a story could be told, beginning with the cliff-like facade of Chartres, a design that hardly seems to be architecture: too flush and barely articulated, with openings that are too few and too small, as if crushed and partly sunk into the ground by the immense weight of the masonry. At Notre Dame, on the other hand, symmetry and consistency prevail. The facade seems to have been subjected to an academic exercise in composition, each large-scale motif or series of motifs fitting neatly within its own compartment. This west front was much loved by Le Corbusier, who used it to demonstrate the application of *tracés régulateurs*.

At Reims the horizontal storeys are still strongly marked, but the process of disintegration is well advanced.

No gothic facade is more colossal (as anyone who has stood beside one of its statues in the adjacent Musée du Tau can testify), but it is full of crevices and ligaments, battered on the outside and as if corrupted from the inside. For architecture, it is the ultimate *écorché*, a model of immense power and pain. This, together with the extraordinary liberties taken by its sculptors in the central portal, is reminiscent of Michelangelo, even if the *terribilità* here is on a scale that would be inconceivable in the work of an individual artist.

Henceforth, the sense of compositional balance becomes uncertain. Though I lived for much of my youth in the shadow of Amiens cathedral (my ophthalmologist's consulting room stood opposite its main facade), I still struggle to find order in its composition. It is as if the neat compartments of Notre Dame's facade had been slid around on the face of a pocket puzzle game. The rose has been moved up, while the kings' gallery has been moved down to a position immediately above the arcade. Above the two lateral porticos, just enough height has been reserved for a lunette. Only the upper storeys of the two towers, which differ in height and in detail, break the symmetry.

The sense of awkwardness in the arrangement persists, even though the complicated circumstances of the construction are now well understood.[32] However, the greatness of Amiens's facade lies in the porches, which offer ample compensation for any reservations. Few forms in the history of architecture have achieved a greater sensuousness or a keener sense of drama. Their canopies are shaped like gigantic shells from whose depth incomparable statues speak to us in a voice that comes from times immemorial and seems almost audible. Still today, I cannot approach them without trepidation.

At Bourges the line of porticos (of which there are five) also stands proud of the main facade. But above them everything seems to be in a state of disarray. Given that the bays of the great nave behind proceed with faultless regularity

Palimpsest of Reims, mid thirteenth century
© Timothy O'Hare

Detail of arcade, Sainte Chapelle of Saint-Germer-de-Fly, Oise, Picardy
© Irénée Scalbert

from end to end, this is all the more surprising. To refer to the west front as a facade is almost a euphemism. Six massive buttresses rise like monumental candles, with no setback whatsoever. Between them, with the exception of the unusually fine tracery in the central bay, the wall is almost entirely windowless. The space is filled instead with deep arcades, some arched and others ogival. Above this gallimaufry rise two rather squat towers, ungainly and unequal in size. Although the arrangement is not beautiful in any conventional sense, the west front of Bourges exudes strength and character. Its awkwardness may clash with the grace of the nave but no one has argued that this is detrimental to the overall effect of the building. The cathedral remains – to borrow Ruskin's phrase – an unaccusable whole.

Such inconsistencies are integral to gothic architecture. At Amiens, site restrictions resulted in shallow towers that appear, on the west front, like a 'constructional *trompe l'oeil*'.[33] The facade was flattened against the pre-existing nave. As in the case of Milan cathedral, no feature above the level of the triforium – neither the Gallery of Kings, nor the rose, nor the towers – had been designed at the outset. As construction proceeded, a succession of formal accidents was concealed by improvised solutions.

At Rouen no fewer than six architects were employed on the west front over a period of 350 years. At Strasbourg the design of the tower evolved over a period of eighty years in the hands of a succession of masters, notwithstanding what Goethe wrote about its 'countless details melt[ing] together into a complete whole'.[34] In gothic architecture the dimension of time cannot be separated from its aesthetic. In a true sense, Gothic cathedrals have no beginning and no end. Records might provide dates for the start of the building campaign, but the laying of the first stone seldom marks a clear start. Records might provide the date of the consecration of a church but, here again, completion is regularly prevented

by fire, collapse, extension, shelling and, in our own time, creative restoration.

The notion of a unified gothic style reaching maturity in the Rayonnant style, and ending with the fireworks of the Flamboyant style, is a fantasy – a legacy of the nineteenth century, when gothic was defined in opposition to, and in parallel with, classicism. Strictly speaking, each cathedral develops its own aesthetic in the process of its making; each is a kind of precipitate arising from an admixture of intentions and events. Unlike classical buildings, gothic cannot be understood in the light of a particular model or theory. Unlike classicism, it does not submit to the authority of a language, a grammar or a vocabulary.

The expectation of uniformity and consistency in the design of buildings did not exist in medieval times. Common sense suggests that there was at least some vision of the whole, but there is little evidence that this original idea was considered sacrosanct. As the facade of Rouen demonstrates, architects were anxious to keep up with changing fashions, even at the cost of a loss of symmetry. Moreover, the possibility that a design might survive without modification during extended periods of construction simply did not correlate with medieval expectations. 'The concept', Peter Draper has argued, 'insofar as one can suggest an articulated notion – was, rather, one of coherence than conformity to an original design.'[35]

But cathedrals defy even notions of stylistic coherence. Defined by their ability to respond to or resist circumstances, they embrace inconsistency and are tolerant of mistakes. A cathedral's character, like that of a person, could be described as the sum of its distinguishing qualities. And, like the latter, its essence is moral. Ruskin understood this when he attributed to gothic qualities such as rudeness, obstinacy and generosity. Character is the expression in one object of its passage through time. It is the result of a multitude of events, random and planned, contingent and rational, natural and human.

It defines the forms of a cathedral as much as it does the process and the values by which these forms were created. The moulding of character, like the construction of a cathedral, needs time.

Modernism struggled with gothic. The conception of architecture as the fulfilment of human *needs* found no resonance in religion, and there was no middle ground between the 'house as a machine for living in' and the house of God. Efforts to establish minimum standards or to achieve an economy of means were hardly compatible with the urge to build cathedrals. Yet, in a fundamental, existential way, gothic is functionalism reduced to its purest form, based not on physical or social needs but on belief. The thirteenth-century theologian William Durandus wrote that, 'in the Temple of God, the foundation is Faith, which is conversant with unseen things'.³⁶ In the building of cathedrals, faith was the programme.

Programme

Treatises played a minor role in gothic architecture, but there was a theory, in the form of the Bible. More particularly, this theory was founded on the Gospels and on the life of Christ: theory as biography. A gothic cathedral is in effect a re-enactment of the Passion – the final events in the life of Jesus Christ. The death of Jesus was at the core of all medieval life and art. 'Life', wrote one grim doctor of the Church, 'is but the shadow thrown by the cross of Christ, outside that shadow is death.'³⁷

Nowhere was this devotion to the life of Christ more fully represented than in the relics of Sainte Chapelle in Paris which included, most precious of all, the Crown of Thorns; the purple robe of an emperor in which Herod's guards derisively clothed Jesus; a fragment of the Holy Reed which they placed in his hands in lieu of a sceptre; the linen with which he washed the feet of his apostles during the Last Supper; a fragment of the Cross as well as the 'titulus' affixed to it;

the Holy Lance which pierced the heart of Christ; a phial containing the water, mixed with blood, which seeped from this wound; the Holy Sponge used to wet Christ's lips with gall and vinegar; a fragment of the Holy Shroud; and a stone from the Holy Sepulchre. To this were added a flask of the Virgin Mary's breast milk, and her coat; the swaddling clothes of the infant Jesus; and the rod with which Moses caused the Red Sea to open and then to close. There were also many relics of saints, including a fragment of Saint John the Baptist's skull; the foot of one of the Holy Innocents; the skulls of Saint Clement, Saint Blaise and Saint Simeon; a rib of Saint Nicaise; a knee of Saint Aignan; and a tooth of Charlemagne.[38] Given the exceptional, not to say surreal, nature of these relics, it is no surprise that the Sainte Chapelle itself should have been conceived of as a reliquary. Much of the masonry and many of the statues were gilded, suggesting the gold and enamel work of the goldsmith.

No aspect of a church was too insignificant to be used as a means of commemorating the Passion – Durandus, for instance, ordained that a cross be engraved on the first stone to be laid in the building of a church. And none was too large. The plan of a cathedral, in the form of a cross, serves as a reminder to the faithful that they should 'tread on the steps of The Crucified'.[39] Above all, the Passion was celebrated in the Mass and in the sacrament of the Eucharist, an adaptation of the life of Christ, a drama combining fiction with reality, in which the events of the Last Supper – Christ's blessing and his sharing of bread and wine with his disciples – are repeatedly commemorated together with the exhortation: 'All take and eat of this. For this is My Body ... All take and drink of this. For this is the chalice of My Blood, of the new and eternal covenant. Mystery of Faith: which shall be shed for you and for many unto the remission of sins.'

In medieval times the congregation's desire to witness the priest's elevation and blessing of the host was so powerful that a dark curtain was sometimes placed behind the altar to enhance the visibility of the host. This prompted visions – that it shone like the sun; that the priest held aloft, not the host, but the infant Christ. It has been said that people sometimes ran from church to church to prolong the experience.[40] The rehearsal on the altar of a bloody sacrifice – the crucifixion of Christ – draws on what is most primitive in religion ('host' derives from the Latin *hostia*, or 'sacrificial victim'). And the fascination with and belief in transubstantiation, in the actual presence of God in the host, before which the assembly kneels in adoration, has affinities with the world of magic.

During the consecration, the priest exceptionally turns away from the congregation to face the altar. He then adopts the ancient attitude of the orant, turning the palms of his hands upwards, to 'seek the things which are above', as counselled by Saint Paul. The action takes place in silence. The upward movement of the host, the stillness, the sense of mystery combine to create an atmosphere that seems to expand to fill the interior of the cathedral, illuminating its meaning. It would be hard to overstate the sense of drama that accompanies the presentation of an object as small as the host – a two-inch wafer, like some radioactive nugget, holding out the promise of eternal life – in a space as vast as a cathedral.

In the late medieval period the appetite for gruesome details of the Passion became insatiable. 'Jesus no longer teaches, he suffers,' Emile Mâle writes. 'Whereas the death of Jesus Christ had been a dogma addressed to the intelligence', he adds, 'now it is a stirring image which speaks to the heart.'[41] The degree of one's absorption in this dolefulness became a measure of religious piety. In sculptures of the Pietà and of the Entombment, and in the *Christ Seated Waiting for Death* in the church of Saint-Nizier at Troyes (a sculpture Mâle singled out for praise), the pain appears to be absolute, in a manner befitting the approaching death of Jesus.

The emotional charge of late gothic sculpture found an equivalent in the increasingly complex foliation of late gothic architecture. The virtuosity must have been fascinating in its own right but the sensibility was new. Architectural forms now possessed a keener susceptibility to emotion. This is visible, for instance, in the upper storeys of the Tour de Beurre at Rouen cathedral, where the foliation is so intricate and brittle as to suggest that the surface of the masonry has itself acquired the power of sensation. It is visible, too, in the increasingly fine modelling of columns and tracery, which together form the pattern on 'the right side of the cloth'. Whereas faith had been dominant in the early phase of gothic, the emotion faith aroused now became increasingly active. Emotion became the programme.

At root an architectural programme is an allegory, a parable. It is founded on a recollection of experience. Norman Foster's terminal at Stansted Airport (today sadly compromised) sought to recapture the clarity of early air travel when 'on one side there was a road and on the other a field'.[42] A church, in turn, is founded upon the commemoration of the Last Supper. Even when a designer closely follows the prescriptions of Ernst Neufert's *Architects' Data* (the book includes a measured drawing of a priest celebrating the Eucharist), there remains in every programme something irreducible. It is this enigma, residing at the core of the creative rehearsal of experience, that determines the particular height and form of the vaults of a cathedral, or the 'trees' at Stansted. It informs every aspect of a building, is what that the architecture critic strives to understand.

The relation between the sacrament of the Eucharist and the form of a cathedral is like the relation between a tungsten filament and a light bulb: necessary, mutually defining. Without the Eucharist there would be no cathedrals. The Passion, as celebrated in the Eucharist, was the blueprint. The successive stages of the Passion – the Last Supper, the prayer

Nave looking east, Amiens Cathedral
Photograph
Henri Deneux
© Médiathèque du Patrimonie / RMN-Grand Palais

on the Mount of Olives, the Arrest, the Judgement, the Crucifixion – were obsessively incorporated in the fabric of cathedrals. In stone and in glass, in metal and in wood, artists reproduced what they knew by heart.

Outside the church episodes from the Passion contributed a rhythm to everyday life. Durandus describes the unfolding of the day in this way: 'At *Matins* bound: at *Prime* revil'd: condemned to Death at *Tierce*: Nailed to the Cross at *Sexts*: at *Nones* His Blessed Side they Pierce: They take Him down at *Vesper*-tide: in grave at *Compline* lay who thence forth bids His Church to keep Her sevenfold Hours always.'[43] Events in the life of Christ, especially the Nativity and Easter – the birth and the death which mark the mysterious thresholds of his incarnation – lent their meaning to the passing of the seasons.

Though seen as originating with God, time was associated with humanity and mortality. Human existence was but a short interval, a hiatus in eternity. Likewise, the incarnation of God in the person of Jesus was a hiatus in the reign of God. In his great essay on art in the Middle Ages, Michelet stressed the central role of the Passion. 'The Middle Ages as a whole', he wrote, 'are contained within Christianity, and Christianity as a whole is contained within the Passion. Literature, art, the manifold developments of the human mind from the third to the fifteenth century, all hangs on this mystery.'[44] He further emphasised the moment when Christ withdraws to the Mount of Olives to pray in solitude. There he implores his father to spare him what he knows is to come: 'Please take this cup of suffering away from me.'[45] Once crucified he cries out in agony: '*Eloi, Eloi, lema sabachthani?*' ('My God, my God, why have you abandoned me?')[46] For Michelet the anxiety of doubt, the fear of abandonment by God, was the essence of medieval thought.

Christ's doubt is like a breach in the Gospels, the moment when Christ, now alone with his conscience, doubts his own faith and experiences what it is like to be human.

Made incarnate by his father to redeem mankind, then abandoned by him in his last hour, Jesus fears becoming human himself. The moment is not without suspense, nor is it without irony. Having taken a human form to give humanity a chance to redeem itself from sin, Christ contemplates the loss of his own godliness.

In dwelling on the Passion the aim is to stress that gothic architecture cannot be understood in isolation from the religion which gave rise to it – any more than, say, Islamic architecture can be isolated from Islam, or Renaissance architecture from humanist culture. Writers in the twentieth century privileged a secular conception of gothic, focusing mainly on its form and structure. Yet Christianity – its rituals, its beliefs and its values – constitutes the anthropological basis of gothic. Gothic architecture is human, not in spite of religion, but because of it. The doubt, the anxiety, the suffering in the Passion – what Michelet called 'the night of the soul' – are human feelings. As such, they are universally understood and are the means by which gothic forms are made intelligible to all.

These feelings, this 'passionate vegetation of the mind', underpinned gothic and the foliation of its lines. From them arose a man-made order parallel to that of nature, its flora, its rocks and minerals. Improbably, this order combined passion and mind, emotion and intellect, instinct and logic. If, in early gothic, the ribs were believed to carry the vaults, in the more extravagant examples of late gothic, ribs became detached from the surface of the vaults and carried nothing but themselves. In the chapels of the Cathedral of Our Lady at Ingolstadt, ribs imitate branches and fork into cusps that are sharp like brambles, and the bosses bear thistle-like spikes, causing the apex of the vault to assume the aspect of a crown of thorns. The passion displayed in this fantastical outgrowth seems itself a prolongation of the Passion of Christ.

Gothic is not conventional in a classical sense. To this day there is no easy answer concerning the nature of the order by which it can be recognised. The acts of devotion which brought a church into existence took precedence over the formal unity of the building. These acts took many different forms – the gift of a new chapel, the rebuilding of a tower, the offering of a window – and they were not soon exhausted. Thus a cathedral encompasses many projects and it is in its nature to accommodate differences. Moreover, as its construction often lasted for as long as gothic itself (and sometimes beyond), it was open not only to new additions but also to random events which could either curtail or engender new projects.

In this respect, there is much that resonates with current preoccupations in architecture. Gothic is open-source, like the software whose code is freely available and modifiable. It was contingent, in that, more than other styles of architecture, it was open and responsive to the vagaries of time. Faced with unprecedented tasks, it was often improvised, like some giant work of *bricolage*. It was collaborative, in that design decisions were seldom if ever concentrated in the hands of a singular author. Lastly, in spite of its scale, it was, and remains, almost entirely the work of dedicated craftsmen. Open-source, contingency, *bricolage*, collaboration, craft – these topics are frequently discussed today and they all share related motives: that of finding a meaningful engagement between the profession and the building's users, between invention and situation, between the plan and the effects of time.[47]

Christ Seated Waiting for Death, Church of Saint-Nizier, Troyes, sixteenth century © The Courtauld Institute of Art, London

In time gothic found an ally. Its pace was not a 'dynamic from hell', but rather the composure of heaven.[48] It showed no anxiety about originality and remained imperturbable in the face of events large and small. Much of its fabric has been repaired, removed and replaced over the course of centuries. For instance, only half to two-thirds of the original stained glass survives in the great windows of the Paris Sainte Chapelle, mingling the coloured specks of its glass with those of subsequent restorations. Not merely great in their design, gothic cathedrals have demonstrated a rare capacity to adapt to transformations, additions and maintenance. Unlike so many familiar monuments, they have not merely weathered the passing of time but have embraced it. Hence their immense and immensely fragile shells have endured to remain among the few great works of art and architecture which are still freely accessible to all.

Originally published in AA *Files 72, 2016*

Thanks to Richard Plant for reading a draft of this essay; to Mary Crettier for her exhaustive comments on the text; to Merritt Bucholz, who first invited me to lecture on gothic; and to Marie Scalbert for offering transport, hospitality and trust.

1. Eugène Viollet-le-Duc, *Dictionnaire Raisonné de l'Architecture Française du XIe au XVIe siècle*, 1854–1868, vol 9 (Paris: A Morel, 1902), p 214.
2. James S Ackerman, '"Ars sine scientia nihil est": Gothic Theory of Architecture at the Cathedral of Milan', *Art Bulletin*, vol 31, 1949, p 103.
3. Wolfgang Schöller, 'Le dessin d'architecture à l'époque gothique', in Roland Recht (ed), *Les Bâtisseurs des Cathédrales Gothiques* (Strasbourg: Musée d'art moderne, 1990), p 232.
4. Werner Müller, 'Le dessin technique à l'époque gothique', *ibid*, p 237.
5. See Jean Bony, 'The Genesis of Gothic: Accident or Necessity?', *Australian Journal of Art*, 1980, vol 2.
6. Jules Michelet, 'La Passion comme Principe d'Art au Moyen Âge', in *Histoire de France*, livre IV, 1833, reprinted in Jules Michelet, *Oeuvres Complètes*, vol IV (Paris: Flammarion, 1974), pp 592–610.
7. Gilles Deleuze and Félix Guattari, *A Thousand Plateaus: Capitalism and Schizophrenia*, translated by Brian Massumi (Minneapolis, MN: University of Minnesota Press, 1987), p 156.
8. *Ibid*, p 157.
9. James S Ackerman, *op cit*, p 107.
10. Robert Branner, 'Drawings from a Thirteenth-Century Architect's Shop: The Reims Palimpsest', *Journal of the Society of Architectural Historians*, Winter 1958, vol XVII, no 4, p 15.
11. Lon R Shelby, 'The Practical Geometry of Medieval Masons', *Studies in Medieval Culture*, vol 5, 1975, p 143.
12. Roland Recht, 'Les "traités pratiques" d'architecture gothique', in Roland Recht, *op cit*, p 280.
13. Eugène Viollet-le-Duc, *op cit*, vol 4, p 197.
14. Jean Bony, *The English Decorated Style: Gothic Architecture Transformed, 1230–1350* (London: Phaidon, 1979), p 43.
15. Jean Bony, *French Gothic Architecture of the Twelfth and Thirteenth Centuries* (Berkeley, CA: University of California Press, 1983), p 361.
16. John Ruskin, 'The Nature of Gothic', in *The Stones of Venice*, 1853 (Boston, MA: Da Capo Press 1985), p 187.
17. Eugène Viollet-le-Duc, *op cit*, vol 5, p 391.
18. Auguste Choisy, *Histoire de l'Architecture*, vol 2 (Paris: Gauthier-Villars, 1899), p 526.
19. Wilhelm Worringer, *Form in Gothic, 1912–1927* (London: A Tiranti, 1957), p 107.
20. Eugène Viollet-le-Duc, *op cit*, vol 2, p 520.
21. John Ruskin, 'The Bible of Amiens', in *Our Fathers Have Told Us*, part I, 1881, p 7 of the travellers' edition (Orpington: G Allen, 1890). The work was translated into French by Marcel Proust in 1904.
22. Irénée Scalbert, 'The New Architecture: The Yokohama International Port Terminal', *Casabella*, no 708, February 2003, pp 30–41 (English translation, pp 109–13).
23. Jean Bony, *op cit*, note 15, p 273.

24 Eugène Viollet-le-Duc, *op cit*, vol 1, p 76.
25 Jean Bony, *op cit*, p 396.
26 John Ruskin, 'The Bible of Amiens', *op cit*, p 13.
27 John Ruskin, 'The Nature of Gothic', *op cit*, p 156.
28 Robert Venturi, *Complexity and Contradiction in Architecture* (New York, NY: Museum of Modern Art, 1966), p 88.
29 John Ruskin, 'The Nature of Gothic', *op cit*, p 168.
30 Peter Kurmann, 'Gautier de Varingroy et le Problème du Style Personnel d'un Architecte au XIIIe siècle', in Roland Recht, *op cit*, p 187.
31 Eugène Viollet-le-Duc, *op cit*, vol 2, p 322.
32 Alain Erlande-Brandenburg, 'La Facade de la Cathédrale d'Amiens', *Bulletin Monumental*, 1977; Jean Bony, *op cit*, p 280; Anne Prache, 'Remarques sur les Parties Hautes de la Cathédrale d'Amiens', *Gazette des Beaux-Arts*, vol 127, 1996.
33 Jean Bony, *op cit*, p 280.
34 Johann Wolfgang von Goethe, quoted in Paul Frankl, *Gothic Architecture*, 1962 (New Haven, CT: Yale University Press, 2001), p 219.
35 Peter Draper, 'The Bane of Consistency: Nineteenth-Century Legacies in the Study of Gothic Architecture', in F Salmon (ed), *Gothic and Gothic Revival* (London: Society of Architectural Historians of Great Britain, 1998), p 12.
36 William Durandus, *The Symbolism of Churches and Church Ornaments* (London: J G F & J Rivington, 1843), p 25.
37 Emile Mâle, *L'Art Religieux de la Fin du Moyen Âge en France* (Paris: Armand Colin, 1908), p 222.
38 Sophie de Sède, *La Sainte Chapelle et la Politique de la Fin des Temps* (Paris: Julliard, 1972), p 18.
39 William Durandus, *op cit*, p 26.
40 Rev Joseph A Jungmann, *The Mass of the Roman Rite: Its Origins and Development* (London: Burns & Oates, 1959), pp 424, 426; see also Roland Recht, *Seeing and Believing: The Art of Gothic Cathedrals* (Chicago, IL: University of Chicago Press, 2010).
41 Emile Mâle, *op cit*, p 86.
42 David Jenkins (ed), *Norman Foster Works*, vol 3 (London: Prestel, 2007), p 29.
43 William Durandus, *op cit*, p 91.
44 Jules Michelet, *op cit*, p 592.
45 *The New Testament*, Mark 14:32–36.
46 *Ibid*, Mark 15:34.
47 See for instance, and respectively, Mario Carpo, *The Alphabet and the Algorithm* (Cambridge, MA: MIT Press, 2011); Jeremy Till, *Architecture Depends* (Cambridge, MA: MIT Press, 2009); Irénée Scalbert and 6a Architects, *Never Modern* (Zurich: Park Books, 2013); Richard Sennett, *The Craftsman* (London: Penguin, 2008).
48 The expression was adopted by Rem Koolhaas from Jean-Paul Baïetto, the president of Euralille, to describe the momentum needed to bring the development to completion.

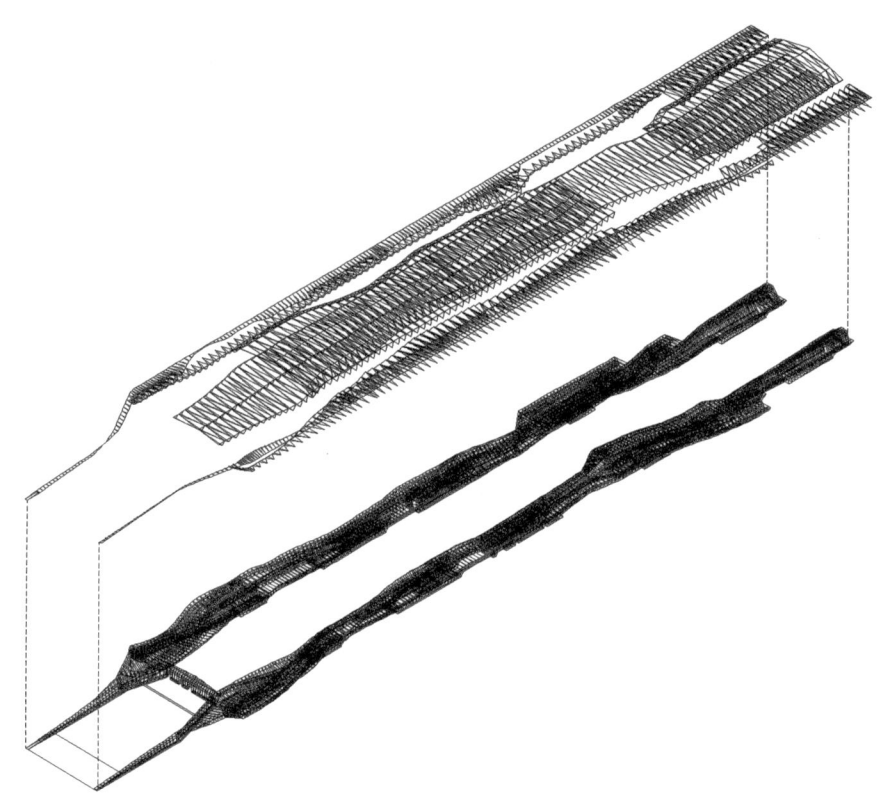

Building in Japan

In *Bauen in Frankreich* in 1928 – a book that features some of the most visionary pages written by an architecture critic in the twentieth century – Sigfried Giedion demanded that life be grasped in its totality. Industry, construction, art, architecture: all, he claimed, are part of a single life process and none can make sense in isolation. For Giedion, industry is the inner expression of this process, with construction constituting, in his words, the unconscious of architecture. This, he went on to argue, interconnects not only with the built fabric but with the forces that hold and reshape human nature. Architecture, in this sense, is without beginning or end, and part of a continuous movement. It is integral to a life process in which space and time are indissociable.

This intuition underpins the thinking of an emerging strain of contemporary architectural practice. For Foreign Office Architects (FOA), for example, and a growing number of other young offices, buildings are not plans translated into space or ideas turned into stone. They are not even creations of the mind. Instead, they are the effects of time. Similar concepts have been elaborated before, by figures like Ilya Prigogine among scientists, and by Henri Bergson and Gilles Deleuze among philosophers, but nothing more may have been heard on the subject among architects without Benoit Mandelbrot. Architects may not have read his books of mathematics, notably *The Fractal Geometry of Nature* (1982), but the geometry which he invented and the sensational images which he produced (pioneering the emergence of computer graphics in the 1970s) provided the essential relay, aesthetically and practically, between nature and architecture, between scientific knowledge and the imagination of space.

For Mandelbrot, drawings are essential means to the development of an intuition. Whereas a mathematical formula relates only to a small aspect of the relationship between reality and its model, the eye, he claims, has enormous powers of integration and discrimination. Moreover, his digital

Girders and folds, FOA, Yokohama International Port Terminal Courtesy Farshid Moussavi reconstructions of the complex shapes of clouds, mountains, coastlines and trees flatter geometry: once regarded as arduous and abstract, it now seems playful and sensuous. For the architects who explored the creative possibilities of computers in the 1990s this was a revelation.

Mandelbrot foresaw the aesthetic possibilities of the new geometry, and in the process distinguished between 'scalebound' and 'scaling' objects. Miesian buildings, for instance, are 'scalebound'. They are objects in which elements of scale, such as a window grid, are few in number and each have a distinct size. They represent to Mandelbrot a throwback to Euclid. On the other hand, Tony Garnier's Opera House in Paris, with its proliferation of details and its craggy outline, is a 'scaling' building. Like the mountains and coastlines which Mandelbrot studied, it has many different scales which interact confusedly and merge in a continuum.

Instances of scaling were also found in the visual arts, for example in Leonardo's drawing *Deluge* (1518) and in *The Great Wave* (1832) by Hokusai, an artist 'fascinated by eddies and whorls of every kind', and much admired by Mandelbrot. Alejandro Zaera-Polo and Farshid Moussavi, partners in FOA, have also called upon the authority of Hokusai. They consulted books on his work during the competition in 1995 for the Yokohama International Port Terminal. Later on, needing to sway a Japanese audience struggling to understand their winning entry, they invoked with great effect the spirit of the artist and referred to the same print which had so appealed to Mandelbrot.

In his own reflections on time and irreversibility, the chemist Prigogine had sought scientific answers to the same philosophical questions posed half a century earlier by Bergson, and to a lesser extent two centuries before that by Leibniz. A few years after FOA's victory in the competition in Yokohama, Sanford Kwinter and Jeffrey Kipnis – both of them critics who championed new, digitally inspired architecture – again referred to Bergson and Leibniz, even if their preferred philosophical reference was the more spatially evocative and often incomprehensible writings of Deleuze, notably his trio of titles *Bergsonism, The Fold: Leibniz and the Baroque*, and *Mille Plateaux*. Out of this intellectual melange new words entered the architectural vocabulary: surface, fold, topology, organisation, singularities, coherence, deterritorialisation, reterritorialisation, etc. New techniques were also developed: topological grids, intensive tiling, diagrammatic performance among them. In the process, the search for complexity in architecture was matched by a no less complex and often abstruse architectural language.

But with the completion of the Yokohama International Port Terminal in 2002 this semantic fog began to lift, and so the theory behind the building could be evaluated against a structure of considerable size and startling appearance. Indeed, as soon as images of the completed design were released to the press, the roof surface quickly became an icon for a new kind of architecture, a sort of frontispiece which described a vast, exposed, boundless space steeped in Deleuzian nomadology. Beneath it, in the ferry terminal proper, the theory was exposed to a first set of constraints associated with planning. Further below, in the car park, it faced a second set of constraints linked with building. The configuration of the project in three distinct surfaces – roof, terminal and car park – presents the equivalent of a cross-section cut through the history of the project, ranging from still barely formed speculations in the competition entry to hard-headed construction.

From the beginning, FOA intended to bring together ferry passengers and the people of Yokohama in 'a machine of integration'. They wished to establish a 'seamless connection' with the ground of the city. In addition, there was to be no separation between envelope and structure in a building where stresses are absorbed by 'singularities within a material continuum'. Not only was the building to have no columns – a feature which caused disbelief among engineers – not only was its space strangely continuous: it also seemed to be made in a single substance, as yet neither the paper of origami imagined during the competition nor the steel of shipyards later used in the construction, by a kind of alchemical process only known to computers.

FOA's vision recalls the views expressed by Giedion in *Bauen in Frankreich*. In four magnificent pages boldly titled 'Architecture', Giedion doubts that the discipline can survive under the weight of its own monumentality. Architecture is no longer spatial or plastic. Its boundaries become blurred, fields overlap, moving elements like elevators become parts of buildings. No longer distinct from the city, buildings seek to connect with it, to fall in line with the indivisible life process of which architecture is only a part, 'even if a special one'. The exalted task of the architect, then, is to transform the surface of the earth, to envision new grounds which are artificial and continuous. Above all, the architect must imagine forms which are neither abstract, neutral nor homogeneous like the pioneering steel structures of the nineteenth century, but are instead concrete and differentiated.

Despite the power and ambition of these words, in Yokohama, however, the sponsors of the project wanted something else. In the concept of *ni-wa-minato* ('very-bright-with-the-sunshine'), highlighted in the competition brief,

Roof plan
Courtesy Farshid Moussavi

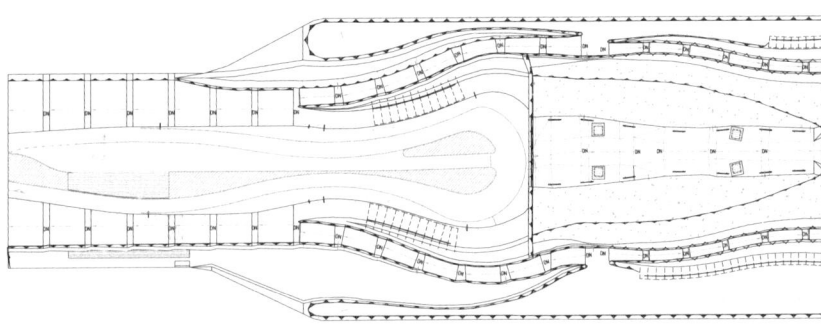

they had made explicit their desire to see a great symbol. The new ferry terminal should be able to achieve for Yokohama what Kansai International Airport did for Osaka, perhaps even what Utzon's Opera House did for Sydney. It is no accident, then, that the commentary provided by Arata Isozaki, who was vice-chairman of the jury, is almost exclusively concerned with symbolic matters, and was also reflected by the schemes which made it through to the final shortlist: a shape relating to that of a Japanese sword (Matsumoto and Shinohara), a rational plan crowned by a large symbolic glass box reminiscent, to Isozaki's mind, of a traditional oriental roof (Rikken Yamamoto), the back of a whale (Ryoji Suzuki) and FOA's scheme which curiously did not register on Isozaki's symbolic scale: 'an innovative idea cutting through', he wrote, 'the style/anti-style pluralism'. FOA's entry appeared to mean nothing by itself. The jury emphasised the radical simplicity of its appearance. The design, they wisely concluded, would set off the boats moored along the pier. Reciprocally it would be made more attractive by the presence of the ships.

FOA's masterstroke, however, was to transform the 500m2 garden specified in the brief into an 18,000m2 open space on a scale with the nearby Yamashita Park. They could not have known at the time that given the political sensitivity of

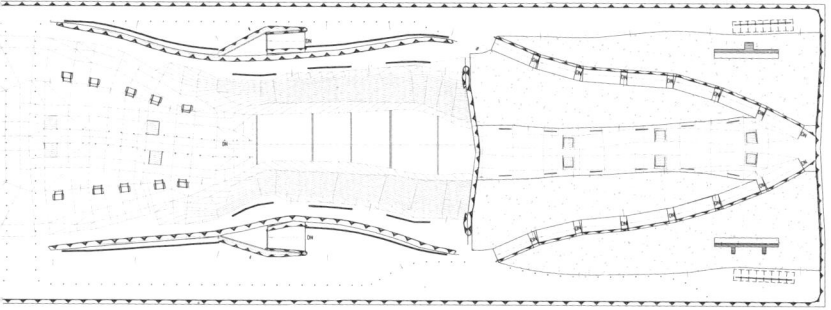

building at the interface between city centre and harbour, this move was just right. Growing competition with other Asian ports led the City of Yokohama to launch an aggressive development policy seeking to transform its harbour into the hub port of East Asia. Vast container terminals were recently completed or are under construction on land reclaimed from the bay. These developments are in effect cutting the 3.6 million inhabitants of Yokohama off from the sea – the nearest beach is now several kilometres away – and putting pressure on the politicians to attach to these large-scale industrial facilities amenities designed for the enjoyment of the local population.

The 270 hectares of container parking which make the Honmoku Pier were supplemented with the little appendage of a fishing jetty projecting into the sea. The even larger and newer Minami Honmoku Pier will be contained on two sides by a green belt, helping to transform Yokohama, in the words of an official brochure, into 'an energetic harbour leading the world' as well as 'a port full of charm for our citizens'. Given this context, it is not hard to understand why the lay members of the jury, all of them politicians, should have leapt on the proposal for a large public space on the site of the terminal, and why the client, the Port Harbour Bureau, is not overly keen (unlike the architects) to bring together passengers and citizens.

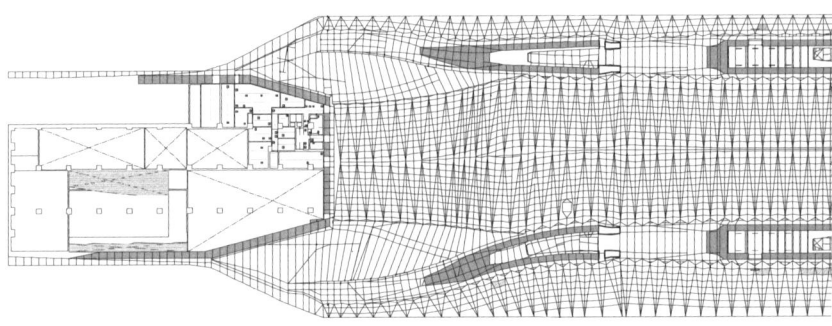

Roof structure
Courtesy Farshid Moussavi

The connection between the new terminal and the town centre is far less equivocal. The terminal stands at one end of the artery with which the centre is identified, with a city stadium marking the opposite end. The pairing of these two buildings represents a great deal more than a symbol, for the new terminal was a key element in Yokohama's bid to host the 2002 World Cup final. It gave the city an advantage over Saitama, its less accessible but better equipped rival to the north of Tokyo. According to Kunio Watanabe of the Structural Design Group, the charismatic structural engineer for the new ferry terminal, the timing of the World Cup was decisive. It prompted understandably nervous city officials to go ahead with a project for which there was no precedent and to complete its construction before the start of the tournament.

These two key factors which defined the context of the project – the bid to host the World Cup final and the fear of alienating citizens through excessive industrial development – therefore shed a particular light on the seamless connections envisaged by FOA. In addition, there was little in the immediate surroundings to legitimise a sensitive response to the local fabric. Where, then, could FOA's 'new grounds' intersect with the context? Could the gospel of continuity ever be more than a metaphor? Within the framework of the competition, FOA could do no more than dig in and develop a feeling for the brief

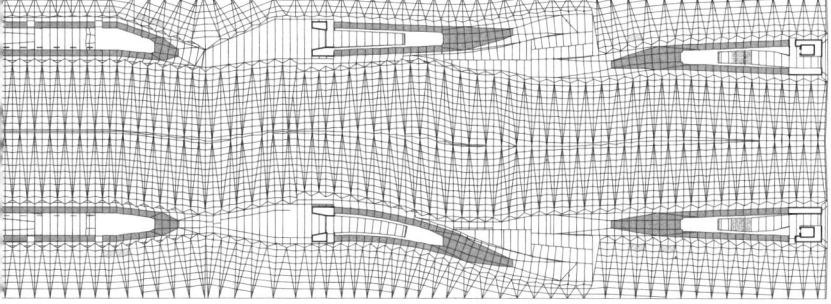

and for the presence of the sea. In the event, both provided powerful alibis for the seamless forms with which their new architecture had become infatuated.

Given the aim and the sophistication of the theory, the building at Yokohama is surprisingly reticent. It presents itself as a datascape without data, as a construction whose story became unretrievable as if to prove that it can stand on its own merit without the props of reason. The access drive rises gently to the level of the plaza and the main entrance, leaving one unprepared for the spaces beyond. On either side projecting belvederes reach forward to enclose the forecourt and overlook the incoming traffic. The strangeness of the scene gradually takes hold. Broad timber pavements rise on either side of the drive, their wooden kerb sitting directly on the asphalt. The access road widens on the ascent, suggesting by a chance optical effect that it is slightly arched (it is not). As one reaches the forecourt the space appears to dip slightly as if, having climbed something like a forearm, one had landed in the palm of a hand. The setting makes an inviting gesture to the sky and leads one, quite appropriately, to anticipate the presence of the sea.

Hemmed in between the bus shelters and the belvederes, valleys lead onto the roof. True to expectation, one finds

Terminal level plan
Courtesy Farshid Moussavi

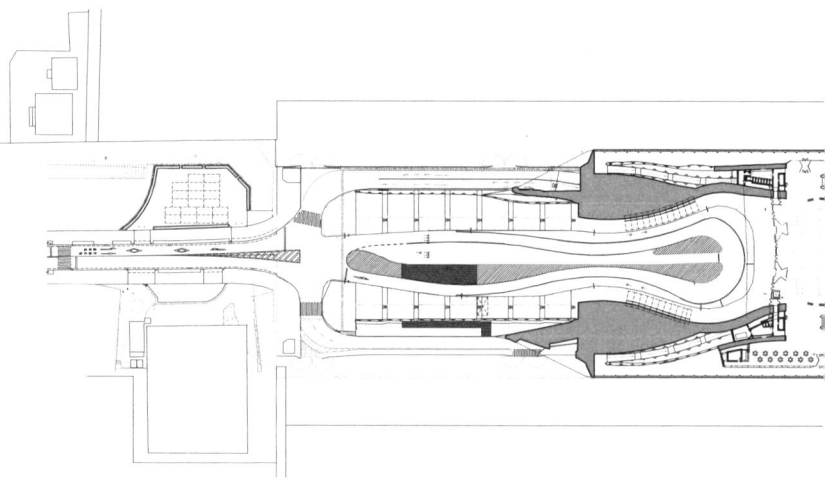

the sea beyond a broad timber deck running in a straight line for a cool 350m. Treading further across the roof is like venturing onto the body of Gulliver: it remains cautiously alien. Neither scalebound nor scaling, it recognises only two scales: the micro-patterns of the timber deck and the macro-forms of its undulations, skin lines and body lumps. Perhaps as many as 10,000 people will gather here to watch Yokohama's bi-annual fireworks. Little else is known about the uses of this 24-hour public space which, the architects acknowledge, will grow over time.

Most furniture is out of plumb, as if blown by the wind in the barren, desolate place which the roof will at times inevitably become. A theme emerges in which an assortment of ideas – water, grass, dunes, beach, deck, boat, etc – produces a strong maritime resonance. Like in the original design, bits of uncertain use and unfamiliar form are dotted across the space and signify its intended nomadic character. But how could a building be truly nomadic? How could it be like a landscape, at once wholly open-ended in its occupation and exhaustively determined in its form? As if to echo a recurrent problem in the sciences of nature, how could it be the result of both chance and necessity? City officials did rise to the

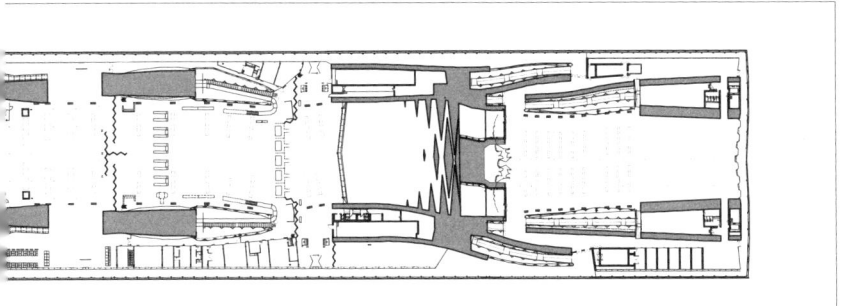

political opportunity presented by the new public space, but not to the extent of supplementing it with a meaningful brief. As a result the basis for its necessity must be found in the plan of the terminal below it.

The complex forms of the building are widely understood to be the outcome of an experiment with computers. In turn the fascination with the generation of complex forms helped to conceal the project's ideological content. In an interview conducted in 1994 for *El Croquis* by Zaera-Polo with Peter Eisenman, the discussion between them comes to a head on a fundamental issue. Zaera-Polo reiterates his commitment to a rule-based design method of the kind employed by Eisenman. But, unlike Eisenman, he argues that the first move should not be arbitrary, that architects cannot produce anything relevant unless some intention be declared from the outset. Rules need purpose.

Accordingly, the rules deduced by FOA from the brief for the terminal were carried out with a sophistication, a force of conviction and a raw coherence seldom seen in the functionalism of old. Throughout the modern period, functionalism followed one of two paths: for the majority form followed programme, while for a minority, including Mies van der Rohe and engineers like Nervi whom the modern movement co-opted, form followed structure. This distinction between function and structure, between humans and materials, was central to the humanist tradition of modernism. But in the Yokohama project this distinction is superseded. Programme and structure became fused and determine jointly the form of the architecture. The originality is in fact more profound: function has become atomised, digitised, architecture now being produced by a kind of unitary operation repeated as many times as necessary.

The operation retained by FOA for the Yokohama competition is the fold. At a large scale the fold helped to bring the 'flying carpet' of the roof in contact with the ground, providing points of support and a principle for organising circulation in the building. At a small scale it aimed to introduce rigidity in surfaces by turning and returning them again onto themselves. Crucially, the fold was consistent with the intellectual atmosphere – fractals, Deleuze, Kipnis, etc – which prevailed in FOA's milieu.

In a lecture delivered at the Architectural Association in the wake of their competition success, Zaera-Polo and Moussavi showed a figure drawn for the Rorschach psychological test (a favourite image at the time). The image presented a striking resemblance to the Yokohama cross-sections, complete with freely formed roof, cavern-like interiors, projecting boarding decks and recessed supports below. Like the Yokohama project, the Rorschach test originates in a fold which is the means by which ink is spread on the two halves of a sheet of paper to produce a figure. Inevitably the figure is symmetrical, even if – as Rorschach, a Swiss clinical physician, tersely observed – there is 'very little difference between the two halves'. Rorschach's experiments in the interpretation of accidental ink blobs showed that elated individuals 'perceive' while depressed others 'interpret'. This led him to conclude that there exists no clear boundary between perception and interpretation, and that interpretation is merely a special kind of perception. There is between representations and objects of nature a difference in degree rather than a difference in kind.

FOA justified the symmetry of the terminal building as a by-product of the brief, with ships flanking the pier on both sides. This makes good sense. In addition, it is possible to associate the pervasive symmetry, complete with the 'little difference between the two halves', with a Rorschach-like original fold, and to conceive the project as an imaginative perception of the brief, as if the brief had presented itself to the architects as a test of their perceptive powers. Thus form would follow perception in a way that brings to mind

Overleaf
Determination of the girder geometry
Courtesy Farshid Moussavi

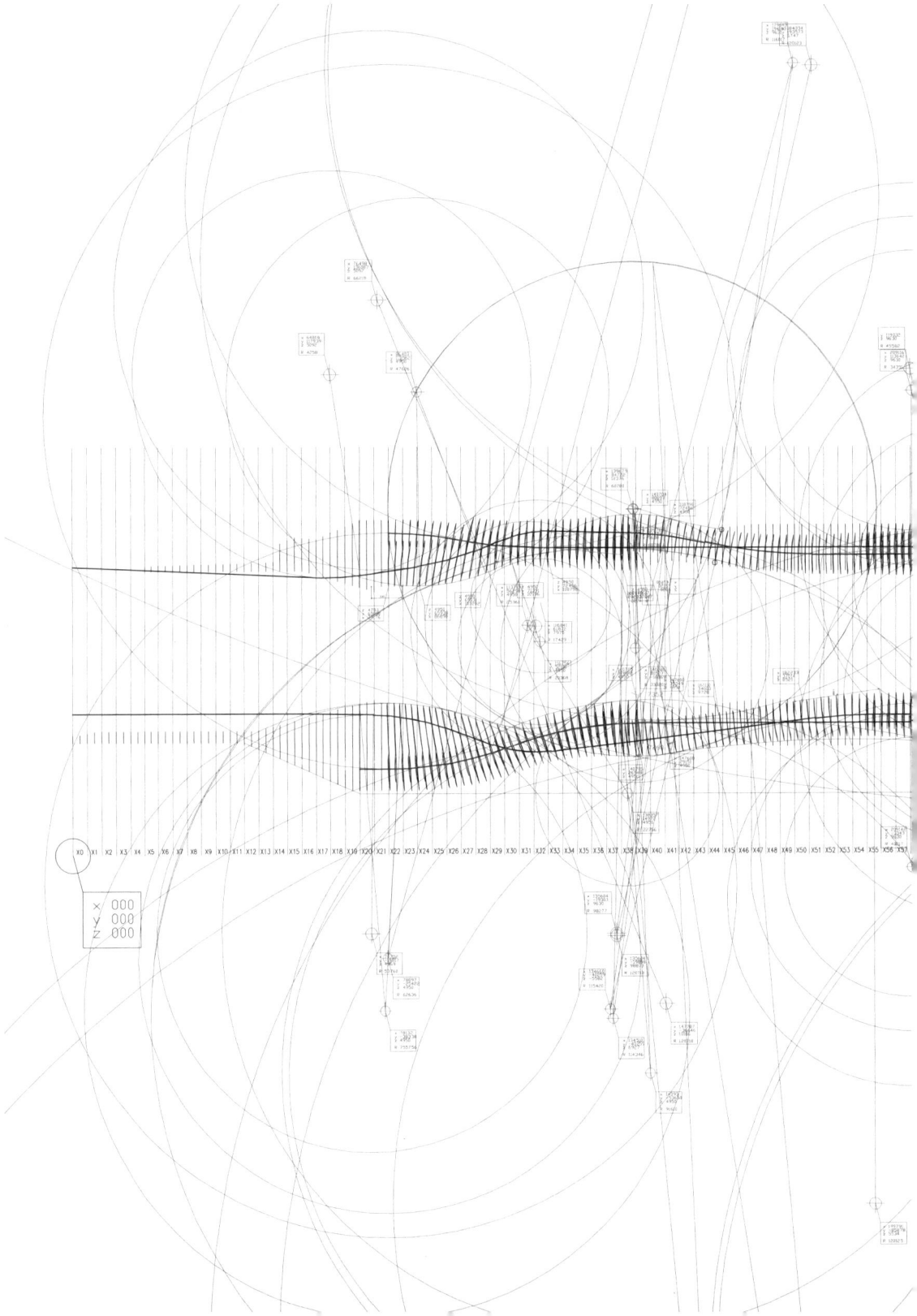

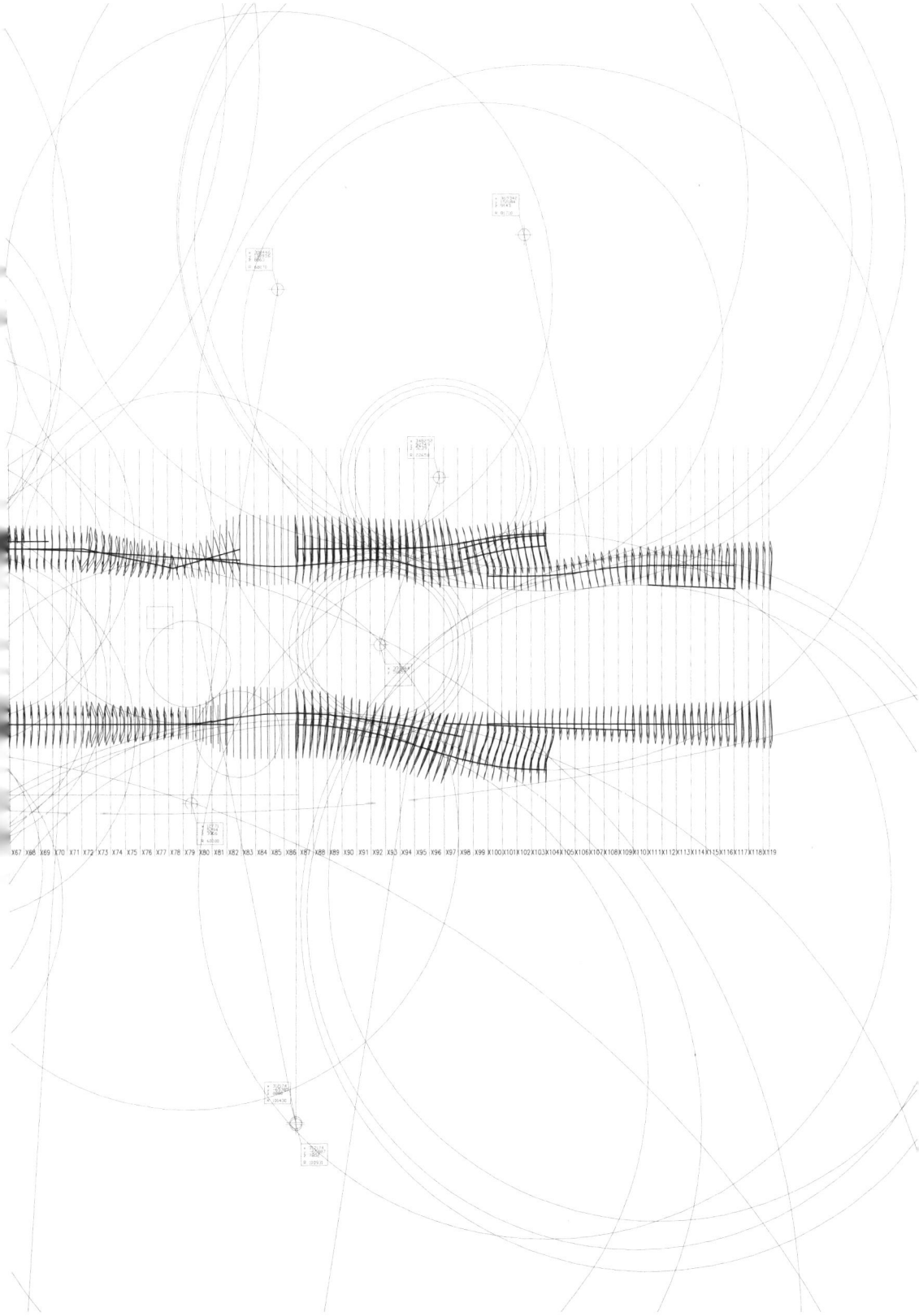

Bergson's discussion of the eye. 'The eye, with its marvellous complexity of structure, may be', he wrote, 'only the simple act of vision', the complexity of the organ being inseparable from the unity of its function.

Nature need not give it a thought, but how were FOA to grapple with this unity of function? How could they, to paraphrase Bergson, feel their object – the shifting brief – so as to get its mobile impression at every instant? In a situation which kept changing almost to the end, the terminal deck offered a stable reference. From the outset, it was imagined as a horizontal layer situated between the apron and the roof piazza. Its level was fixed at 5m, the height required for boarding ships. The six per cent gradient of the access drive and the area required for the traffic plaza determined the position of the main entrance. Points of support for the Terminal needed to be within specified distances from the edge of the apron falling under international control, the distance being shorter on the north than on the south side. Above, the narrow boarding decks running the entire length of the building needed to project further out towards the water edge to connect with the movable fingers of standard length leading onto the ships. These restrictions imposed by administration, structure, technical equipment and common sense caused he ramps to swerve – which they do more sharply on the south side where the distance between the points of support below and the boarding decks above is at its widest. In addition, the superimposition of the ramps leading onto the roof occasioned further deflections to allow for head clearance on the ramps below.

Along the sides of the building, the intricate arrangement of brief requirements and site constraints caused a kind of turbulence and gave the plan the character of necessity. Yet the terminal building is essentially a shed. It consists literally of two rooms of haunting immensity, like nave and chancel, lifted above the ground to make space for the car park. At

170m, the length of the terminal alone far exceeds that of most cathedrals. Yet at never more than 10m, its height is less than that of most churches. As one becomes accustomed to the relative darkness of the space, one notices not the nervous swerve of the ramps which separate the nave from the aisles, but their shallow inclines. The complexity proposed by the theory and described by the plan gives way to regularity, moderation and a kind of saturnine dimness. At the end of the terminal, where an uplift might be expected in the form of a transept or a tower, there is of course nothing of the kind. On the contrary, the ceiling which until then sloped imperceptibly, falls sharply and draws the eye through the looking glass to the car park below which, from here, vividly recalls the hold of a ship.

The citizens' facilities occupying the end of the building are responsible for this downlift, pressing down as it were on the roof surface to bring it in line with the 5m boarding level. Including at first a Hall of Civic Exchange flanked by restaurants, shopping and exhibition areas, they were later substantially reduced. But the idea of a hall for public and commercial use survived, flanked to the north by a restaurant and to the south by a belvedere including VIP facilities. Though on rare occasions the hall will be open to passengers to celebrate the arrival or the departure of a ship, it will be reserved for local events, for instance graduation ceremonies, weddings, gymnastics competitions, market fairs and public dances. From the outset it was envisaged that the position of the hall would draw visitors to the end of the pier and help bring the roof piazza to life. But the parochial and intermittent uses presently under consideration are unlikely to achieve this aim and take the measure of the exceptional situation.

The large areas of glazing at both ends of the hall and the comparatively modest length of the hall – at 75m, it is slightly shorter than most cathedrals – brings more light in than in the terminal below. While the terminal may be said to be Romanesque in character (a character which Victor Hugo described as 'sombre, mysterious, low and as if overwhelmed by the weight of the semi-circular arch'), the hall appears by contrast tall and airy like a gothic church. The folds, being fewer in number, appear larger and their faces, being closer to the natural light, are more contrasted and contribute a powerful monumentality to the space. It is here that the likeness with a cathedral, further aided by the current uncertainty concerning its purpose and by the vast window overlooking the sea (even if not quite a rose) is most irresistible. In its form, situation and character, the hall recalls Schinkel's powerful romantic fantasy *The Gothic Cathedral by the Water* (c 1814).

In a building which is allegedly moulded upon the outline of a brief, the multi-purpose hall presents a paradox. While the design became increasingly precise as it was rushed towards the completion date, the brief for the citizens' facilities was becoming increasingly vague. Ultimately the hall reflects less its own necessity than its history. It provides a somewhat mordant illustration of FOA's conception of the plan as 'simply the state that it is, given the level of intelligence it has reached'. According to this definition, a building must not be judged by external standards (for this would reflect a Platonic bias) or even by those set by its plans. If the origin is merely the point where a project happens to start, completion is the point where design happens to end, and they have no further significance. In a theory which recognises the smooth, seamless passage of time and the coherence of its effects, a project can be declared complete at any stage of its process – a view which is hard to reconcile with the notions of accountability and professionalism.

Inspired by the new sciences of nature, this understanding rests on the assumption that nature and architecture belong to the same material world. But it overlooks a fundamental difference between both. Building projects may, like nature, be developed and realised in real time, but the rules which guide their developments exist outside real time. The entire conception of architecture is based upon events which, it is assumed, *will* take place. Events being to some degree unpredictable, architecture projects are, unlike nature, essentially speculative. As Zaero-Polo reminded Eisenman, they are 'intentional'. Moreover, architectural forms are inert: they ignore the cycle of seasons, they neither create nor die. However great the temptation exerted by computer animations, architecture remains, to adapt Goethe, frozen motion. This is why FOA must refer not merely to the time and to the history of a project, but to its 'accelerated time', to its 'micro-history', in an attempt to dissolve the sugar of architecture into the water of nature.

Bergson himself never claimed (architecture theorists, please note!) that architecture could be absorbed within the perpetual becoming of life. On the contrary, he made a fundamental distinction between the 'organisation' of nature and the 'manufacture' of men. Manufacture, he wrote, 'consists in shaping matter, in making it supple and in bending it, in converting it into an instrument in order to become master of it'. It consists in 'assembling parts of matter … in order to obtain from them a common action' which is constituted in an ideal. Moreover (and crucially), this assembly follows a 'plan' which 'closes the future whose form it indicates'. Plans represent this absence of future, the essential stillness of architecture. Construction alone can manifest the passing of time. But to accomplish this, a project must transgress its plans. It must, as it were, jump ahead of itself, in a field where events are not governed by some external purpose but are instead unpredictable and irretrievable. It is in such rare and brief moments, when a project becomes a spontaneous becoming, that a new architecture can be said to be fulfilled.

In the new sciences even rules are expected to change under the effect of time. Mandelbrot, for instance, did not want to solve equations. These were not static descriptions that could be verified at any time. Rather, by a process of

Overleaf
Roof plan, detailed setting-out drawing
Courtesy Farshid Moussavi

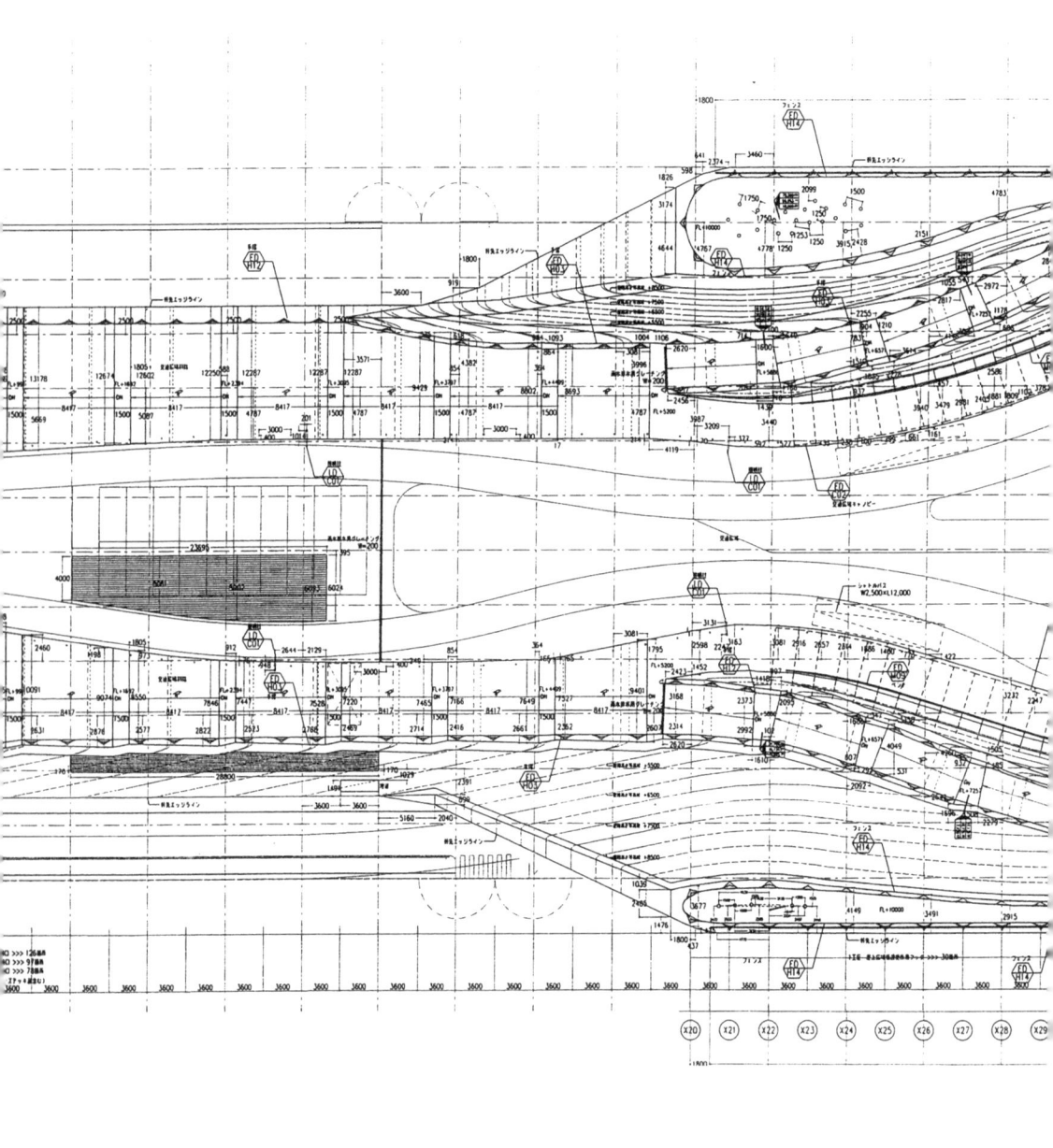

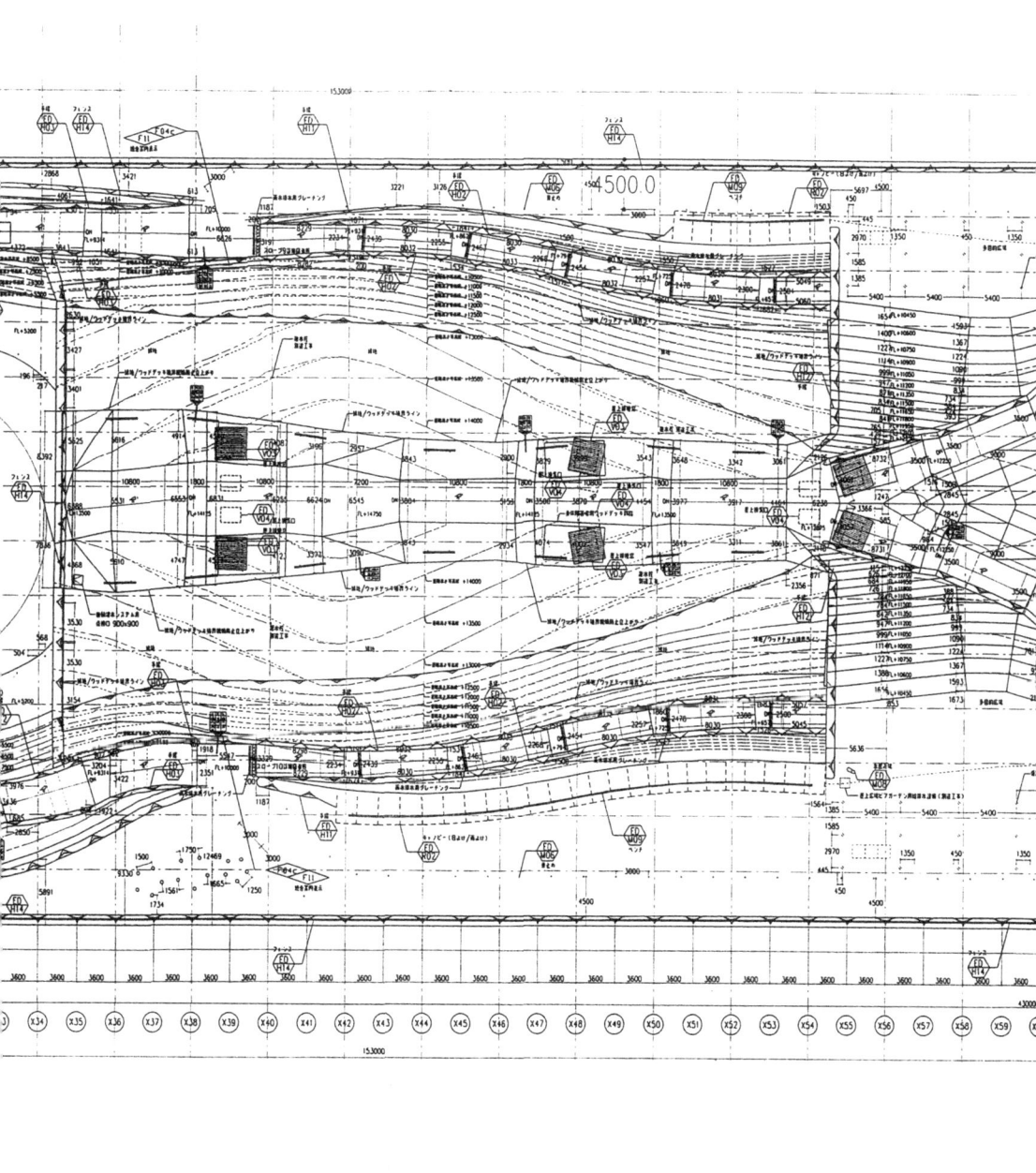

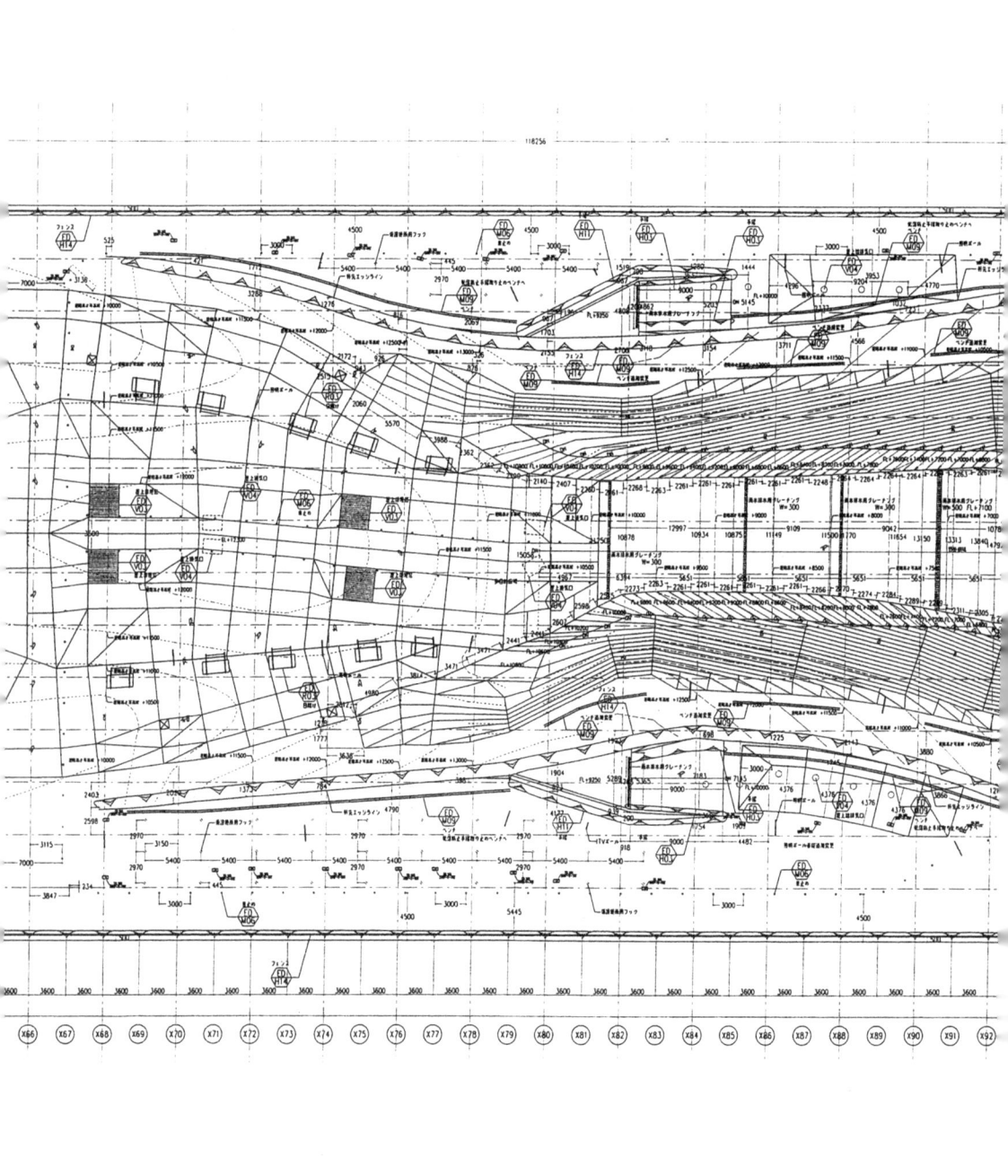

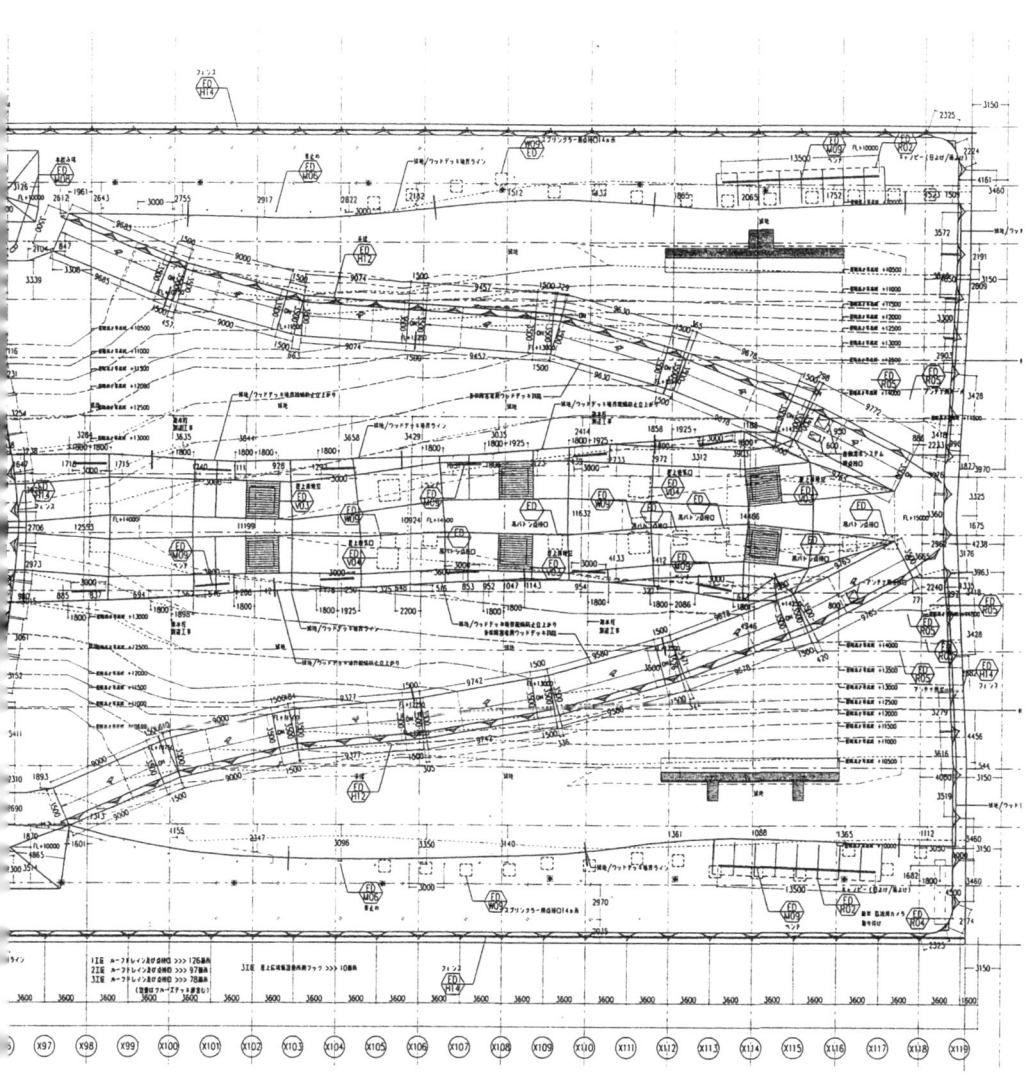

iteration, by repeatedly feeding a particular number into them, each time equations produced a new number. They became dynamic processes. Likewise in the new architecture. FOA did not want a definitive plan. They sought, instead, the iteration loop, the 'no-return' diagram which, when repeated, would produce the specific order of the project. They imagined their project as a microcosm of nature, as an organisation of matter engaged, like nature, in productive activity.

The small sketch of a 'self-similar structure' shows how direct the impact of these ideas actually was. It was rushed by FOA without the assistance of an engineer in the last 20 minutes before the dispatch of the competition documents to Japan. At this early stage the drawing was intended as a mere concept that imitated the structure of corrugated cardboard. But having started as a pure geometry, as a scaling set in the architects' eye, the structure became then gradually more 'oriented'. It came to describe a geometry of situation (as topology used to be known). For instance, gravity introduced a verticality by which surfaces, with the underside made in steel and the upper side clad in timber, became differentiated. Local characteristics further contributed singularities: ramps swerved to make specific connections, trusses were inserted within certain folds as reinforcement, corrugations were introduced in the tall glazing areas which could not support their own weight. As Giedion said of the Galerie des Machines, built in Paris in 1889, materials were not held in a closed system but floated in a field of shifting forces. The progressive connection between components gradually defined the structure. 'Construction became form'.

FOA sought out the moments when new configurations emerged. They experienced these developments not as the unwitting and sometimes unwelcome consequences of their plans, but as revelations which came from within the project as if from the depths of nature. One moment, in particular, was memorable. For several months FOA had struggled with the geometry of the project. The number of cross-sections had increased dramatically from the initial 32 in the competition entry to 248 corresponding to the basic 1.8m width of a fold. It soon became clear that increasing the level of definition of the sections was not going to work and that another approach was needed. The key was the invention of 'control lines', which described in three dimensions the undulations of the girders. The steel plates forming the floor and sides of the ramps, and the U-shaped stiffeners to which these are welded were rotated in plan as well as tilted in elevation to adhere to these lines. Increasingly the parallel cross-sections became irrelevant. They had been replaced with circles of different sizes rolled against the length of the control lines which defined the girders. Together they formed bubbles on the plans as if to suggest that the project, taking a subliminal cue from Prigogine's thermodynamics, had passed from a liquid state to one of ebullition. Nothing was straight any more. The project had reached an apparently chaotic state in which all that seemed to remain of the plan, of the closure referred to by Bergson, was a point in the future: the completion date.

There remained the search for an elegant solution for the lateral folds. A first attempt consisted in setting them perpendicular to the face of the girders. This worked well for the cantilevers of the boarding decks. The two plates of each fold had become symmetrical and identical, and the number of different parts was halved. In the median section, however, the folds were framed by two sets of girders which were never symmetrical at any point along their length. No rule emerged to help determine how and where, if fixed at a right angle to both girders, they were to meet in the middle. If, on the other hand, the folds were parallel to one another, they intersected the face of the girders in random ways, making each plate of each fold a special case and adding significantly to the cost of construction. It became clear that the configuration of the folds was not going to be deduced from that of the girders.

View of the main entrance under construction, *c* 2001
© Ramon Prat

It was instead necessary to proceed from the centre outwards, from a line equidistant to both sets of girders. This gently curving line became a 'spine' on either side of which the halves of each fold were strictly symmetrical. In this way the regularity of the folds was optimised, and the remaining irregularities were absorbed in the intermediate folds.

At this moment everything seemed to fall into place as if of its own accord. Neither the control lines nor the folds were set in reference to an orthogonal grid. They defined instead a 'topological grid', a kind of local grid specifically adapted to the forms of the project. Instead of referring each part to a particular band or square, the new grid established functions or vectors that connected the parts between themselves, thereby diminishing the amount of information required for the determination of the form. Construction became form, though in a reverse movement from that envisaged by Giedion. Architecture no longer needed to be shorn of its tradition and its monumentality in order to expose a well-engineered ossature. On the contrary, construction could now be reclaimed for architecture. It could become plastic and spatial in ways that had been until then unattainable in conventional building. If, according to Watanabe, the design of the structure had by convention been the responsibility of engineers, it was now led by the feeling of the architects. FOA's instinct, he suggests, are closer to those of Antonio Gaudí than of Félix Candela.

With hindsight, the sequence of events leading to a mixed solution (cantilevered perpendicular folds to the sides of the building and parallel folds in the central areas) presents a convincing rationale. But the alternative, in which all folds would have been made perpendicular to the girders, continues to nag, the more so because neither options, being equally unprecedented, were ruled out by the engineers. It may have produced a spatial order in which there would have been no systemic discontinuity between girders and folds, between lateral supports and transversal arches. In short, a complex

order in which the rises and swerves of the ramps would have fanned outwards to produce the kind of seamless efflorescence which characterises the vaults of gothic cathedrals, the fractal sets of Mandelbrot and Edward Lorenz's turbulent models of the weather.

 As built the spine is unnoticeable to the naked eye, especially in the car park, where the folds are for the most part horizontal and repeat with almost unbroken regularity. The space is neither scalebound nor scaling. The parts relate neither to the observer nor to each other: they have no scale. Owing to the extreme disproportion of the length to the height (350m to about 5m), the folds attain a fabulous size. They seem to be as short as they are deep, and to be almost close enough to be touched with the hand. The light coming from the sides barely reaches the middle folds which peak downwards for greater strength.

 Here is a crypt where knights and bishops might rest, its space necessarily compressed by the edifice above. Time which had dominated the conception of the project comes to a stand-still as if it were too weak, too insubstantial to resist the triumphant march of space. Here the ramps fall to the sides like recumbent figures, their bodies filled with concrete, twisting and turning in their sleep, casting long sheaves of steel which brush against the vaults as if in a dream. Nothing suggests that they were made to carry. At the far end of the building a ramp reaches inwards with a swerve, while another, lying as if head to toe, rises by not touching, stretches to the light and out of sight. In this moment the building confounds the predictions described in its plans. Seldom has architecture appeared more nonchalant, more like a vision, rising from the bed of its foundations not to carry a prescribed load but rather to trace by a feat of engineering the most graceful line from the car park to the roof, from dead matter to live speculation.

 'Architecture', FOA like to say, 'is the engineering of material life'. We saw the confusion which the idea of material

View of the terminal under construction, *c* 2001
© Ramon Prat

life, applied indiscriminately to nature and architecture, introduces in the conception of the plan. Another conflict stems from the desire to align architecture with engineering, with the practical application of scientific knowledge. Its source lies in an ambiguity at the heart of FOA's interest in science. If the architects chose to apply the new sciences of nature in the field of construction, it would not be unreasonable to expect that the turbulent effects described by the girders might be further deployed in the vaults. But the design of the vaults suggests (the curving spine notwithstanding) the application of another kind of knowledge: that of engineering. While the girders proliferate effects, all of them unique, the folds demonstrate on the contrary the necessity for repetition. It is as if, at the junction between girders and folds, a theory originating in the sciences of nature was forced into making the concessions required by building science. As if the spontaneous emergence of nature were thrown in disarray before the concerted efforts necessary to marshal a plan. As if the dunes of the roof were undermined by the repeated undertow effect of the folds.

Repetition, Ove Arup argued in the context of the Sydney Opera House, is the key to economical construction. Repetition, Zaera-Polo claimed on the basis of his experience in Yokohama, must exist in order to meet the deadline. All this, it may be. Still, doubters will see in the embrace of repetition a retraction by FOA of their early aims, a necessary coming to on the part of young and relatively inexperienced architects. They will mind the inconsistency. But great adventures in the building trades are seldom rational. They are, like the big cathedrals, capricious concretions of time.

In the last resort FOA's cathedral for a material age is not founded upon scientific knowledge (no adventure could be) but upon an act of faith. It stands on the belief that in the near future computers will provide the invisible reason of architecture. Computers conceal a whole eschatology of creation. They lead us into conceiving spaces which are no longer homogeneous, but are, like nature, continuous, coherent and differentiated. They open our eyes to the proliferation of nuances and they fine-tune our sensibility. There need be no more discontinuity between design and manufacture, between CAD and CAM, between information and matter – so long as manufacturers, Watanabe argues, stop fabricating by hand and adapt their methods to the computer. There need be no further discontinuity between conception and vision. The computer has instaured, in James Gleick's felicitous phrase, 'a new mathematics of the eye'.

Some will compare the combination of mathematical speculation and visionary imagination with the rhetoric of the baroque. Others will draw parallels between the minor asymmetries of its plans and the sensibility of the rococo. Still others will be reminded by the development of its structure of the spirit of the gothic. But comparisons with the art of the past merely gloss over FOA's achievement. More than a new aesthetic, the Yokohama project points to another relationship between fabrication and seeing, between the mathematics of pragmatic construction and its seldom ideal but often beautiful effects. While equations are indeed productive, vision remains central to the process for it is the eye which, *pace* Mandelbrot, integrates and discriminates.

*Originally published as 'The New Architecture'
in Casabella 708, February 2003*

Overleaf
View of the car park under construction, c 2001
© Ramon Prat

This article is based on interviews with Alejandro Zaera-Polo and Farshid Moussavi held in February 1995 and October 1995, and lectures given by them at the Architectural Association in London in June 1995, December 1999 and October 2001. Other interviews were held in April 2002 with Kunio Watanabe and Taro Yokoyama of the Structural Design Group, Tokyo, Toshio Kumakura of the Port Harbour Bureau, Yokohama, and Masao Ohtaki of the Yokohama City Assembly. With thanks to Kenichi Matsuzawa and Keisuke Tamura of FOA.

A Real Living Contact with the Things Themselves

Previous
Claude Lorrain, *Mercury Stealing the Herds of Admetus from Apollo*, 1660
© Trustees of the Wallace Collection, London

It was once common to distinguish between two kinds of landscape. One was wild and full of surprises, and lent itself especially well to painting. The other, lacking in such effects, made up for them in its fertility and abundance. Although not considered suited to painting, it did at least afford excellent places in which to live. Paolo Pino, for one, presented this view in a treatise on painting published in Venice in 1548;

> The northerners show a special gift for painting landscapes because they portray the scenery of their own homeland, which offers more suitable motifs by virtue of its wildness, while we Italians live in the garden of the world, which is more delightful to behold in reality than in painting.[1]

The distinction between beauty and delight, between art and experience, was hardly a natural one. Why should places that are more deserving of our admiration be assumed to be too remote and strange for human life? Or indeed why, conversely, should places where life is pleasant be deemed not beautiful enough to merit painting? In a few words Pino defined the situation preceding the gradual transformation in landscape painting over the next 250 years: the transformation from a cosmic landscape representing God's creation in its diversity and completeness to a personalised landscape in which the artist transcribes a deeply felt experience.

The pivotal figure in this development was Claude Lorrain, a man born in 1600 or 1604 in the relative wilderness of northeastern France (Lorraine, from which he takes his name). Having elected to live in Italy, first in Naples and then in Rome (where he died, in 1682), Claude was among the first to recognise the pictorial virtues of the garden of the world. In his painting *Mercury Stealing the Herds of Admetus from Apollo* the atmosphere is instantly affecting. The shade seems delightfully cool, and the air exceptionally calm. The mood, to which a few lines from Ovid offer a kind of decorative pretext, is one of distraction. We feel sympathy neither for Apollo's lovesickness for a nymph nor for the loss of the cows in his care. If we rush after the angel-like figure of Mercury, it is not in the hope that someone might retrieve the stolen herds, but that he may guide our eyes to the landscape's distant shore. Claude's figures exist in and for the landscape, a landscape that, in a diffuse sense, was a recollection of the artist's own experience.

After Claude, artists increasingly sought subjects not in history but in life. This did not make them realists in a modern sense. Rather, by the early nineteenth century they sought to constitute aspects of real experience into a living ideal. Biography became the new mythology. This evolution did not affect landscape painting alone. The discovery that actual experience rather than conventional learning could provide the material for creation transformed architecture as much as art. Out went the plaster casts of classical columns and statues. In came the air of the country and of modernity, the essential joys – in the words of Le Corbusier – of light, air and greenery.

Claude Lorrain, *View from Monte Mario*, c 1640
British Museum, Department of Prints and Drawings
© Trustees of the British Museum

In the process, some architects fell under the spell of Goethe's *Italian Journey.* Others were directly influenced by the landscape painters they met in Italy. They may still have consulted Charles Percier and Pierre François Leonard Fontaine's *Choix des plus célèbres maisons de plaisance de Rome et de ses environs, mesurées et dessinées* – a choice of the grandest and most classical villas – but they were no longer satisfied with ancient models, be they actual ruins or their reconstructions on paper. Instead they found inspiration in the Italian landscape, in its ordinary constructions and in the Italian way of life. If experience could be transcribed and to a degree re-enacted through painting, then it should also be possible to discover in it a *modus vivendi* – a lifestyle – and to devise an architectural programme to match. This belief sustained the invention, by John Nash, Karl Friedrich Schinkel and many lesser architects active in the mid-nineteenth century, of an architecture directly inspired by the Italian vernacular.

Whatever the value of this new Italianate craze (about which opinions vary), whatever the corruption of its forms, there can be no doubt as to the boldness of the enterprise.

Claude Lorrain, *Wooded Scene*, from the Tivoli book, 1640–45
©Teylers Museum, Haarlem

In time, aligning art with life, matching forms with functions, was no longer enough. Art was to be made directly from life. For the Dadaist poet Tristan Tzara, 'La pensée se fait dans la bouche' (thought happens in the mouth). For Alison and Peter Smithson, architecture was 'the direct result of a way of life'. For MVRDV, the formal art of architecture implodes in the concept of datascape. To this day, the proposition that architecture can be modelled upon lived experience or a particular lifestyle remains as current as it is elusive. It must contend with vulgarity because a lifestyle, owing to its generality, often lacks distinction. It must reckon, too, with imprecision, because lived experience, unlike the column orders of classicism or the functions of modernism, is resistant to reason and measure. When it does succeed, however, when art and architecture attain the lack of concern commonly associated with everyday life, the enhancement of delight handsomely compensates for the tarnishing of beauty.

Few landscape painters have inspired more affection than Claude. And few have achieved a comparable commercial success. Yet among the rare artists with whom one likes to be intimate to the point of calling them by their first name – Raphael, Leonardo, Michelangelo, etc – none has become more problematic than him. The critic John Ruskin despised his art, claiming that the classical ideal had blinded Claude to the truth and variety of nature. Indeed, for Ruskin, the feebleness of the artist's work resided precisely in the realism for which he had previously been praised. More recently, the critic Roger Fry echoed Ruskin's criticism in an essay that otherwise tries hard to be conciliatory, finding the artist guilty in turn of naivety, timidity, childishness, incapacity, superficiality and perfunctoriness as well as platitude. Claude is only redeemed *in extremis* by the concession of a moderating and genial charm. The painter was in effect proscribed by modernists together with the *naifs* and peasants, all of whom would have shared a comparable 'natural habit of mind'.

Yet Claude's drawings from nature are another matter altogether. Their essential quality is their spontaneity. Unlike the paintings, they are not landscapes that we can instinctively recognise as views, with intimations of distance and well-known sites. Even today, they often surprise in their apparent arbitrariness, as if the artist merely drew what lay in front of him as he sat for lunch or for a rest on the way to somewhere else. And while they reveal little about the *campagna*, their subjects are real places and actual moments.

Thus when Ruskin dislodged Claude from the official canon, when the paintings came to be seen as contrived and retrograde, the drawings offered a precious plank upon which Claude was able to reach to the modern side of art. He became a pioneer – if not of open-air painting, then of open-air drawing. And in this small regard he no longer prefigured the academic tradition of landscape painting, but the experimental art of Corot, Turner, Constable and Cézanne. So his drawings were no longer the lifelong source of subjects for painting that they had clearly been. Instead painters and critics sought to retrieve in the paintings beneath the triviality of Claude's ideal the true rendering of space and light, of a real atmosphere. They appreciated his paintings so long as they could recognise in them the spontaneity of his drawings. Choosing to disregard the fact that some were composed and laboured, and others less so, they associated the naivety of the paintings with the spontaneity of the drawings, as they might have primitivism with automatism in the work of the surrealists. Thus Claude was transformed into a noble savage *avant la lettre*, as if his acculturation were to give the precise measure of the authenticity of his art.

The central difficulty presented by Claude's work resides in the ambiguity between his naturalness – the word was used by Joachim von Sandrart, his biographer and friend – and naturalism, a category in which he has since been placed. Sandrart relates how Claude, having contemplated either

Claude Lorrain, *The Grotto of Neptune in Tivoli*, c 1640 © Musée du Louvre

sunrise or sunset, immediately prepared his colours before returning home. Back in the studio, he applied them to the work he had in mind 'with much greater naturalness than anyone had ever done'.² The critic Lawrence Gowing first emphasised the oddity of this practice, which, he claimed, had no precedent. This literalness, Gowing suggests, was the source of Claude's naturalness. It enabled him to keep his eye firmly on a reality that he apprehended originally and directly. The scenes in his paintings may have been ideal and imaginary but the space and the light in them were real.

Given this convergence between painting and experience, it is surprising that Claude painted no more than ten topographical views. Only in his drawings, in those made directly from the subject, do we find a consistent avoidance of the baroque conventions that separated the foreground shown as a proscenium from the actual view shown as a stage. His drawings of the Campo Vaccino, for example, are not records of its archaeology (as for instance Maarten van Heemskerck's had been). They do not show the ruins that had been popular subjects with Cornelis van Poelenburgh and Bartholomeus Breenbergh, Claude's immediate forerunners, but its space. When Claude sketches at the Villa Madama near Rome he shows not the villa but the trees and the distant view of the Tiber. Yet even his drawings, for all their naturalness, are no less removed than his paintings from what we now understand as realism. Their hallmark lies not in resemblance but in Claude's saturation of his observations with personal feeling – a quality that is far more responsible for the ideal character of his work than any literary or mythological association.

Among the sites Claude visited Tivoli was special. To this small town in the foothills of the Apennines, Claude, Nicholas Poussin, Peter Van Lear and Sandrart (who mentions the journey) rode together to paint or draw from nature. In sheer concentration of talent and in symbolic significance, the episode would be hard to match – as if Picasso, Braque and Derain had set out together for L'Estaque to invent cubism. Already in

Claude Lorrain, *View of Tivoli*, 1640 Courtesy J Paul Getty Museum Open Content Programme

the 1620s, Filippo Napoletano and Van Poelenbergh had painted Tivoli's smaller waterfalls or *cascatelle* seeping out of the rock and pouring into the Anio. Unusually for the times, they and Breenbergh also described in great detail the ordinary buildings massed at the top of the hill.

Yet it was Claude who offered the clearest sign of the growing importance of Tivoli. His interest in the place is at its most visible in his drawings, above all in the 'Tivoli book' made between 1639 and 1641. The set of drawings include neither Hadrian's Villa, which was already known at the time, nor the gardens of the Villa d'Este, which guidebooks then commended in enthusiastic terms. Rather, at Tivoli the artist preferred to draw nature from observation. Claude especially enjoyed the banks of the Anio above the falls, where the riverbed is shallow and wide, and where the mood is particularly still. Nothing in these beautiful drawings indicates the presence of the great cascade only a short distance away before the arching bridge – nothing except the Temple of Sibyl, as if suspended above the gorge with its great doorway facing the falls.

Established first by religion, the pairing of temple with falls was confirmed by tourism. Already in Braun & Hogenberg's survey of world cities, *Civitates Orbis Terrarum,* Tivoli is included, surprisingly given its small size. In the accompanying engraving of 1578 it is celebrated not for its wealth or its culture but for its nature, to which the Temple of Sibyl (clearly captioned together with the falls) lends, by its association with the classical past, an intellectual and moral authority. The scheme adopted by Claude in his *View of the Campagna from Tivoli,* now in the Queen's Collection (as distinct from other versions in the British Museum), is broadly similar. In Claude's *View,* however, the flat *campagna* is more prominent on the horizon and the town barely stands within the frame. The Temple of Sibyl, hardly more than 50m to the left, is not included perhaps because it features prominently on the pendant with which this painting formed a pair. Claude also took striking liberties with his subject. The water of the Anio, for instance, runs deep in the floor of the valley and cannot be seen from where the artist stood, and the water mill in the foreground seems expressly made to inspire Ruskin's contempt. However, in what is one of the earliest topographical views of a natural landscape, Claude's desire for accuracy is manifest notably in the convent of San Antonio to the right, still in existence today, and in the forms of the hills – a preparatory squared-up drawing testifies to it.

View of the Campagna from Tivoli has since been rehearsed by dozens if not hundreds of artists, both famous and anonymous, in drawings, paintings, prints, even poems. Tivoli became the Mecca of landscape painters, who came seeking revelations about their art. It became the model for gardeners and planners who sought to replicate it in wildly different countries and climates. By the mid-eighteenth century, its landscape was the most famous in the whole of Europe. Claude, Marcel Roethlisberger claimed, invented the lasting idea of the *campagna*. In reality, he did far more than this: he created the first generic landscape. Eventually it came to signify the entire land of Italy, and it set the standard for the appreciation of all landscapes.

Only after taking the measure of the passion for landscapes, for the hills of Tivoli and the Bay of Naples, does it become possible to understand the desire, some 200 years after Claude, to recreate them by architectural means. But how could one ensure that such recreation would at least equal the original experience? What means could guarantee the transcription of experience except Goethe's capacity for sensitive perception and for creating value? What skill except Schinkel's versatility could dissolve rational method and allow experience to shine forth unadulterated? Why did Schinkel succeed so famously in his design for a gardener's house in Potsdam, while Nash failed so miserably in his own version of an Italianate villa at Cronkhill? Why does the one convey an

Claude Lorrain, *View of the Campagna from Tivoli*, 1645 British Museum, Department of Prints and Drawings © Trustees of the British Museum

appreciation of the Italian way of life, while the other gestures in vain under the burden of picturesque conventions?

The villa at Cronkhill, which John Nash completed in Shropshire in 1802, participates in 'that mixed style' – as it was unappealingly but accurately named by Richard Payne Knight, a friend of Nash's, as well as the owner of no less than 273 drawings attributed to Claude – 'which characterises the buildings of Claude and the Poussins'. Knight further describes the style as 'taken from models which were built piecemeal during many successive ages; or by several different nations, it is distinguished by no particular manner of execution, or class of ornaments; but admits of all promiscuously, from a plain wall or buttress, of the roughest masonry, to the most highly wrought Corinthian capital'.[3]

Mixed, piecemeal, promiscuous: these terms are hardly the kind to enhance the reputation of Claude, and Cronkhill, canonised by Nikolaus Pevsner and others after him as the first building in the Italianate style, is no masterpiece. From afar its silhouette, powdered and well-dressed according to Georgian propriety, is not without grace. Close up, however, much of it transpires to be a cheap makeover at pains to conceal a weak design. The square tower, which offsets from a distance the round one, recedes so far into the main body of the house as to leave the last isolated and disproportioned. It is flanked on one side by a single-storey arcade and on the other by the entrance porch, both of which are crowned by an improbably rich balustrade. To the left, the brick dressing of the service wing tries but fails to hide the timber-framed gable of a seventeenth-century farmhouse. To the right, the white paint breaks off behind the porch, where every manner of brick extensions and lean-tos set about their appointed task.

Much has been made of Nash's debt to Claude in the composition of this mixture. There are those who have even found in Claude's *Pastoral Landscape*, now in the Birmingham City Art Gallery, Nash's immediate source for Cronkhill. Like Nash, Claude combined a round tower with a square one in a structure that might be a farmhouse or a monastic building. But all things that are Italian in the painting – the unpainted brickwork, the square windows, the shallow eaves – are contradicted at Cronkhill. Nash's vision of Italy was a picturesque fantasy summarily executed with Georgian details, white paint being employed as a substitute for sunshine, and deep eaves as a substitute for shade. Most of the effort went into making the building seem what it was not. Nash struggled to restore a vague two-dimensional image to a three-dimensional reality. In the process everything that might conceivably be Italian or even Claudian was undermined by pictorial values.

What held true for the picturesque – that the reality of nature was a picture – was fundamentally alien to Claude, for whom (as his biographers have testified) the reality of a picture *was* nature. Between the one and the other the divide is no less essential than that which separates the modern from the postmodern. In this, if nothing else, Claude remains closer to Ruskin, his chief detractor, than he was to the picturesque theorists who had admired him most, or to Nash, who crucially never went to Italy.

To understand the higher value ascribed to nature and to life one must look not only at the method but also at the motivations that led artists and architects to discard the authority of classical forms and pay tribute instead to ordinary vernacular settings. For example, the Welsh painter Thomas Jones came to Italy in 1776, but his originality came into its own only following his move to Naples, in 1782. In the course of this year (his last in Italy) he made a dozen works that, even if on a minute scale, suggest that the repertory of landscape painting had been revalued and transformed since the age of Claude. Gowing even sees greatness in this tiny oeuvre, its impact gathering force as the works became smaller and their subject more ordinary. Thus *A Wall in Naples* (only 16cm across) is described by him as one of the great microcosms of painting. The grubby and stained expanse of wall, the window punched more or less in the middle, the slit of blue sky jammed between the parapet of the wall and the edge of the canvas: together these amount to no particular subject 'except just that'.

But what was it that Jones painted? And what was it a microcosm of? How could a painter who was admittedly not a theoretician but certainly not a *naif*, and who was educated with Richard Wilson, one of the best landscape artists of the time – and, moreover, a friend of some of the best and the better-connected artists of his generation (including John Robert Cozens and Giovanni Battista Lusieri) – come to value his

Overleaf
Thomas Jones,
Rooftops in Naples, 1782
© Ashmolean Museum,
University of Oxford
/ Bridgeman Images

studies so much more than his finished works? How are we, in particular, to understand the following entry in his journal, dated 17 May 1780?

> I began a *View of my Kitchen* on a 4 palm Cloth, this being the first attempt at Still Life. The Subject was prosecuted and finished *con Amore* – when tired of other things, i painted on my *Kitchen Scene* by way of Relaxation & Amusement, and I still keep this picture by me as a pleasant remembrance of Times past.[4]

What could have prompted an artist versed in Claude and Dughet to paint, of all things, his kitchen, except the pleasure of living? Did Jones not express a feeling shared by Goethe – but for an interval of four years the two could have met – writing that while in Rome he had been glad to study, while in Naples he wanted only to live. More than Paestum, Pompeii and Herculaneum, more than the fashionable Court of Naples, it was the enjoyment of the countryside that, having first diverted the affections of the likes of Jones from Tivoli to the Alban Hills, enticed travellers from Rome to Naples. The same enjoyment encouraged them further south across the Strait of Messina. Once in Sicily, even the ruins of Girgenti – where, Goethe wrote, 'there seemed nothing here for a draughtsman to do' – could not compete with the view from Palermo or, better still, from a terrace at Taormina, 'looking over this beautiful seashore, seeing roses and hearing nightingales which, we are told, sing for six months without stopping'.

Even when it was as plain as a wall, no subject remained indifferent or neutral. Indeed, ordinariness – for instance, when Jones painted the view from *his* window or the scene of *his* kitchen – bordered on insignificance and concentrates one's attention on the artist's intimacy. Landscape painting remained what it had been in the seventeenth century: a way of penetrating nature and of recording the sensations it inspired.

Goethe believed that Claude, Salvator Rosa and Poussin had sought a *true* vision of the relationship between nature and art, to which he added: 'I shall never rest until I know that all my ideas are derived, not from hearsay or tradition, but from my real living contact with the things themselves' (this last expression rendered more expansive in W H Auden's classic translation).⁵ How more pressing than for Claude this 'real living contact' had become for Jones and his contemporaries. In its quest, artists left their studios and invented open-air painting, for which no means were to be proscribed. Jones often undertook his drawings while in transit (he referred to those executed on his way to Naples as 'flying sketches'). Far from impeding contact, the rapidity with which they were made testified to their authenticity, to the kind of virtue ascribed today to *cinéma vérité* and the photography of a Henri Cartier-Bresson or a Brassaï. 'The things themselves' were judged to be of far superior value than their image, which constituted merely their souvenir.

Representing the fulfilment of a long and gradual development, no construction was too humble, no prospect too familiar or ordinary, no angle on a ruin too insignificant. Even the *lazzaroni*, who, Goethe tells us, 'work not merely to live but to enjoy themselves' and led the careless life of a fool's paradise, were co-opted to participate in the spectacle of nature. There is probably no other city in the world except Naples where the poor are thought to offer a pleasing sight, and where a visit to the Spanish quarter, one of the poorest in the city, continues to be worth a detour. The 'Magick Land' that Jones recognised in Italy, constituted by the late eighteenth century a realm even more magical than the Roman *campagna* had been for Claude. For the first time, perhaps, the ideal was thought to reside neither in religion nor in art but in life itself.

Schinkel first visited Italy in 1803, one year after Nash completed the villa at Cronkhill. During his journey, Schinkel's curiosity was aroused by objects far removed from the classical

Overleaf
Jacob Philipp Hackert,
Veduta di Capri con il Monte Solaro, 1792
© Reggia di Casserta, Naples

architecture with which his name continues to be associated. He sketched the cathedrals of Siena and Milan, *cinquecento* brick buildings in Ferrara and Bologna, and, perhaps not surprisingly for someone who was also a painter, landscapes. In a letter to his master, the architect David Gilly, he wrote that 'when it comes to antiquity, it offers nothing new to an architect, because one is from childhood familiar with it'. He, too, wanted to see through the conventions of his time and to apprehend 'the things themselves'.

In Schinkel's own *Reisen nach Italien*, one of the few enthusiastic entries concerns his visit to Capri. After describing the ascent of the stairs that separate the harbour of Capri from the village of Anacapri, he expresses his surprise at finding himself on a beautiful and fertile plateau high above the sea. Here, he continues, 'stand the most lovely houses, which surpass every vernacular construction I have ever seen in terms of form and cleanliness. Only a kitchen and a few rooms for sleeping. The rest of the spaces are outdoors,

Karl Friedrich Schinkel, *Farmhouse at Anacapri*, 1804
© Kupferstichkabinett, Staatliche Museen zu Berlin

set under pergolas laden with vines. For practical reasons the little houses are painted white every year. The people in this wine-growing country are really the simplest in Europe. They have neither judges nor soldiers because everyone lives in the greatest harmony... Here lives a people who are completely uncorrupted. There are only a few families, unmixed with outsiders... I shall never forget my stay among them.'[6]

Not even Le Corbusier could have dreamed a more perfect utopia. What could antiquity have contributed to this plateau where custom and dwelling, vegetation and climate, were gathered as if in a stoup, contained to act as a foil for creation? Such a landscape transcended the unity of vision advocated by the picturesque and created a unity that embraced the totality of experience.

The places that painters chose to represent were no longer the conventional prospects framed by *repoussoirs* of the baroque landscape nor the vast panoramas affected by the romantics. They were topographies such as the island of Capri or, at a more intimate scale, the interiors of ordinary streets and houses where one might conceivably live. Between 1814 and 1816, the Danish artist Christoffer Wilhelm Eckersberg painted a courtyard in Rome. It seems natural to assume that it was related to a place the artist had personally experienced (we know that his lodgings were in the vicinity). The format of the painting (30cm square) is much the same as that favoured by Jones, although it could hardly be more unlike the latter's 'flying sketches'. But its emotive quality is no longer veiled by the semblance of painting 'just that'. Every aspect of this painting has been carefully premeditated. Everything about it is small, intimate and man-made. Everything has been carefully placed. The scene is so still as to seem airless, were it not for the patch of sky (paler and smaller than in Jones's *Wall in Naples)* that ventilates an intensely private world. No one is present to animate the stage. Even though every window is open, the only presence is our own.

Christoffer Wilhelm Eckersberg, *Roman Courtyard*, 1813–16 Ribe Kunstmuseum / Bridgeman Images

Although we do not know the whereabouts of this courtyard, the sense of location is so overwhelming as to make us think that a real courtyard must exist. The sense of time in the painting is no less categorical, shadows falling upon the walls as if on a sundial. It could not be much earlier than noon or much later than two. A well and a fountain stand at the centre of the canvas. Water is the discreet subject of the painting, and it is made all the more subtle when it is realised that the spout is, for the time being, dry. In the furthest corner of the space, plant pots mark the edge of the terrace, which provides a symbolic horizon. The picture as a whole presents itself as a microcosm of the Italian landscape, as a man-made analogue to the topography of Tivoli. The generic pair of waterfall and temple has been replaced by another, consisting of fountain and pergola, while the easel that the eighteenth-century painter placed before it has become a window. Whatever survives of the dramatic, of the sublime and of the historical has been absorbed in ordinary life to make the contact with things more vivid and real.

Jones and Eckersberg were not alone in finding even in the poorest houses in Italy a compelling beauty. In his *Eléments de perspective pratique* of 1800, Pierre-Henri de Valenciennes recommended vernacular constructions as worthwhile subjects for composition. By the early nineteenth century, artists were painting the ordinary fabric of Rome 'as Cézanne did his apples'.[7] In the park of the fashionable Villa Borghese, specifically recommended by de Valenciennes for practice, artists drew neither the trees (as Claude had done repeatedly at the Villa Madama) nor the villa itself. One after the other they chose instead, in a gesture so often repeated as to seem ritualised, to represent the humblest sight in the grounds. Close to the Porta del Pincio, built right against the wall of the park, there existed a house known alternatively as the Porter's Lodge, Casino del Pineto (lofty pines grew in its vicinity), Casa Cenci (after a noble family in sixteenth-century Rome),

Previous
Christoffer Wilhelm Eckersberg,
La fontana dell'Acqua Acetosa, 1814
© National Gallery of Denmark

and, as recorded on an engraving dated 1623, *Casetta per il Giardiniero* – little house for the gardener.

If Tivoli had been a shorthand for the garden of the world, the gardener's house was now the essential place from which to lavish care upon it. Friedrich Weinbrenner, an architect from Karlsruhe, drew this last structure in the mid-1790s. During his first visit to Rome, Schinkel made a sketch of it, which David Gilly reproduced soon afterwards on the title page of a treatise published in 1805. Pierre Clochar included an accurate view of it in his *Palais, maisons et vues d'Italie* of 1809. Furthermore, the following artists drew or painted it: J M Rohden in 1798, Eckersberg between 1813 and 1816 (his canvas now lost), Scheffer von Leonhardshoff in 1815, Johan Christian Dahl in 1821, J Schirmer in 1839–40, Jørgen Roed in 1840, Georg Busse in 1841 and Heinrich Buntzen in 1843, as well as M C Rørbye, Frederik Rohde and Bertel Thorvaldsen.[8]

Give or take five degrees, the angle of view remained the same throughout the 50-year period, and the various paintings present a by and large consistent description of the place. Beyond a stretch of bare ground, immediately behind a ramp used for loading carts (as Weinbrenner's sketch indicates), a blind brick volume carries a first-floor loggia high enough to afford views above the wall of the park. Plant pots stand on the parapet. Two massive pillars at the corners of the loggia support a hipped roof for shade. Behind, a sheer tower rises to about twice the loggia's height. Openings are few, details are rare and the ancient brickwork is drawn with immense care – seldom could the texture of buildings have meant so much, and so much more than architectural details. A bread oven stands in a recess to the left. In two or three views, a door and windows are visible along the side of the house to the right.

In the coupling of loggia and tower, the gardener's house captured in a single image the simplicity and the nobility of life in Italy. There is about it, in the exceptional height of the pines, in the solitude of the alley and in the association with the powerful name of the Borghese, the kind of atmosphere that shrouds such fantastical constructions as Claude's *Enchanted Castle*. The image is precise and sparse: at once an evocative monument and a functional vessel with the signature umbrella pines frothing in its wake. Upon it could be pegged every fantasy of Italy. Many believed, for instance, that it was Raphael's studio, and the replica that Buntzen made of his earlier painting even received the fanciful but desirable title *Raphael's Studio in Tivoli Near Rome*. The truth of history and geography was clearly not on a level with the careless subjectivity attending to the things we love.

The affection for Italy could easily turn into an affectation for the Italianate. In the translation by artists and aristocrats of peasant life into villas and chalets, the authenticity of the passion was easily lost in the banality of its consumption. A good example of this can be found at Clisson, a small town in the French province of Vendée, where the sculptor Lemot wished to recreate all at once the conviviality of the artistic community in Rome, the architecture of the gardener's house at the Villa Borghese and the landscape of Tivoli.

In 1805 Lemot bought a large piece of land in a meander of the River Sèvre to create a place for landscape painters to meet and work. Around the villa, which he planned for his retirement, follies were to be scattered throughout the park, including a replica of the Temple of Sibyl perched on a craggy escarpment – here of granite rather than limestone. Though scaled down as well as simplified (no expensive fluting or Corinthian capitals, just a simple Doric order), the project's effect is not without charm and would have been more realistic had Lemot's plan for a cascade fed by the drainage water from the surrounding fields been realised. The sculptor further purchased the considerable ruin of the castle of Clisson, across the Sèvre and within sight of his future villa. He did so not merely to honour, like the romantics, the glory of medieval France, but because it evoked – at least it did to one

Overleaf
Johan Christian Dahl, *Villa Borghese*, 1821
Photograph KODE / Dag Fosse
© KODE-Art Museums and Composer Homes

of his friends, the artist Pierre Cacault – the Colosseum and the still-greater glory of ancient Rome.

Close to the main entrance of his estate, adjoining the boundary wall, Lemot built his own version of the gardener's house at the Villa Borghese for the accommodation of a guardian and, until the completion of the villa, himself. Like its Roman equivalent, a first-floor loggia flanks the main facade. But here the similarities end. The tower (now serving as a dovecote) was plucked from the main body of the model and moved to the side, where it marks the corner of a small, seemingly fortified courtyard. As a consequence, the scale and the enigmatic character of the original were lost. Arcades were opened beneath the loggia to form a porch, thus making a nonsense of the crenellations of the courtyard wall. Unlike its more sturdy precedent, much here is skin-deep or, in the case of the plan, room-deep – the accommodation being stretched along the perimeter wall of the courtyard, which it seems at pains to justify.

The gardener's house at Clisson comes a close second to Cronkhill in the genealogy of poor examples of the Italianate style. It is on a level with the many publications that, from the beginning of the nineteenth century, featured the humbler class of Italian buildings. Charles Parker, for instance, included in his *Villa Rustica* of 1848 the elevations of the gardener's house in the Villa Borghese in which the gain in precision matches the loss in poetry. However, when it came to design proper, the author thought it wise to embroider upon the underlying scheme. Where plain walls had sufficed, surfaces were now deadened with frames and panels. Where steps once led to a landing *inside* the porch, they now projected outwards with balustrades and piers. The loggia was reduced in size and deprived of its pillars. To compensate for the loss, the face of this mere balcony was ennobled with an escutcheon. Nothing was lacking except, perhaps, the railway tracks and the name of the station.

Parker believed that the Italian genre was best suited to the design of houses. The exteriors could be made to correspond with real locations in Italy (the house design mentioned above was found, according to the author, in the vicinity of Florence), and the actual plans could be adapted to the needs of the British. In a similar vein, J C Loudon claimed in 1833 that the Italian genre, owing to its inexpensive details, suited 'a people of average condition, a democracy'. Above all, it suited landlords, mortgage lenders and builders, for whom 'the only incentives to quality … were either in the nature of safeguard or rapid marketability'.[9] However well suited to the accommodation of the middle classes, the Italian genre was progressively diluted with the coming and passing of other fashions. Its forms became sufficiently ambiguous for John Summerson to call them nondescript and to perceive in them the 'absence of creation [which] is at once the horror and the fascination of the suburb'.[10] Nothing could be further from the Italy visited by Goethe, Jones and Eckersberg. The real living contact with things that Goethe so ardently desired had been lost before another kind of contact: with the expanding middle classes aspiring to a cultivated and vaguely bohemian lifestyle.

By his talent and his social position, Schinkel was best able to resist the corruption of the Italian ideal. He was deeply moved by his visit to Anacapri. He recalled the motif of its vernacular dwellings in a small drawing on a sheet for the *Architektonisches Lehrbuch*, a treatise he never completed. On the rest of the sheet he combined its basic elements – plain walls, arcades, pergolas and vaults – for the design of a far grander villa in Capri. In one sketch the villa is shown standing on the ledge of a cliff with trees reaching towards a distant mountain behind it and a valley winding down before it to the sea. Clearly the situation owes as much to Claude as it does to its geographical location.

On 30 May 1804 Schinkel made another visit that was to have more tangible repercussions. We know from his diary

Karl Friedrich Schinkel, sketch designs for a country house near Syracuse, 1804 © Kupferstichkabinett, Staatliche Museen zu Berlin

that on that day he visited the villa of an Englishman near Syracuse, that the villa was situated in a ravishing site on the flank of a hill, that it was graced by a grotto and a pool, and that the ruins of an episcopal castle stood above it. The place was recently identified as the Villa di Tremilia, built on the flank of Monte Epipoli some 3km to the northwest of the Sicilian city. In addition to the features described in the diary, Schinkel would have found on the lower levels a large enclosure, a house and a store (accommodated in the remains of a Byzantine church), a hermitage, a little church and a few other ancillary buildings.[11]

Most of these features are repeated, possibly from memory, in a design for a country house near Syracuse, made by the architect while he was still in Italy, and which he planned to include in the *Lehrbuch*. On a sheet of wonderfully versatile sketches, Schinkel placed the grotto at the centre of his composition and confirmed its importance by listing it first in the index. Now designated as a bathing place, the little building includes a niche cut into the mountain rock, and it faces the garden of the house on the other side. A pergola connects it to a cave (presumably referring to the pool mentioned in the architect's diary). In the finished design the pivotal role ascribed to the bathing place is further clarified. The pool has become a square basin open to the sky, and communicates directly with the cave. Moreover, it is now aligned with the axis of the main house which rises above it, where the old episcopal palace would have been.

In the sketch design, next to the grotto to the south, Schinkel proposed a 'milk salon', a structure that had become a fashionable adjunct to country houses during the eighteenth century. From here a covered platform leads to a compact two-storey dwelling block for the servants. Two flights of stairs connect this platform to the main courtyard of the farm below. Along the opposite side of the servants' quarters, a separate courtyard accommodates the animals and faces

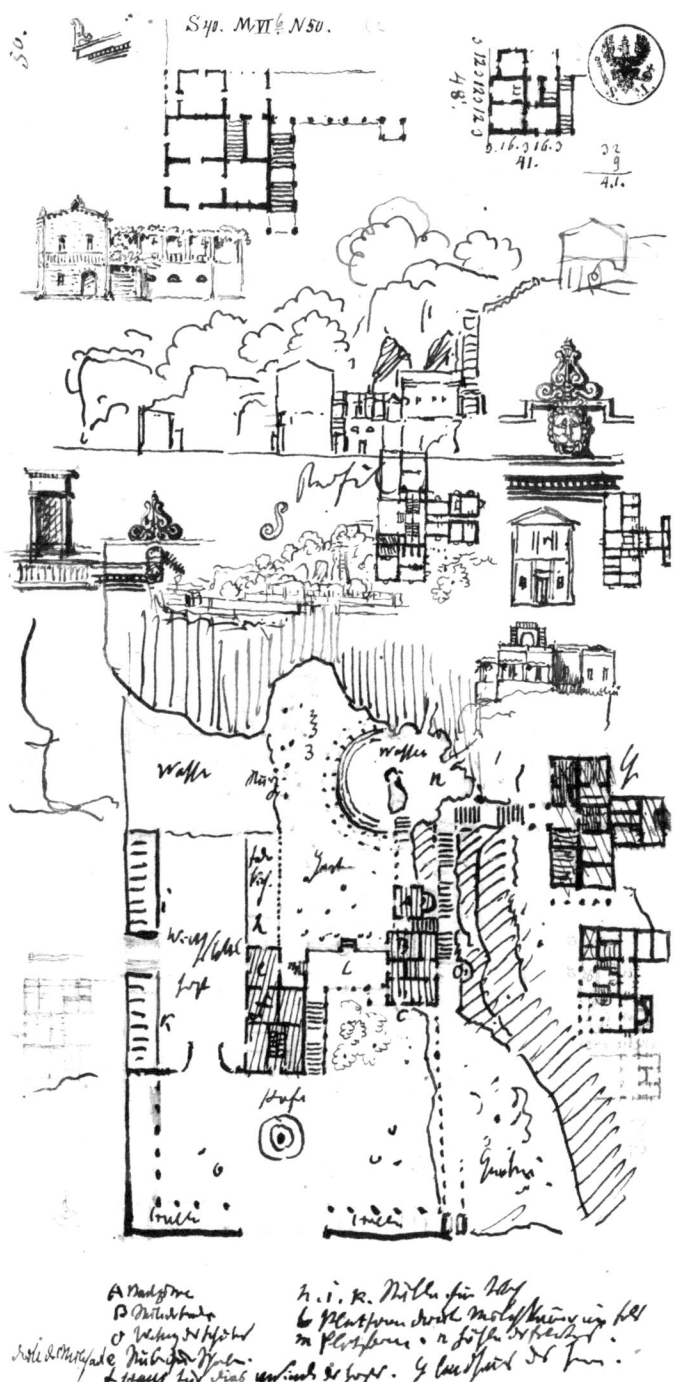

towards the plain. The site plan and section (rather than the many sketch plans for the villa) dominate the sheet. They were clearly drawn first and indicate, like Schinkel's carefully rendered Claudian perspective, that the relation of the buildings to the landscape was uppermost in the architect's mind. The designs for the bathing place, the servants' house and the villa are of little interest in themselves. They are accessory to the site and make no attempt to offer, as Summerson said of Cronkhill, a comment on the landscape in which they stand. Rather, they compose with it, they organise and divide it, creating a complex structure within which the mind is at ease to wander.

The culmination of this work is the gardener's house Schinkel built in Postdam between 1829 and 1836. In all essentials its plan replicates one for the country house near Syracuse, *but in mirror image.* The grotto/bathing place has become a Pompeian atrium, but the basic configuration of a square room terminated by a niche is retained. The same is true of its position in respect to the garden, and the proximity of the house to the palace of Sanssouci may have put the architect in mind of the old episcopal castle. An arcade rather than a pergola runs in front of the atrium, and leads not to a cave but to the water of the Schafgraben. The dairy is where one expects it, almost adjoining the Pompeian atrium, and faces the upper floor of the gardener's house across a terrace that offers views of the garden. On the far side of the garden, the Schafgraben is shaped, as on the plan of the finished project for Syracuse, into a small canal and flows into the freely formed reservoirs, lake or pool. The plan of the gardener's house proper consists of two rooms in one direction and three in the other, like the servants' house near Syracuse. A staircase, also protected by a pergola, reaches from the terrace to the entrance court (now much reduced in size but of superior spatial subtlety).

Schinkel also made a few notable changes. Between the house and the lake he added a salon in the form of a Greek temple adapted from James Stuart and Nicholas Revett's *Antiquities of Athens*. Where there used to be a yard for farm animals, a memorial garden to the parents of Crown Prince Friedrich was created. Sensibly the animals were removed to a vine-covered courtyard adjacent to the dairy farm. Most conspicuously, Schinkel downgraded architectural details from the Grecian to the Italian, perhaps playing on the ambiguity of the *Landhaus* designation (meaning either country house or farmhouse) and no doubt gladly responding to the affection in which Italian vernacular constructions were then held in Potsdam and elsewhere. He also added a high tower, which helps secure the unity of the composition, in effect doing *en plein* what the landscape at Syracuse did *en creux*.

On the even land of Potsdam, the rugged topography of the villa near Syracuse is preserved as if in model form in the many changes in levels that are responsible for so much of the charm of the house. Stairs lead into the sitting area adjoining the forecourt. More stairs lead to the main floor of the house. Still more stairs lead to the milk salon and the terrace, from which, according to Schinkel's entry in the *Sammlung*, a pleasant view over the whole site can be enjoyed. The topography of the villa is further preserved in the informality of the plan, the many parts of the house being at first scattered as if to adapt to imaginary variations in level, before being reassembled by chance alignments and offhand symmetries.

In a literal sense the experience of the Syracusan landscape survives in the design of the gardener's house, and the effect is liberating. Unlike the architecture models canonised in the classical tradition, landscapes cannot be learnt. Ever since Claude, the best have been experienced as revelations, and they have endured in sketches and studies – that is, in the impression they first made. By the turn of the eighteenth century, landscapes like the valley of Tivoli and the Bay of Naples were the principal means through which the munificence of Italy and its way of life were recognised. In the new

Overleaf
Karl Friedrich Schinkel, perspective and plan of the Potsdam gardener's house, 1834
© Kupferstichkabinett, Staatliche Museen zu Berlin

scheme of things architecture merely provided the details in a vast topography. Its form and its style continued to matter only insofar as buildings were intermediaries (like the Temple of Sibyl had been in Tivoli) in the accession to the landscape and to a particular mode of existence.

At Potsdam–Syracuse Schinkel did not wish to design a place that would provoke our admiration and stimulate our intellectual curiosity, but one in which we might be inspired to live. Certainly, he was alert to the visual appeal of buildings – anything less would be surprising from an architect who was also a painter. Did he not declare in the *Sammlung* that he had sought to create with the gardener's house a picturesque setting that offered beautiful views? Yet it is the secret resting places, the snugness of the rooms, the open spaces for the enjoyment of country life that he chose to emphasise in the text. Indeed, each place encourages one to pause and take a seat – no less than the Roman *campagna* did for Claude while on his way to Tivoli, the Alban Hills or Frascati. Each place demands not a single visit but the daily familiarity that alone can reveal the underlying reason of the design.

Schinkel imagined the constant growth and enrichment of the building, and there were indeed as many phases in the seven-year period of construction as there are parts in the design. In this way, 'the constant joy of producing and creating can be maintained'. In a setting that aspired to equal the garden of the world, building was akin to gardening. What better tool for the metamorphosis of experience into design than the delicate mobility of mind displayed by Schinkel in his sketches for a villa near Syracuse? What better demonstration of fertility than the unexpected back-to-front reversal of its plan in the gardener's house? A gardener learns in contact with the plants themselves and knows no greater purpose than life. Schinkel, the architect-gardener, condemned 'the error of pure arbitrary abstractions'. Theory, he felt, appeals to the aspects of trivial function and construction, and cannot

Claude Lorrain, *A Group of Trees*, c 1640–45 British Museum, Department of Prints and Drawings © Trustees of the British Museum

answer to the wealth of experience. It kills in the bud the freedom and the poetry without which there can be no architecture worthy of the name.

Architecture had long been discussed in the terms of iconography, as an art that represents certain ideas or images. It could now be conceived in the terms of biography, as an art that seeks to replicate and enrich actual experience. Like the landscape painters who became increasingly committed to open-air painting, architects had in the early nineteenth century the intuition of an open-air architecture: an architecture grown not from the models offered by its own intellectual and stylistic tradition but, to repeat the expression that Claude prompted in Goethe, from the real living contact with the things themselves. The widespread devotion to the landscape of Italy made it possible and legitimate to circumvent centuries of learning and to draw directly from the living spring of the senses.

It became possible and legitimate to conceive of architecture as a sum of imaginative perceptions, as a functionalism of a kind in which experience and memories overrun principles and reason. Most architects, especially those who take pleasure in travelling, have been affected by the discovery. For some, like Gordon Cullen of 'Townscape' fame, or Christopher Alexander, the inventor of Pattern Language, or the situationists (who prefer, admittedly, to create rather than replicate atmospheres), the discovery was determinant. The wildness that Paolo Pino admired in Flemish paintings 500 years ago has long since disappeared, and we have come to appreciate that the garden of the world is not only beautiful in paintings, but that its experience in reality is a source of delight that no painting, however beautiful, can equal.

Originally published as 'A Real Living Contact with the Things Themselves: Landscape Painters and Architects, 1600–1850' in AA Files 50, 2004

Thanks to Kathryn Barron, assistant curator at the Royal Collection Trust, for taking the time to show me Claude's *View of Tivoli* while it was undergoing restoration; to Christoph Grafe, Sarah Wiechmann and Architectural Association students Francesco Brenta, Maria Kouloumbri, Igor Gottschalk and Henrik Lonberg for helping with translations; and to Emanuele Fidone of the University of Syracuse for providing information on the Villa di Tremilia and Schinkel's journey to Italy.

1. E H Gombrich, 'The Renaissance Theory of Art and the Rise of Landscape', *Norm and Form* (London: Phaidon, 1966), p 116.
2. 'The Life of Claude by Sandrart', in Marcel Roethlisberger, *Claude Lorrain: The Paintings* (New Haven, CT: Yale University Press, 1961), p 47.
3. Richard Payne Knight, *An Analytical Enquiry into the Principles of Taste* (London: T Payne, 1805).
4. 'Memoirs of Thomas Jones', *The Walpole Society*, vol 32, 1946–48, p 103.
5. J W Goethe, *Italian Journey, 1786–88*, 27 June 1787, translated by W H Auden and Elizabeth Mayer (London: Penguin, 1992), p 347.
6. Karl Friedrich Schinkel, *Reisen nach Italien* (Berlin: Rütten & Loening, 1979), p 73.
7. Lawrence Gowing, *The Originality of Thomas Jones* (London: Thames and Hudson, 1985).
8. William Gelius, curator at the Thorvaldsens Museum in Copenhagen, kindly drew my attention to several paintings representing this building.
9. John Summerson, 'The Beginnings of an Early Victorian Suburb', *The London Topographical Record*, vol XXVII, 1995, p 34.
10. John Summerson, foreword to Harold James Dyos, *Victorian Suburb: A Study of the Growth of Camberwell* (Leicester: Leicester University Press, 1961), p 9.
11. Emanuele Fidone, 'Schinkel and the Mediterranean: The Landhaus bei Syrakus', in Susan M Peik (ed), *Karl Friedrich Schinkel: Aspects of his Work* (Stuttgart: Axel Menges, 2001). Ten years after writing this essay, on 1 September 2014, Emanuele Fidone drove me to the villa. As we approached the gate, we found that the entire estate of the villa was on fire. The fire must have started a few hours before we arrived.

Mind into Matter

Few modern buildings have expressed quite the same relish for formal play, while none have flaunted their functions with less modesty, than the Leicester Engineering Building by James Stirling and James Gowan. As a result, on completion it caused more confusion than it did scandal. The building *was* well received by the college staff and by most critics, for whom the complexity of its forms acted as a powerful stimulant (while leaving their functionalist beliefs intact). But to the more morally inclined modernists, the mix of intellectual discipline and formal hedonism was frankly offensive. A tutor from the Architectural Association would even say that it strove to 'invent a reason for its own existence', while a student from the same institution accused its architects of being 'only concerned with human function as it provided them with excuses for formal expression'.[1]

Yet in spite of the novelty of the forms, the theoretical views of Stirling and Gowan fell in line with the ideology of the time. Far from wishing to undermine the values of functionalism, the two architects saw these same values as gravely compromised and aspired only to rejuvenate them – specifically, that the rationalisation of postwar reconstruction and the widespread use of prefabrication had made architecture characterless; the infatuation with the arts and crafts movement and the tide of picturesque planning influenced by Swedish examples seemed sentimental and politically safe; and the blend, typical of the Welfare State, of statistical calculations, elevated moral values and benign practice appeared hopelessly parochial. In addition, brutalism, following the publication of Rudolf Wittkower's *Architectural Principles in the Age of Humanism*, had become smothered by neo-Palladian finesse, and had degenerated into 'the kinkiest school of elegance that architecture affords'. In such circumstances, standards against which to evolve one's own position could best be found abroad.

Yet at the same time a small number of architects came to resent the 'tyranny' exercised by Le Corbusier over

Stirling & Gowan, block model, Engineering Building, Leicester University, 1959
© James Stirling / Michael Wilford fonds, Canadian Centre for Architecture

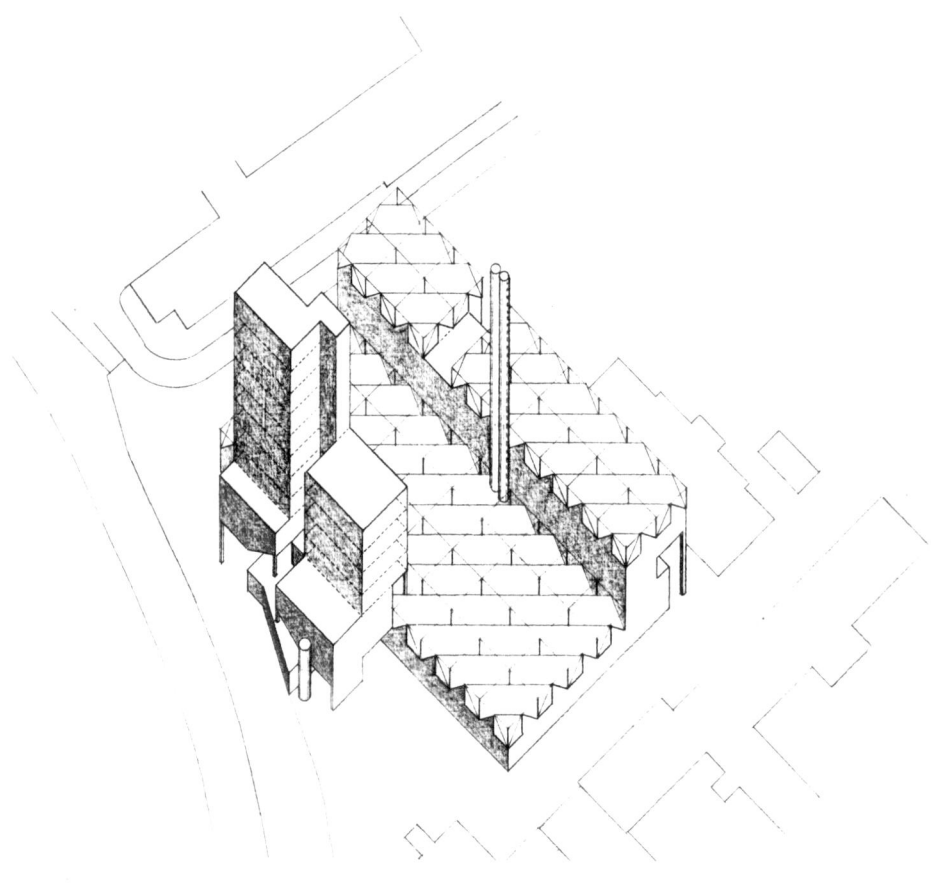

Stirling & Gowan, axonometric sketch, February 1960
Gift of James Gowan to the author

English design, among them Gowan, under whose influence Stirling tempered his own Corbusian training and dared to openly criticise (often at the expense of shocking even his closest friends) the work of the Swiss architect. To the study of works by Aalto, De Stijl, Wright and Kahn, Stirling and Gowan then added unfashionable local sources – for instance, they praised Owen Williams's industrial buildings which, being as much engineering as they were architecture, displayed a convincing matter-of-fact boldness. But they also despised the refined aesthetic to which Eric de Maré's photographs of nineteenth-century mills and warehouses often testified in the pages of *The Architectural Review*. Though Stirling and Gowan participated in the taste for such structures, their understanding of the vernacular did not emphasise repetition, horizontality or transparency – the canonical attributes which Mies and his followers then associated with the works of industry. Instead, their own photographs of Martello towers, oast-houses, brick kilns and railway buildings emphasised verticality, mass and character. More unusually, they collected slides of English country houses and Scottish baronial castles, which they screened after work in front of bemused friends. In this, as in much else, they were influenced by Colin Rowe, in whose coterie Stirling was well known to belong. More particularly, Rowe's exotic comparisons straddling across architectural history, his brushing away of the finery of causation, enabled the two architects to bypass theory and to justify, if only to themselves, form through mere historical precedent – as if the authority of precedent in English Common Law came to replace the enactments of European Codes.

The Commission

Prior to the UK government's major investment in tertiary education in the postwar period, Leicester could only boast a university college whose degrees were ratified by the University of London. But by the 1950s the college was witnessing a massive influx of students, which soon prompted

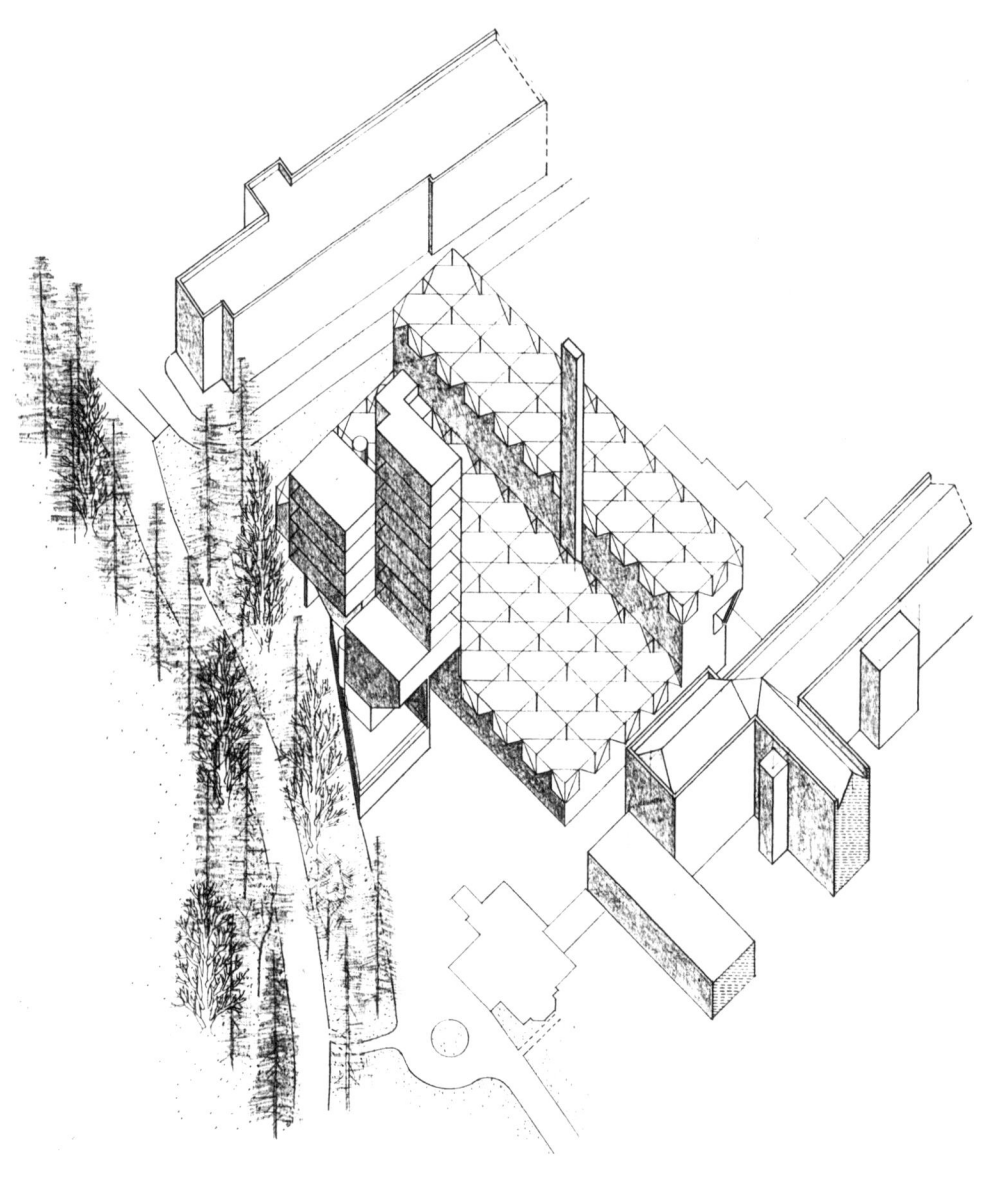

Stirling & Gowan, axonometric sketch, March 1960
Gift of James Gowan to the author

the award of its own university status in 1957. Coming late in this phase of expansion, the newly created engineering department was to be built on the last available plot of the university campus, just a kilometre or so south of the city centre. Contained on three sides by dull neo-Georgian brick buildings, its only real asset was a prospect onto the vast lawn of the adjoining Victoria Park.

When Edward Parkes, then teaching at Cambridge but soon afterwards head of the new engineering department at Leicester, was invited to express his views on the future department, engineering was widely regarded as a set of specialist disciplines resting on the solid foundation of maths and physics. To Parkes, and other members of his upcoming generation, this compartmentalisation seemed arbitrary, and the conception of engineering as applied science fundamentally mistaken. Moreover, future directions in the field appeared largely unpredictable. Such views led Parkes to propose, unusually for the time, a unitary department offering maximum flexibility. For a new engineering school with ambitions (soon satisfied) to compete with Cambridge, this meant a comparatively small faculty, a limit of 200 students, and with much of the teaching carried out on an individual basis in private rooms, or 'monastic cells', ascribed to each member of staff. The importance of lectures was to be downplayed, and alcoves for group work were to be provided within the main laboratories.

Stirling and Gowan were appointed in mid-1959 on the recommendation of Leslie Martin, then masterplanner for the campus as a whole. Together with Parkes and with Frank Newby, of Felix J Samuely & Partners, whom they themselves proposed as structural engineer, they formed an ambitious quartet, all in their early thirties, tasked with the production of the new engineering department.

The briefing document for the design was not issued until September that year and, remarkably, consisted of just a single A4 page. The building was to be divided into laboratories

Overleaf
Stirling & Gowan, sketch studies, undated
Deutsches Architekturmuseum, Frankfurt am Main
Photograph Uwe Dettmar
© Stirling & Gowan

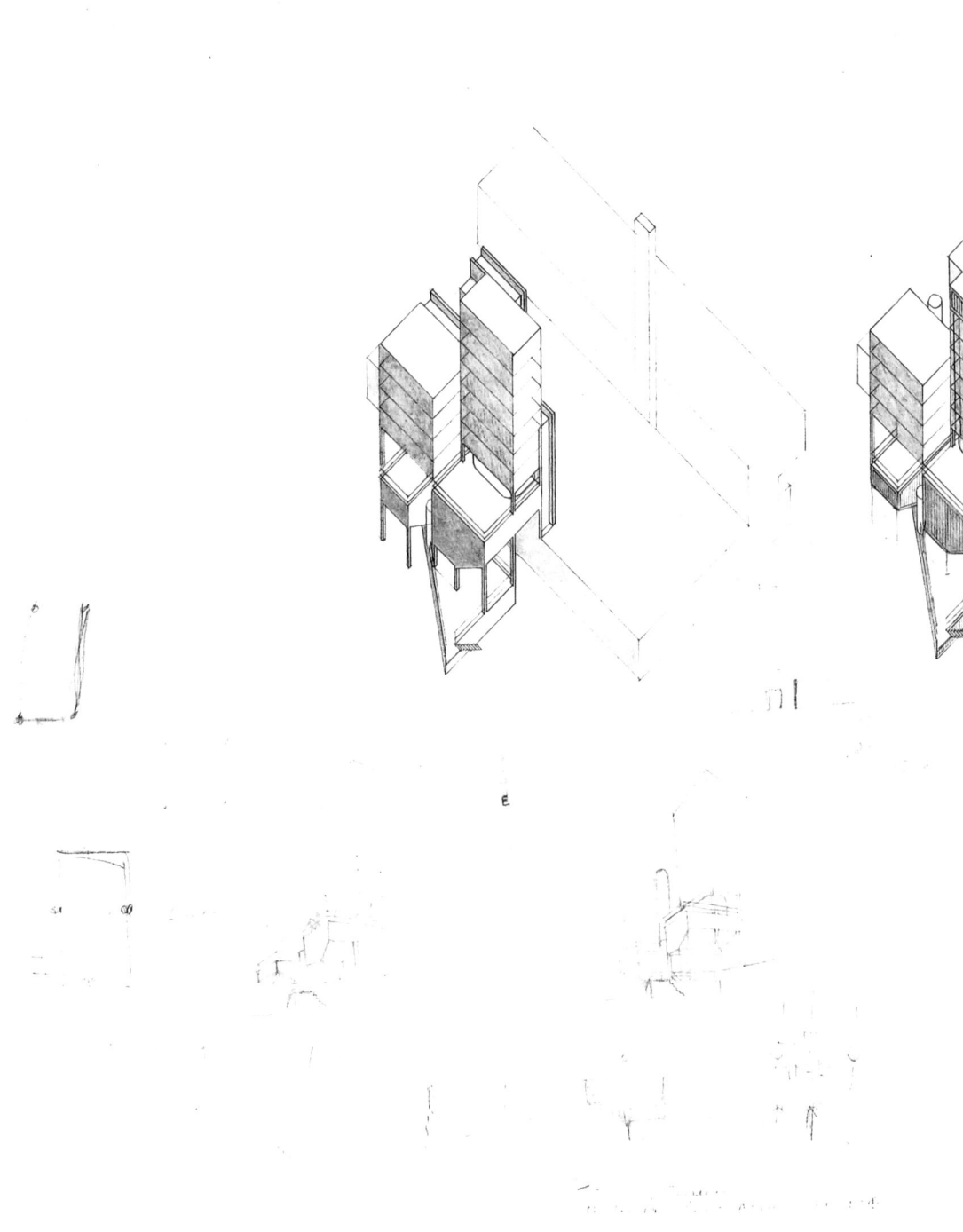

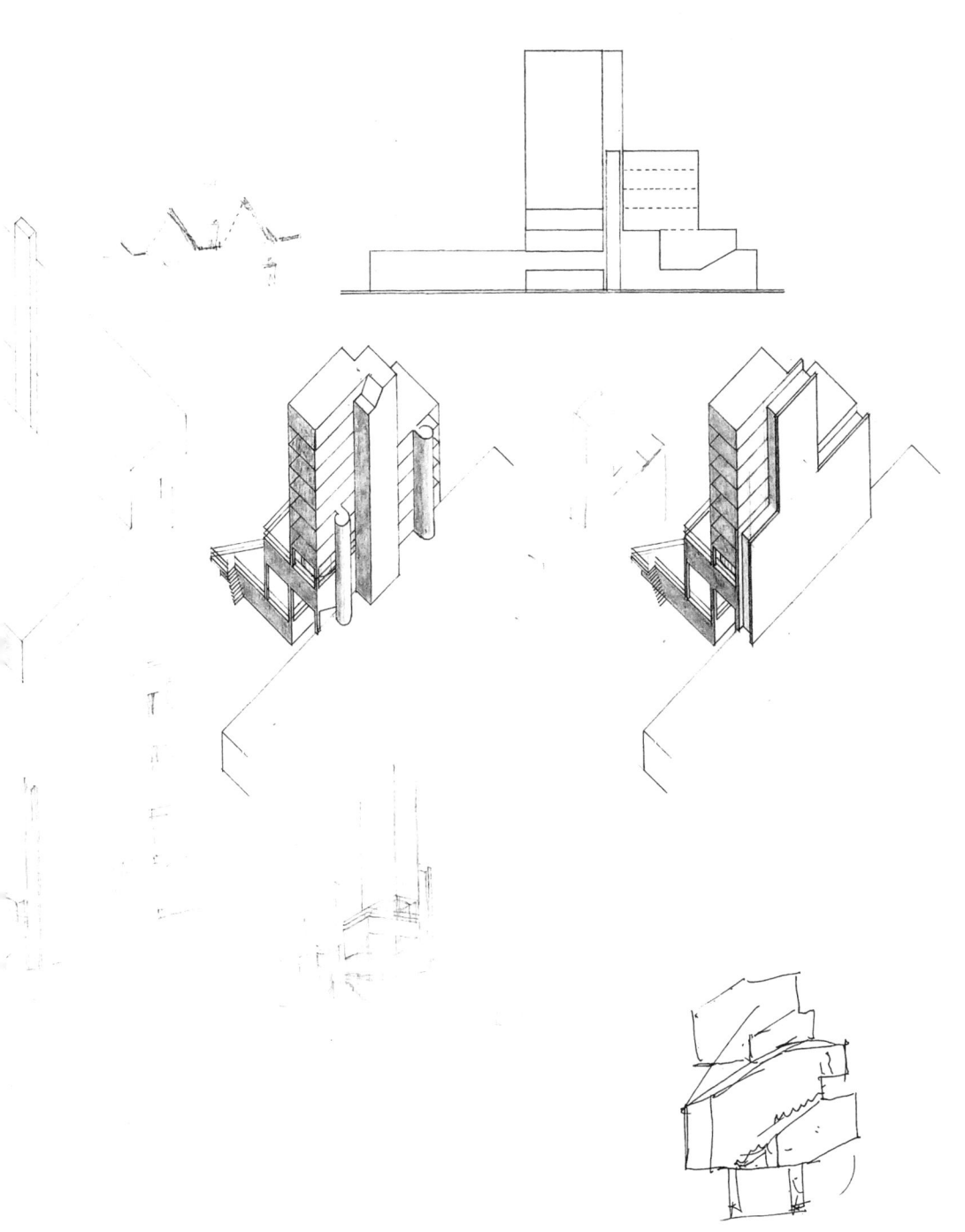

(which for structural or servicing reasons needed to be on the ground floor), high-level laboratories (a response to the constricted site), lecture theatres and small rooms for academic and administrative staff. No stipulation was made by the client, either then or later, as to the form of the building.

Preliminary Drawings Few preliminary drawings survive, and the reconstruction of the various stages of the design must therefore rely in part on sometimes contradictory recollections. But one crucial early decision is clear, recorded in a photograph of a block model, and consisted in bringing together lecture theatres and offices, the use of which was not expected to change. On the suggestion of the client, these were then placed at the front of the site so that they would benefit from views onto the adjoining park. The brief had specified the provision of a high-level 30m head-water tank for hydraulic experiments, which soon led to the accommodation of the offices within its structure, enabling both architects and client to bypass the planners' objections to high-rise development. At ground level the laboratories – upon which was imposed the discipline of a grid – were allowed to spread over most of the restricted site, providing a horizontal 'cypher' against which the more specialised elements of the tower could be played off. Equally few traces survive of the next stages of the design in the second half of 1959, during which at least two abortive plans and three models (all lost) were presented to the client.

As shown in a sketched axonometric dated 25 February 1960, the research laboratories which rested uneasily on top of the raised section of the workshops were then moved to the front of the building, thus clarifying the contrast between modular shed and atypical tower. While the module of the workshops remained unchanged, the ridges of the rooflights were shifted to run at 45 degrees to the dominant geometry, so as to exclude all but indirect north light from the interior of the laboratories.

Here, as elsewhere, the influence of an AA fourth-year student project – the SPD warehouse of 1957 by Edward Reynolds – is already on record. Like the Leicester building, Reynolds' project (for which Newby acted as structural consultant) displays a freely formed tower rising to the side of a deep shed, and a crystal-like roof geometry which resolves itself in the sawtooth profile of a brick perimeter wall. But while its diagonal trusses alternate with long space-frames aligned with the gutters, at Leicester the configuration of the roof, whose skewed rooflights span between a two-way grid of trusses, is far simpler. And while Reynolds's tower is marked by a high degree of organic articulation, Stirling and Gowan merely propose two rectilinear blocks linked by vertical circulations, standing as if on some pedestal on one of the two lecture theatres. These are then supported on a conventional frame structure and face each other on separate levels. Their arrangement, if not quite overlapping, recalls Stirling's Sheffield University competition project of 1953.

In a further axonometric sketch, probably dating from March 1960, the general massing of the tower approximates the final design. Here, the location of the two high-level blocks is reversed, so that the tallest element of the offices now stands astride the entrance hall, unequivocally marking the main access into the building. The lecture theatres were also turned around, their raked underside progressively compressing the space of the entrance, and the cantilever of the main auditorium appears for the first time. While the inefficient diaphragm walls supporting the lecture halls indicate that the engineer's involvement was as yet marginal, the columns at the rear of the high-level workshops were canted at Newby's suggestion. Besides freeing the already constricted drive, this effective structural solution is consistent with Newby's idea (then running against established practices in the building industry) that loads need not be transferred vertically, but could instead follow a complex three-dimensional route to the ground.

Stirling & Gowan, Engineering Building, Leicester University, 1963
©John Donat/RIBA Collections

When the first perspective was produced, only minor changes had occurred in the workshop block. The low perimeter wall, its sawtooth profile now suppressed, forms together with the podium a continuous, windowless brick datum above which rise the exuberant forms of both tower and workshop roof. A ramp cuts into the podium, leads to a first-floor entrance, and prolongs the discordant, bevelled geometry of the lecture theatres to the ground. Turned at 90 degrees, the tapering side of the small auditorium also now projects beyond the perimeter wall. As has been highlighted many times before, this decision draws on Konstantin Melnikov's Rusakov Club (1928), which Stirling and Gowan almost certainly knew through illustrations in Bruno Zevi's *Spazi dell'Architettura Moderna*. Yet Melnikov's influence has been overemphasised, for the character of the monumental cantilevers at Leicester is more forbidding than it is heroic, and evokes Burke's sublime far more readily than it does Bolshevik zeal, which frankly never entered into the architects' preoccupations.

Massing and Routeing

Above the smaller of the two lecture theatres, the architects proceeded to cut a corner of the research laboratories at 45 degrees along the site boundary, which may have suggested the systematic splaying of corners elsewhere. Newby then proposed a diagrid structure for the floors of this block. More famously, he also devised the canted joints at the base of the office block, through which loads coming down on pairs of columns are transferred at an oblique onto single supports. This deceptively logical design, by which penetration into the space of the main lecture hall was avoided, would no doubt have pleased Viollet-le-Duc and lends much expressive power to the structure.

At the same time, Stirling and Gowan spent considerable effort on the planning of the building's circulation systems which, like their arts and crafts predecessors, they regarded as the armature of the plan. To this concern for economy, they then added a mathematical zeal which, in its comical evocation of speed and shop-floor precision, recalls the single-minded conviction of early functionalists.

> Stirling: 'There are about 300 students in the building and, by making it like an iceberg, the bulk of student movement is limited to the lower three levels, where large numbers are changing lessons on the hour, every hour. (Over a five-minute period there is a mass movement and it is essential to concentrate this where the ground coverage is the greatest.) As most of the teaching spaces are at lower level the students tend to dash up and down the stairs, leaving staff to catch the lift to their room at the top. In this way you contrive to keep the staff and the students from colliding.'[2]

The massing of the tower itself was partly inspired by a De Stijl artist's house project, with the plan also inheriting the single stairs of this same domestic source. Seeming at first concise and elegant, this detail soon conflicted with the demands placed upon a multi-storey college building, and eventually the fire-escape stairs were brought onto the landings, reluctantly prompting the duplication of the main stairs (Stirling still managed a minor victory here, arguing that there could be no fire risk in the absence of combustible materials, meaning he could dispense with fire doors between stairs and landings). The resulting choice of routes and the multiplicity of views aptly reflects the pin-wheel succession of floor plans as if slung on the skewer of vertical circulations.

The same perspective also shows large sheets of plate glass on the front section of the building, and much cheaper patent glazing over the workshops. This distinction, favoured by Stirling, who seemed to have envisaged the tower as a kind of frontispiece to the project, implicitly condoned a separation between intellectual work in the lecture theatres and offices and manufacture in the laboratories. It was

Stirling & Gowan, detail of 'undercroft', 1963
©John Donat/RIBA Collections

strongly opposed by Parkes, who felt that the factory aesthetic of the workshops was inappropriate for a school. Patent glazing, whose internal appearance was admired by Stirling and Gowan in such buildings as the Palm House at Kew Gardens, was already considered to be spartan, even cheap and shoddy. The limited budget eventually settled the issue and patent glazing was applied to tower and workshops alike – as it turned out, to both great visual effect and persistent physical inconvenience.

The Workshops The development of the tower was eventful in its waywardness and was Stirling's responsibility (Newby is categorical on this point), while the design of the workshops – developed by Gowan – was painfully slow but more consistent. Early in the design, the roof structure of the shed consisted of two-way girders aligned with the main structural grid, with glazing running at 45 degrees within their depth. In a later balsa, wood model Warren girders are laid diagonally, at right angles with the roof valleys, their upper chords running above the ridges. They are then raised above the perimeter ring beam on diagonal struts whose triangular configuration resembles Wright's monumental trusses in the draughting room of Taliesin East – also illustrated in Zevi's *Spazi dell'Architettura Moderna*. The spectacular diamond forms with which the workshops roof is associated are essentially a strictly logical outcome of these two last decisions.

Responding to the difficulty of making watertight the many intersections between glazing and structure, Newby then suggested that trusses be turned around to line up with the valleys, and be inclined to form the kind of folded-plate structure for which the late Felix Samuely, who died in early 1959, was famous. Glazing could then be fixed directly onto the girders. Still today, and regardless of certain environmental failings, the workshops roof continues to impress through its faultless ingenuity, and by the directness and rare sensitivity

Stirling & Gowan, spiral stair, rear of the large lecture theatre, 1963
©John Donat/RIBA Collections

Stirling & Gowan, 10th-floor landing, 1963
©John Donat/RIBA Collections

of its structural performance. The university itself must also have been convinced, for it approved this initial design in March 1960.

At Leicester the raw material seems to consist not so much of bricks and glass – unrhetorical in their details to a degree approaching insignificance – but in the programme and functions which it listed. Every room or set of rooms that could be prescribed in kind is given a form of its own, and as far as possible is made distinct from others by the interval of glazed circulations. This approach is in many ways entirely cogent with what came to be regarded as the alternative modern tradition – stemming from Häring and expanded by the likes of Aalto and Scharoun – even if the more sensitive understanding these architects were able to bring to function and the complex configurations of space in their work were alien to Stirling and Gowan. Leicester's individual volumes remain abstract in form and archaic in character. They are sustained by a predominantly quantitative, primitive idea of function, which contributes to the early-modern flavour of the building.

Functionalism and Sensibility

Yet sensibility and a measure of self-consciousness were not completely excluded, as this passage by Stirling indicates:

> A few years ago Luigi Moretti illustrated in *Spazio* the plaster castings taken from inside accurate models of certain historical buildings. By treating the external surface and the inner constructions of a building as a three-dimensional negative or mould, he was able to obtain solidified space. If space can be imagined as solid mass determined in shape and size by the proportion of a room or the function of a corridor, then an architectural solution could be perceived by the consideration of alternative ways in which the various elements of the programme could be plastically assembled.[3]

By 1959, the notion of architecture as a mould of spaces determined by function had of course lost its novelty. But the idea that solidified space might result from this operation is a striking idiosyncrasy and, from the point of view of functionalism, an aberration. Nevertheless, it is in this idea that one can recognise the spring of Leicester's particular manner: simple solids struck with the blunt sign of their function, like a child's blocks stamped with letters of the alphabet, assembled for maximum plastic effect. While the result is indeed playful and would cause Colin Rowe to exclaim 'What a beautiful little toy!', there remains an earnest belief in the rules of the functionalist game.

Stirling and Gowan also drew liberally from their broad architectural culture. Some specific precedents are already on record, in addition to the Reynolds warehouse and Melnikov's workers' club. For instance, Frank Lloyd Wright's Johnson Wax building, like Leicester, consists of a tower offset against a single-storey building in which glass crowns a band of red bricks. While in Louis Kahn's more contemporary Medical Research Building, slender brick towers serve a cluster of laboratories. Yet according to Gowan, the key influence on the form of the tower is an artist's house project of 1923 by Van Doesburg and Van Eesteren, made available yet again by Zevi, but this time in his *Poetico dell'Architettura Neoplastica*. A series of cubes, each accommodating a particular room, are assembled on the prismatic shaft of a central stair. Around this core, rooms appear to hover, at once sliding and gyrating, producing in alternance cantilevers and terraces. Similarly at Leicester, the massing of the tower suggests a complex movement around the vertical circulations. On each floor, spatial units seem to seek their natural orientation while remaining tightly pressed against the core. The geometrical centre thus appears to waver between a centralised whole and autonomous parts, not unlike the vicissitudes of the subject in cubist representations.

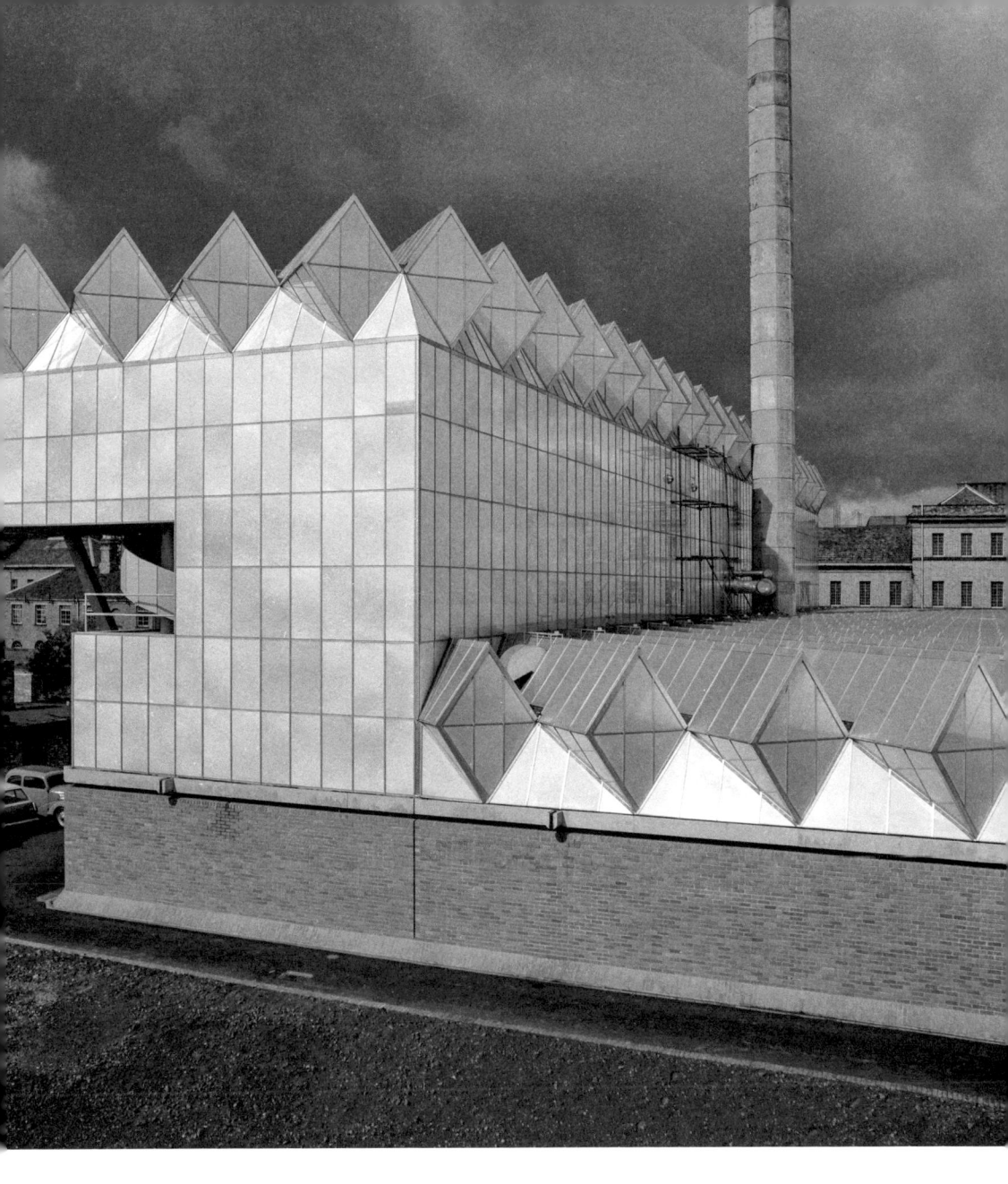

Stirling & Gowan, workshop block, 1963
©John Donat/RIBA Collections

Stirling & Gowan, workshop block, 1963
©John Donat/RIBA Collections

Such abstraction, grounded in twentieth-century art, amplifies the highly cerebral character of Stirling and Gowan's functionalist order, which seems not so much drawn as thought. The architects' reticence to compromise the purity of the functional diagram with visual judgement can even be illustrated with an opaque, quasi-alchemical account of its translation into form. 'At this moment of coagulation', Stirling stated, 'the cerebral loses its abstract value as it is necessary for it to materialise as substance; the successful transition from organisational pattern into structure and materials is dependent upon the author's structural vocabulary. Through its selection the method of support should assist the ideogram of the space organisation.'[4] Though it is clear from the result that visual judgement of the diagram's formal potential was not absent, it is withheld from the scrutiny of others, perhaps even repressed. Instead, the account of the design leaps from the functional diagram to considerations of structure and construction, directed by nothing more specific than 'necessity'.

Coagulation

It is characteristic of Leicester that this precipitate of functions into solids is delayed for as long as possible, and when it is at last envisaged, what was initially a process of assembly becomes one of modelling. In the process, most of the tower's vertical corners were then truncated. The resulting bevels, consistent with the raked forms of the auditoria and the geometry of the workshops' roof, contribute to a sense that the building was hewn out of a single, solid substance. Nothing like a window is allowed to suggest that surfaces might conceal a void. Instead, glazing, mostly reflective by day, glowing by night but seldom transparent, appears as a wrapping to the would-be solids within. The ideogram of function at last acquires sculptural presence, as if the fleeting De Stijl neoplastic composition had suddenly seized into mass.

Indeed, when seen from afar, the building seems toy-like and impossibly small – just the kind of image which graduates to postage-stamp status, as it once did. But in approaching the building, this benign vision is surreptitiously turned on its head. What was diminutive and immaterial now overwhelms with a sense of its formidable weight. The office tower, poised on its four brittle concrete columns, threatens, with the prospect of collapse. The smaller auditorium, wedged beneath the research laboratories, seems to have been thrust into position following some geological hiccup. And the workshop 'diamonds' loom like enormous cyclopean eyes as one emerges on the first-floor landing of the tower.

Such inflation of mass finds its converse in the provocative display of vertiginous voids. On the landings of the tower, railings were provided in front of the curtain wall following the insistent request of the client. Large ducts shoot straight past these railings from the water tank to the bottom of the main stairs, one causing water to pitch to a shrill octave, much to Stirling's delight. Meanwhile in the office tower, a six-storey-high perimeter void was provided between the glazing and the edge beam of the floor slabs, this last being also meant as a seat!

Separation of Function and Form   Unaffected by this perverse play with gravity, a common misconception of Leicester's achievement is that it realised a fusion between function and form. While a concern with both performance and beauty is evident, these were not fused but, on the contrary, pulled apart, and came into play in succession. First, the brief was interpreted in the assembly of basic volumes, guided by the criteria of economy. Adjustments were then made to the form of the resulting diagram, inspired by an aesthetic sense and the knowledge of precedents. Form, then, did not 'follow' function, insofar as the one could not logically be inferred from the other. Rather, both terms, in being set apart, were able to stimulate each other. Functionalism became as much a theory as a method of composition.

If a still archaic conception of function led to somewhat inert interiors in sharp contrast with the vitality of the exterior, Leicester's novelty consisted in the release of what had become an emaciated formal vocabulary within the pen of modernist ideology. Gowan's expression, 'the style for the job', aptly conveys this rehabilitation of form as a partly autonomous value, by which the building was able to be far more expressive of functionalism and twentieth-century abstraction than of engineering and education.

In this sense Leicester presents a fragile paradox: while it considerably enlarged the expressive field of functionalism, it achieved this through a corresponding relaxation of the yoke binding form with function. Hence it could be equally interpreted as a reassertion of the theory of functionalism and as the Trojan horse of postmodernism. Some 30 years ago it acted as a stimulant for architects who eventually jumped the fence, and who were to evolve an architecture whose art became its prime purpose. But as its ambivalence is subjected to the balancing movement of history, Leicester now suggests that a renewed reflection on architecture as service can usefully contribute to the beauty of its form.

Overleaf
Stirling & Gowan, teaching laboratory, 1963
©Sam Lambert
/ RIBA Collections

Originally published in French as 'Le Leicester Building', Le Moniteur-AMC 46, November 1993. This English translation was originally published as 'Cerebral Functionalism: The Design of the Leicester University Engineering Building', Archis, May 1994

This essay is based on interviews held in September and November 1992 with James Gowan, Michael Wilford and Malcolm Higgs, from James Stirling & James Gowan Architects, Edward Parkes and Richard Float, from Leicester University, Frank Newby and Peter Paul, from Felix J Samuely & Partners, Denis Spooner, Colin St John Wilson and Edward John.

1 *Architectural Association Journal*, December 1963, p 142.
2 James Stirling, 'An Architect's Approach to Architecture', *RIBA Journal*, May 1965, p 233.
3 James Stirling, 'The Functional Tradition and Expression', *Perspecta 6*, 1959, p 91.
4 *Ibid*.

The Rococo Revolution

Previous
Olof Fredsberg,
Ulla Tessin in her Study, 1763
© Nationalmuseum, Stockholm

Countess Ulla Tessin had fashionable tastes. Some of the objects in her study, for example the commode and the seventeenth-century Dutch landscape, may have been inherited, but most were new and exotic, from the Chinese wallpaper to the Persian rug, from the rococo desk and the clock above it to the porcelain *objets d'art* scattered across the room (the appliqué flowers around the fireplace, the Chinese vase on top of the bookcase and the porcelain dogs next to the writing desk). In the corner of the room, what appears to be a medley of artlessly arranged objects is, in fact, a *trompe-l'œil* based on a print by François Boucher. This small engraving was the painter's design for the trade card of a well-known Parisian dealer in art and luxury goods, Edme Gersaint. In a shop situated on the Pont Notre-Dame, Gersaint sold, as his card advertised, 'toute sorte de Clainquaillerie Nouvelle et de Gout'jewels, mirrors, paintings, *pagodes*, Japanese porcelains, shells, stones and 'generally all Curious and Foreign Merchandises'.[1] The print itself features a Chinese lacquer cabinet with a leering *pagode* seated on top and a confusion of corals, shells, a teapot and other disparate artefacts. Its appearance on the wall of the countess's study suggests the extent to which, by the mid-eighteenth century, French taste ruled all of Europe, and how eclectic and international this taste had become.

The countess's engaging little study is every bit as intimate and intricate, as lacking in affectation, as full of gaiety, as the tiny watercolour which records it. The natural and the artificial, the inherited and the recently acquired, the *rocaille* and the chinoiserie, are all tastefully combined, reflecting not a style but a coherent sensibility that was of fundamental importance to the culture of the eighteenth century. This new sensibility posed the first serious threat to the dominance of classical rule since the Renaissance, and co-opted – as the extraordinary range of merchandise in Gersaint's shop indicated – whatever came within its reach, as long as it expressed a wild fancy. The combination of an anti-classical temperament and the covetousness of anything foreign or merely unusual laid the foundation for the eclecticism that followed. But in one respect the rococo remains unique and incomparably bold: it made no attempt to establish its legitimacy through theory (unlike the advocates of the various styles which were current in the nineteenth century), nor to occupy, as it were, places in the academies. At no other time has western society travelled so light, with nothing save an exquisite taste and a restless curiosity, and ventured so far in its trust of something so fickle, so unpredictable yet so marvellously responsive as a sensibility.

For most architectural historians, the work of the 'revolutionary architects' of the late eighteenth century reflects the influence of the *philosophes*, and a new spirit of reason. Boullée, Ledoux and their followers are seen as the first moderns, their visionary drawings even anticipating work as modern as that of Le Corbusier. Those unfortunate enough to be out of step with this rationalist approach were seen at best to have produced the fireworks which signalled the end of the baroque. In this way some 70 years, from about 1700 to 1770, have been casually dismissed as the regressive, eccentric and mostly irrelevant stuff of the *ancien régime*.

Without doubt the century witnessed extraordinary developments in the sciences, and the neo-classicism which had fully emerged by the end of the century gave rise to a new cult of simplicity. But it was the rococo – derived from *rocaille*, denoting the imitation rocks used in Italy to create the grottoes of the seventeenth century, and the Italian suffix *-occo* (as in *barocco*) – that was at the heart of its sensibility. The rococo was not confined to the voluptuous style that was to be recognised in the nineteenth century. In its maturity it embraced many non-classical forms, from the baroque to the gothic and Chinese, and it is this protean identity that made it so distinctive and prominent in its time. Yet its reputation remains contentious: rococo is seen as charming but frivolous, amusing but superficial, refined but effete, affecting but rootless.

Leading architecture historians in modern times have rarely given it more than a nod. Sigfried Giedion excluded any mention of the rococo from his *Space, Time and Architecture.* Pevsner regarded it as the self-indulgent recreation of a leisured class of *cognoscenti*.[2] For all the significance Wittkower ascribed to the *jardin anglo-chinois*, the rococo remained for him a mere 'interlude' within the great unfolding of classicism.[3] Joseph Rykwert relegated it to one of the eight chapters which comprise *The First Moderns* – the title of a history of eighteenth-century architecture which declares its bias from the outset. Robert Venturi expressed 'a partiality for … rococo especially', though, like Henry-Russell Hitchcock, he confined his research and his sympathies to late German baroque.[4] John Summerson identified a 'remorseless widening of horizons' to which the rococo contributed in co-opting foreign styles, yet he saw its origins not in a crisis of culture and expanding trade but, curiously, in the pre-eminence of the culture of classicism and in the uncheckable growth of history which it promoted. Thus the authority of Rome was displaced by a plurality embracing Greek, gothic, Chinese and Indian. For Summerson this development culminated not in eclecticism, but in the possibility, once historical styles could be compared, of conceiving a new style, whether personal, national or an abstraction of all styles. 'The way is clear', he concluded, 'for architectural revolution in a profound sense', and this revolution was, of course, the modernism that he championed.[5]

Misunderstood and undervalued, the rococo 'interlude' was radical, indeed revolutionary, in its consequences. In the first place, it undermined the universal value that had been claimed for classicism, and more particularly for the discipline of the classical orders, which had endured since the beginning of the Renaissance. Of greater importance still, the aesthetic curiosity of rococo designers, aroused by the impact of foreign trade upon domestic lives, contributed greatly to the rise of eclecticism and to 'the problem of style', which would be the curse of the nineteenth century and much of the twentieth. Thus 200 years before our own time, the culture of the west was driven by the potent combination of a desire for freedom and an incipient trend towards globalisation.

No great personality or extraordinary event marked the beginnings of rococo. It grew out of the fissures of classicism, and was an offshoot of the perennial decorative forms that had survived weeding by the high priests of the Grand Goût. The grotesque was the oldest among these, and was derived from a type of ancient ornament which had been discovered during the Renaissance in subterranean ruins known as *grotte,* or grottoes. The liberal use of the grotesque in Raphael's redecoration of the upper *loggie* in the Vatican Palace ensured that this style of ornament remained influential. But it had a serious weakness: there was little or no structure to connect its fanciful motifs. By the middle of the sixteenth century grotesque ornament was reinforced by the bands of strapwork that were so prominent a feature in mannerist pattern books from Holland and elsewhere, and it came under the brief but determining influence of the arabesque of Saracenic origin. The story of the grotesque and of its subsequent enrichment is one that is often told in relation to the rococo, yet the pivotal importance ascribed to it in these accounts confirms the widely held view of the rococo as merely a decorative style, as a distraction from the more important events of the eighteenth century.

Moreover, it fails to acknowledge that rococo was not the product of a process of evolution in the decorative arts but, rather, took considerable liberties with them. Most strikingly, it sought to evacuate to the margins of the composition – and occasionally to eliminate altogether – the linear, abstract and rhythmic forms, the bands, the straps and the interlacing, of which decoration is usually composed. Dedicated to the pursuit of freedom and pleasure, the rococo sensibility showed

a striking lack of interest in pattern – unless it defined a place where a *galant* might be concealed. In the first three decades of the eighteenth century the whole paraphernalia of classicism – frames, pilasters, columns, cornices, baldachins and pergolas – was overwhelmed by a charming and most extraordinary confusion. Scrollwork, garlands, foliage, often in pale colours, were thinly showered on a background that could be white or gold. Thus the airy, light-seeking and ultimately more vigorous rococo displaced the grotesque and its tributaries.

Jean-Antoine Watteau, *Singerie*, pencil sketch for a wall painting at the Château de Marly, 1709 © Nationalmuseum, Stockholm

The confusion the rococo cast over the body of classicism is mirrored in the agitation of the hypersensitive heroines of eighteenth-century novels. Indeed, the interior world of such heroines could be seen as a metaphor for the new manner of interior decoration: both shared the same polished elegance, the same sentimentality and eroticism. The novel around 1700–20 – the defining moment of the rococo – sought to permeate classical language with that of everyday life and emotions. But classical aesthetics was hardly equipped to provide a framework for ordinary experience, and this resulted in a lack of confidence in the narrative, a sense of emptiness which became a formal characteristic of the work.[6] Content became mobile and vagrant, as if in search of a hospitable form. Stories were discursive and somewhat unreal, much like the arabesque, which was used as a support by every genre for every kind of figure, be it a faun, a Colombine or a peasant. The *scènes galantes* depicted in paintings were likewise cast adrift on the canvas. In Watteau's *Pilgrimage to the Island of Cythera*, by far the most famous example of the genre, it is impossible to determine whether the participants are embarking or disembarking, looking forward to the thrill of seduction or with regret at favours interrupted or as yet unobtained. In these scenes, which were inspired by the amateur performances or tableaux with which the Parisian nobility entertained themselves, facial expressions seem fleeting, as if in search of a definite character and narrative.

The earthy performances of Italian theatre companies provided the model for these *fêtes galantes*. Such companies enjoyed considerable prestige and popularity throughout Europe during this period, and often had access to the inner circles of power – the great actor Tiberio Fiorilli was even authorised to make faces in front of the infant Louis XIV when the latter had tantrums. Although Fiorilli and the other members of the Paris-based company (a dozen altogether) performed entirely in Italian until the end of the seventeenth century, they were so firmly established in the life of the court that in 1680 the troupe, by then known as the Comédie Italienne, was granted the privilege of being the only company to perform in the Theatre de Comédie Française. Their repertoire included none of the comedies, tragedies and pastorals that were inspired by classical forms, and their performances were for the most part improvised. These became increasingly outrageous until 1697, when 'the Italians', as they were commonly known, went so far in the play *La Fausse Prude* as to suggest that Madame de Maintenon was unfaithful to the king and even promiscuous. She was not, and their performing privilege was revoked, in a still much-debated episode that could be regarded as the watershed of rococo.

Harlequin, Colombine, Pantaloon, Blackamoor, Pierrot – the *vecchi* and *zanni* who peopled the Comédie Italienne – were thenceforth obliged to seek their audiences at fairs. And where the Italians went, the nobility followed, finding in the vitality and unpolished character of their productions a welcome relief from the austerity and boredom of the court. Above all, they found it in the parades the comedians used to entice the public into the theatre, in the licentiousness of the short satirical farces they performed, in the deliberately affected and ridiculous postures of the actors, and in their refusal to recognise any rules whatsoever. Such parades were adapted for the *fêtes galantes* that were held in country parks outside Paris. Two hundred years later the parade once again served

Jean-Antoine Watteau, *Gilles and his Family*, c 1716–18
© Trustees of the Wallace Collection, London

as a model, providing relief, not from the court, but from the bourgeoisie. Most famously, Picasso, Satie and Cocteau staged a performance at the Théâtre de Chatelet in 1917 titled *Parade*. Here too the action was set in front of a fair booth, with acrobats, a Chinese conjurer and, to keep up with the times, 'a little American girl'.

For the *honnête homme* or the *galant* who formed the moral background to these entertainments, idleness was not an indulgence but a purposeful resistance to officialdom.

Claude Gillot, *Actors*, c 1710 © Nationalmuseum, Stockholm

The *galant*'s ideal was one of acute responsiveness, of obligingness, pliability and suggestiveness, demanding 'an element of self-portrayal in acting, with its reflection and illusion, perception and understanding, and the dialectic of intellect and sensuality'.[7] Self-portrayal, reflection, illusion, *double entendre, demi-monde:* it is no wonder that mirrors were so prominent in rococo interiors.

Architecture – an art so well suited to the classical temperament – lagged behind these changes. Rococo had been confined to the world of interiors until about 1730, when in Paris three decorators with architectural ambitions, Nicolas Pineau, Jacques de Lajoue and Juste-Aurèle Meissonnier, became chiefly responsible for the development of the *genre pittoresque.* In their mostly unbuilt intimations of what a full-blown rococo architecture might be like, architectonic elements were dissolved in continuous and mostly scaleless ornamental forms. This genre became identified with the use of asymmetry, known as *contraste* (symmetry then denoted proportion and did not acquire its present meaning until the middle of the century). Meissonnier included in his book of ornaments a few highly plastic architectural fantasies, sometimes titled *morceaux de caprice.* He created a scaled-up version of the cartouche, a form that had previously been confined to book illustration and panelling, which he then bent and broke apart into a riot of cornices, volutes and crests, planted like reeds alongside cascades and stairways. Aided by the widespread publication of prints of this kind, the fashion for rococo soon swept across most of Europe.

The tangled undergrowth of rococo ornament, emotional disarray in the novel, the stylistic licence of the Italian theatre, the spirited idleness of the *galant*, the *genre pittoresque:* all deliberately flouted conventions of taste. Exposure to foreign trade and to artefacts and buildings that were remote geographically (Chinese or Indian) or historically (Greek, Roman or gothic) achieved comparable results and undermined long-established, mostly classical traditions.

Of all the imports that were caught in the eddies of the rococo, none were more common than those from China. Commerce with China had begun long before the eighteenth century. As early as 1500, a mere two years after Vasco da Gama's voyage to Calicut, Pope Urban VI's Bull had ceded to the Portuguese 'the eastern half of the undiscovered world'

– a pregnant phrase at once simple in its implied symmetry and full of expectation in its incompleteness. A century later, East India companies were founded, first in Britain (1600) and then in Holland (1602). By the mid-1650s oriental textiles, porcelains and lacquers were flooding the markets of London, Amsterdam and Paris. By 1700 Indian calico and chintz had become so popular with the British that the weavers of Spitalfields, their livelihood threatened, ran berserk in the streets of the City, splashing *aqua fortis* on women's dresses. By the 1720s Chinese tea was no longer the prerogative of the *beau monde*, and the amount imported increased five-fold in that decade. By 1760 it had become the most important item in the company's portfolio, porcelains and other crafts merely providing ballast for its merchant vessels. By 1770 the commerce in tea had achieved a revolution in the field of trade, parallel with the revolution rococo and chinoiserie had achieved in the field of taste.

The close relationship between changes in taste and developments in trade can be appreciated at a glance in the watercolour of Countess Ulla Tessin's study or in the eclectic range of articles sold by Gersaint. The free and easy harmony depicted on the latter's visiting card (etched, it will be remembered, by Boucher) was very much less self-conscious than Robert Venturi's postmodern 'difficult whole'. Lacquer panels from Japan or China were set in the sides of commodes or escritoires and then framed by rococo ornaments without seeming in the least out of place. Likewise, artistic personalities as supremely confident as Boucher, Watteau and Tiepolo were able to co-opt things foreign into their art without compromising its integrity. The rococo was, as it were, a signboard – Watteau's most famous *Enseigne* hung above the window of Gersaint's shop for a period of 15 days – as well as a shop window in which imports, notably those of the East India Company, and all manner of fantasy could be displayed and admired. It not only featured the 'duck' and the shed behind it that Venturi,

Scott-Brown and Izenour identified as typical of the strip in Las Vegas, but also included the merchandise inside. Thus the resistance that local taste would normally impose on the assimilation of foreign artefacts and exotic fashions was suspended.

By the late seventeenth century the Chinaman, complete with drooping moustache, had become one of the stock characters of the Comédie Italienne. He was depicted for the first time in 1707 at the Chateau de La Muette, the official residence of the Captain of the Bois de Boulogne. Here Watteau painted, in his decoration of the Cabinet du Roi, a group of 30 compositions including 'figures chinoises et tartares'. Intriguingly, the female figures were given European features, while their male counterparts were oriental. This earliest example of chinoiserie (now destroyed) set the tone for all such later fantasies in France and Europe. Not long after, the potters of Meissen were busy manufacturing in porcelain the little band of the *commedia dell'arte*.

If the Chinaman could appear in the *commedia dell' arte*, then so could Harlequin in China, as in *The Mandarin, or Arlequin Widower*, a play that was staged in London in the 1750s, at the peak of the fashion for chinoiserie. *Scènes de La vie chinoise*, a series of etchings made by Boucher in 1742, became a source for Beauvais tapestries. Louis XV even presented a set of these tapestries to Quianlong, Emperor of China, who was so delighted that he had a special pavilion built for them.

Jean-Antoine Watteau, *L'Enseigne de Gersaint*, 1720 © bpk / Kupferstich-kabinett, SMB / Volker-H Schneider

China came to represent the mysterious and inscrutable – adjectives that were not yet commonplace in this context – and the role of Chinaman could be worn like a mask on stage or in a *scène galante.* Thus rococo and chinoiserie represented equivalent and often intertwined artifices behind which a greater degree of freedom and enjoyment could be obtained. While the European nobility attempted to eliminate the rules segregating high and low forms of expression – for example those which prevented the Italians from performing at Versailles and at the Comédie Française – the East India Company sought to remove trade barriers between countries and, indirectly, between the particular tastes which prevailed in each. From the inside, the abolition of rules liberated the imagination; from the outside, the expansion of trade promoted the possibility of choice. The ensuing alliance between fantasy and variety – one that was so characteristic of the eighteenth century, and was to be of decisive importance in the emergence of eclecticism – found its greatest fulfilment in the notion of the caprice.

Like the rococo by which it was later absorbed, the capriccio was rooted in the grotesque, and was marked, in the sixteenth century, by the presence of the fantastic, the bizarre and the abnormal. In the mid-seventeenth century Salvator Rosa, following a literary conceit, conceived of the capriccio

Juste-Aurèle Meissonnier, *Design for Centrepiece and Two Tureens for the Duke of Kingston in 1735*, 1742–48 © Cooper Hewitt, Smithsonian Design Museum

as a child, the lack of constancy and the extravagance of whom was felt to be properly capricious, and chose to represent himself as such in an etching, complete with hat and feathers. Though his landscape paintings would not have been described as capriccios, their subjects – deep forests, brooding skies, majestic waterfalls, stormy seas and even attacks by bandits – conveyed a mood of horror (the Italian word *caporiccio*, from which capriccio is derived, meant fright) that was prized by a new class of traveller, the tourist. In combination with the temples, whether Greek or Roman or gothic, that Rosa concealed in foliage, reflected on the surface of a lake, or perched on a cliff, they exercised a considerable influence on the eighteenth-century landscape garden which was England's major contribution to the rococo. 'Capriccio' then denoted a mode of invention which sought to delight the eye, in contrast to the composition which addressed itself principally to the mind. A prime example is the vast architectural settings that the Bibienas created for the stage. Indeed, theatre designers were an influence on several of the painters who produced capriccios, notably Tiepolo and Piranesi, while Canaletto had actually trained as one.

Canaletto made a clear distinction between *vedute prese da i luoghi,* or 'views taken from a site', and *vedute ideate*, which were imaginary. These latter could be designed in a literal sense, as when the painter placed Vicenza's basilica on the quayside at the Rialto in Venice, or when he relocated the horses of San Marco on pedestals in the piazza or, more bizarrely, when he replaced the waters of the lagoon that lies before San Giorgio Maggiore with a forlorn piazza of the kind which can be found on the outskirts of Venice. Yet the distinction between that which was 'captured' and that which was imagined could be a matter of some subtlety. The most impressive of Canaletto's etchings have nothing of the cut-and-paste technique about them. In a magnificent imaginary view of Venice of 1741, everything is invented – the evocative

Overleaf
Canaletto (Giovanni Antonio Canal), *Imaginary View of Venice*, 1741
© Metropolitan Museum of Art, New York

silhouette of the city in the distance, the expanse of the lagoon that triggers so effectively a sense of *dépaysement*, the buildings in the foreground as if charmed into an indeterminate state between architecture and decay. But the sum of its topography, architecture and atmosphere, each in every aspect unique, results in a view that appears compellingly authentic. The entire city seems to have broken out of its old envelope to be improvised afresh into a playful spectacle.

In subsequent years the capriccio became more systematic, more wilfully fanciful. Whole buildings and ruins are removed from the city and recomposed in the setting of the Lagoon. Makeshift timber bridges are thrown across a confusion of mud and water. Gothic and Roman arches reach across the sky, the details of their imposts and architraves overgrown with weeds and vines. Rustic structures neither urban nor authentically rural seem to fit effortlessly into the liminal landscape of the Lagoon, in this wasteland at once wild and civilised, Venetian and Arcadian. Likewise, Watteau's scenery is both of the forest and of the pasture, and the English park, at once *anglo* and *chinois*. By the 1770s the demand for capriccios had spawned an industry. Among the approximately 250 by Francesco Guardi which survive, there are several *Veduta lagunare defantasie con porticciole*, several *Arco in rovina in un villaggio lagunare*, and no fewer *Casa rustica in riva alta lagune*. Little about them remained capricious, save their speedy execution.

The caprice, or folly, became almost as common in the *jardin anglo-chinois* as it was in views of the Lagoon. In 1722 the Italian architect Giacomo Quarenghi marked the entrance of Tsarskoe Selo, the country estate he built for the Russian emperor near St Petersburg, with a folly. The 'Great Caprice' consists of a decaying triumphal arch upon which stands, most incongruously, a Chinese pavilion. A far more enchanting example is the Chinese pavilion the King of Sweden demanded built over a single night to celebrate the birthday of his queen, Lovisa Ulrica, in 1753. It was rebuilt in 1763, on a more lavish scale, in the park of the royal residence of Drottningholm near Stockholm. There was little in the interiors of Kina – as it was affectionately known – that was not Chinese, either imported from China itself or copied from engravings in the Chinese taste by Boucher or William Chambers. As an admiring English visitor observed at the time, 'whimsy and caprice ... spread a grotesque air through the whole'.[8] Here was a *maison de plaisance*, a *solitude* delightfully adapted to the landscape fashion that was fast expanding throughout Europe – a new Arcady, peppered with *pavillons d'amour, bagatelles, sans-soucis, mon bijou, mon repos, favorites* and *ermitages*, of a kind with the cosmetic beauty spots – the *baiseuse*, the *équivoque*, the *assassine* in the corner of the eye, the *majestueuse* on the forehead, the *galante* on the cheek, or the *coquette* near the lips – the *mouches*, or 'flies', that fashion and fantasy planted with an air of randomness on women's faces.[9] Like the *fêtes galantes* later adapted by modernists to serve as a model for their own performances, the Chinese pavilion at Drottningholm

Overleaf
The Blue Drawing Room in the Chinese pavilion, Drottningholm, Sweden, 1763
© The Royal Collections, Stockholm

Elevation of Chinese pavilion, Drottningholm, Sweden, 1763
© The Royal Collections, Stockholm

prefigured not only popular suburban housing but the modern craze for marginal forms of existence – the *dérive* through the urban periphery, on the lookout for the strange entertainments of the mob, or of gypsies, or simply of deviants.

The rococo has been associated in turn with the picturesque of the *jardin anglo-chinois*, the sentimentality of Greuze, the sobs of *Manon Lescaut* and the romanticism of Salvator Rosa and Guardi – as well as with the purely formal qualities which allegedly caused painting to be degraded to the level of decoration. For the more fastidious observer, it was a French style of decoration that was fully realised in the *rocaille*. It was, it is true, particularly evident and effusive in interiors, and perhaps for this reason architectural historians have relegated it to a footnote of classicism, and have overlooked its subtle and real impact on the facades and plans of buildings. Some have recognised in it the dominant mood of the eighteenth century, but most have dismissed the rococo as superficial.

Yet this is to judge the rococo according to standards of form and content that it never claimed. The rococo was truly syncretic, and as a result it has eluded, and will continue to elude, attempts at a rigorous stylistic definition. In its own time it denoted unclassical forms – gothic, baroque, *rocaille* or Chinese – and it prospered under this protean identity. It was unconcerned with naming itself (only in the nineteenth century did the word become identified with a particular style) and, most remarkably, it never developed a theory of its own. Rococo artists showed what Michael Levey admiringly describes as a 'sheer brilliant brainlessness'.[10] In eighteenth-century painting as much as in literature and the polite society of the salons, superficiality, even to the point of frivolity, was held to be a virtue. The profundity of speculative reason, on the other hand, was felt to stifle the pleasures of conversation. The high favour in which the conversational mode was held is reflected by the new fashion in portraiture. The rococo portrait was never profound: it made no attempt to reveal

Jean-Marc Nattier, *The Comtesse de Tillières*, 1750 © Trustees of the Wallace Collection, London

the hidden essence. It triumphed over conventions, but never to the extent that it became fixed in some transcendental expression. The suggestion of an ideal or of an individual identity was proscribed. The artist sought instead to represent the sitter as he or she actually was, with his or her superficial radiance caught in a fleeting moment. There were no incentives to be didactically moral or historically true. If the portrait, indeed the whole of rococo art, had a social purpose at all, it was simply to please.

This expression of content was devalued nowhere more evidently than in the representation of classical antiquity, which had become merely an 'excuse for not wearing clothes',[11] and it met with no compensating appreciation of form. Form itself became spindly, calligraphic and gratuitous – *lignes en liberté*, anticipating, in the spatial or graphic domains, Marinetti's *mots en liberté*. The propensity of the rococo to dissolve the forms that came under its influence, especially those which reflected the structural rigour of classicism, will perhaps appeal to those who champion the formless. On the other hand, the resistance to theory may be less attractive in an age that is found, by its own account, to be lacking in ideology. Yet it is precisely rococo's capacity to thrive without rules which should recommend it to a present that is still weighed down by the debris of modernism.

Giovanni Battista Piranesi, *Design for a Gondola*, c 1744 ©The Morgan Library and Museum, New York / Bequest of Junius S Morgan and the gift of Henry S Morgan

Bereft of an enduring theory, whether by will or by accident, rococo was guided only by sensibility. This in turn called for a state of maximum receptiveness, not unlike that which is today achieved with the computer. Indeed, two of the principal attributes of the computer – instantaneity and accuracy – recall those associated with the ideal rococo artist: 'speedy, prolific, dazzling in colour, assured in draughtsmanship, ever-talented and never touching the fringe of genius'.[12] By its capacity to manipulate increasingly complex geometries and imaging techniques, the computer generates the capriccios of our time.

The rococo prized sensibility far too highly ever to settle into a particular style, or to follow the characteristic signature of an individual. In this respect, a comparison with the work of Frank Gehry would be instructive. Ever since the Vitra Museum, his designs have succeeded well beyond what Meissonnier imagined, and in Germany the Zimmerman brothers, Balthasar Neumann, Johann Fischer and the Asam brothers achieved, in the sphere of architecture. But the parallel threatens to confine rococo to a discussion chiefly of form, and to obscure its innate mobility. Besides asymmetry and other irregularities of form, rococo embraced informality in manners and inconsistency in thought – whatever would allow it to bend the rules and deviate from the routine. No form or genre was too vulgar or too sacred for its purposes. The resulting *mélange* of the high and the low has been claimed as the revolutionary contribution of the rococo, which, unburdened with transcendence, could delight in 'a revelation and enchantment of the earthly presence'.[13]

Yet rococo was more revolutionary still. No longer limited by the demands of theory and internal coherence, it was able to borrow from existing traditions any form, figure or attitude that took its fancy, in a spirit that became truly international and syncretic. Thus it paved the way towards eclecticism – this alone was a major contribution – and it was more daring than any movement in the nineteenth century in that no ideology can be associated with it such as inspired the revival of the gothic or the defence of classicism in the nineteenth century. Nor was it relativist in the sense that postmodern eclecticism is. The rococo flirted with, then flouted styles. At once eclectic and formless, it was the anti-style *par excellence*. Like no art before it, the rococo gave itself up to the will of the moment, to a lust for the endless variety of the present. No art had ever been so contemporary, and it is this – obtained with acute sensibility and a love of the sudden and arbitrary manifestation of the will, of caprice – which makes the rococo so compelling.

1. A type of Chinese figurine that was a travesty of Pu Tai, the god of happiness.
2. Nikolaus Pevsner, *An Outline of European Architecture* (London: J Murray, 1943), p 375.
3. Rudolf Wittkower, 'Classical Theory and Eighteenth Century Sensibility', in *Palladio and English Palladianism* (London: Thames and Hudson, 1974), p 203.
4. Robert Venturi, *Complexity and Contradiction in Architecture* (New York, NY: MOMA, 1966), p 19.
5. John Summerson, *The Architecture of the Eighteenth Century* (London: Thames and Hudson, 1969), p 76.
6. Rene Demaris, 'Les Fêtes galantes chez Watteau et dans le roman contemporain', *Dix-huitième siècle*, no 3, 1971.
7. Erich Hubala, *Baroque and Rococo* (London: Herbert Press, 1976), p 167.
8. William Mavor, *Historical Account of the Most Celebrated Voyages, Travels, and Discoveries from the Time of Columbus to the Present Period* (London: E Newbery, 1797), p 43.
9. Edmond and Jules de Goncourt, *La Femme au dix-huitième siècle* (Paris: Charpentier, 1878), p 321.
10. Michael Levey, *Rococo to Revolution: Major Trends in Eighteenth-Century Painting* (London: Thames and Hudson, 1966), p 25.
11. *Ibid*, p 16.
12. *Ibid*, p 24.
13. Hans Sedlmayr and Hermann Bauer, 'Rococo', *World Encyclopaedia of Art*, vol XII (New York, NY: McGraw Hill, 1958), col 237.

Architecture is not Made with the Brain

The Economist Building (1960–64) is commonly regarded as Alison and Peter Smithson's masterpiece. Some commentators praise the spatial effects of its plaza (though seldom without reservations), others value the principles informing the work, while still others admire the building for being at once well-made and discreet. At the time, this last quality was not associated with the Smithsons. In spite of the familiar classical character of their Hunstanton school of 1954, its minimal detailing was seen as exceptionally brash, while in the House of the Future (1956), the architects attempted to rethink domestic architecture from first principles, and transposed the forms hitherto associated with bathroom fixtures to the moulded plastic of which the interior was made.

What little the Smithsons had built by 1959 was arresting, provocative and thoughtful. These few projects, together with their influential lectures at the Architectural Association and their membership of the exclusive Team 10 'family', had placed them at the forefront of the architectural avant-garde in Britain. In contrast, there is little about the Economist Building that is overtly provocative. So what is it, apart from the signature, that explains and justifies its reputation?

The modern idiom in office design was by then firmly established. Derived from SOM's Lever House in New York (1951–52), it consisted of a low podium building which, at least in theory, addressed the users of the street, and a tower or slab above it which engaged with the podium rather as a cleaver does with the chopping-block. With the exception of four or five such buildings either completed or on site in London during the late 1950s, office design was governed by market forces and building regulations, and architects had to make do with the relatively scarce resources of the postwar years.

Given these circumstances the Economist Building was a notably accomplished performance. The clients received it with great enthusiasm: 'We met Alison and Peter Smithson six years ago with trepidation', they wrote, 'and take leave

Previous
Boodle's Club and Martins Bank (*left*) from a view south down St James's Street, London, 1964
Photograph Michael Carapetian

of them now with affection, and awe'.[1] Reviews in the press were broadly favourable, and praise was extended to the very aspects of the scheme about which the clients were most uncertain. If to a staff-writer of *The Economist* 'the really exciting possibilities of the courtyard [hadn't] yet been realised',[2] the plaza was nevertheless, according to one critic, 'the most successful modern square in London'[3] and, wrote another, felt 'so marvellously right in its place'.[4] Objections were for the most part mere quibbles: some regretted the lack of kiosks and cafés[5] and even of potted plants on the plaza,[6] while for a follower of Mies van der Rohe the travertine dressing of the facades resembled papier-mâché.[7]

But in order to fully understand the success of the Economist Building it needs to be examined in relation to contemporary practice. The vast Comprehensive Development Areas which had been set up to organise the rebuilding of postwar London were widely regarded as the principal achievement of the 1950s, but their application to the whole of the capital was increasingly felt to be crude and unrealistic. It became clear that in some parts of British cities only piecemeal development would be feasible. In addition, the ownership of one-car-per-family had for some years been promoted by industrial lobbies. Yet few roads were being built and there was, until the publication of the Buchanan Report in 1963, almost no coordination between land-use and transport policies.

The design of the Economist Building seemed to succeed exactly where the Comprehensive Development Areas had failed. Modern yet sensitive, it addressed both traffic and urban fabric. Ironically, the most unreserved praise came from the camp to whose views the Smithsons were most antagonistic: the advocates of 'Townscape' at *The Architectural Review*, who, led by Gordon Cullen, strove to reinstate traditional visual values in urbanism. They hailed the building as a masterly picturesque composition.[8] Curiously, the few critics who expressed doubts about the building, in particular the way it deferred to the surroundings, were among those who previously had been the Smithsons' most ardent supporters. Why, they asked, had the architects of a building which clearly presented itself as an urban model failed to conceive of it as part of an extensive redevelopment of the district?[9] After all, it was known that the client representative himself had entertained the vision of a modernised St James's Street, with towers soaring behind the existing buildings along the pavement line, which would be preserved. Such an idea had probably also occurred to the Smithsons, for early in the design stage they made a collage showing replicas of the Economist tower scattered throughout the district, though they refrained from sharing this with the client.

Of all the building's critics Reyner Banham was the most impatient. Lamenting the way the London of the twentieth century still had its feet 'mired in an eighteenth-century street pattern', he compared the Economist plaza to the 'lid of a large dust bin', with modernity swept beneath it to make way for a historicist, Acropolis-like exercise in civic design.[10] These were strong words to have come from a supposed ally.

Such reactions owed something to the Smithsons' own views on the city. In one of their earliest articles they attacked Camillo Sitte and the notion of townscape, criticising his town plans for being visual rather than 'real' – for pertaining more to art than to life. Yet to careful observers the renewed respect for the 'corridor street' and the 'organic' city, which the Smithsons and other members of Team 10 were promoting on social grounds, appeared to be in sympathy with picturesque sensibilities – and, in so far as 'townscape' could be seen as a manifestation of vitality, it was. On the other hand, the Smithsons' love of the contemporary seemed incompatible, for the likes of Banham, with a respect for the clutter of history.[11]

However forward-looking the Smithsons' views, there really was something antiquated about them, and the architects remained strongly attached to the heroic period of modernism.

Overleaf
George Kasabov, photomontage of the Economist Building in its St James's Street site, 1963
Gift of Peter Smithson to the author

As late as 1957, in an article published in *The Architectural Review*, they reaffirmed their faith in Le Corbusier's lyrical vision of the city,[12] and indeed their competition entry of the same year for Berlin Hauptstadt owes much to the Plan Voisin (1925) – a raised pedestrian esplanade punctuated with towers, a view of the car traffic below offered as a spectacle, and an infill of shops and restaurants between the two – though for Le Corbusier's 'gigantic and majestic prisms' they chose to substitute smaller towers grouped in a cluster, a more flexible arrangement adapted from Denys Lasdun.

Also evident in their work of this period is an awareness of Louis Kahn. The Smithsons admired his plan for mid-town Philadelphia (1953), and invited him to the Team 10 meeting at Otterlo in 1959. As with their Berlin Hauptstadt, Kahn's urbanism sought to 'find expression from the order of movement'[13] – a concept that first appears in the Smithsons' writings at the time of the Berlin competition. Surrounding their plan with a monumental 'Chinese wall' of offices (the expression Kahn used for his Penn Centre), they described the town centre as 'a cathedral of the mind'[14] (Kahn had described his own Civic Centre as 'the cathedral of the city').

In Hauptstadt, driving a car was to be a form of leisure, as was the activity of shopping in the raised 'streets of quietude' (the expression is Le Corbusier's, or rather his English translator's)[15] – a provocative assimilation of the material and the spiritual. The two circulation 'nets', one orthogonal and the other irregular, would be connected at various 'pressure points' by 'piazzas' and 'small squarish towers about 30m high' that were to house administrative offices for the shops below. At the suggestion of Peter Sigmond, who worked with the Smithsons on the competition entry, the buildings of an old district which had barely survived Allied bombing were to become, in Team 10 fashion, a Kasbah: 'everything which remains is preserved as far as possible, and between the preserved buildings are new buildings to an increased scale (about double) arranged around courtyards'.[16] This could be a reasonably accurate description of the Economist Building in its own context, which in effect is a realisation, at a smaller scale, of the Berlin Hauptstadt plan.

The premises of *The Economist* magazine had been bombed during the war. After several changes of address a five-storey building of once dubious reputation was bought in Ryder Street, in the heart of London's club land, where the Smithsons' tower now stands. In spite of a relatively modest circulation of 70,000, *The Economist* (established in 1843) enjoyed great respect and exercised considerable influence.[17] Sometimes described as belonging to 'the extreme centre', it was attached to no political party, and strove to offer disinterested analysis. Geoffrey Crowther, then its chairman, had been a formidable editor but, surprisingly for a man who was reputedly obsessed with gadgets and who had virtually designed his own houses, he showed little detailed interest in the new development.

The project originated in a desire to consolidate *The Economist* offices, then scattered in several buildings throughout the district. Its driving force was Peter Dallas-Smith, one of *The Economist*'s two joint managers, a man in his early forties, some ten years older than the Smithsons. Crowther gave him full control of the development, and made only two stipulations: Robert McAlpine & Sons Ltd, whose chairman, Edwin McAlpine, was an old friend, was to act as building contractor, and at the top of a new tower, which had to be at least ten storeys high, there would be a private flat for Crowther himself (who, according to Dallas-Smith, saw himself as a tycoon in the making). This extraordinary request had a major impact on the project. With a local plot ratio of 5:1[18] it could only be achieved through a major programme of property acquisition. Dallas-Smith recalls standing on the roof of their old premises with Crowther, pointing out all the buildings that would need to be acquired in order to generate 10,000m2 of

Overleaf
Alison and Peter Smithson, preliminary plan of entrance level (*left*) and upper floors (*right*), showing clockwise the residential block, the Economist tower, the bank building, and Boodle's Club, 1961

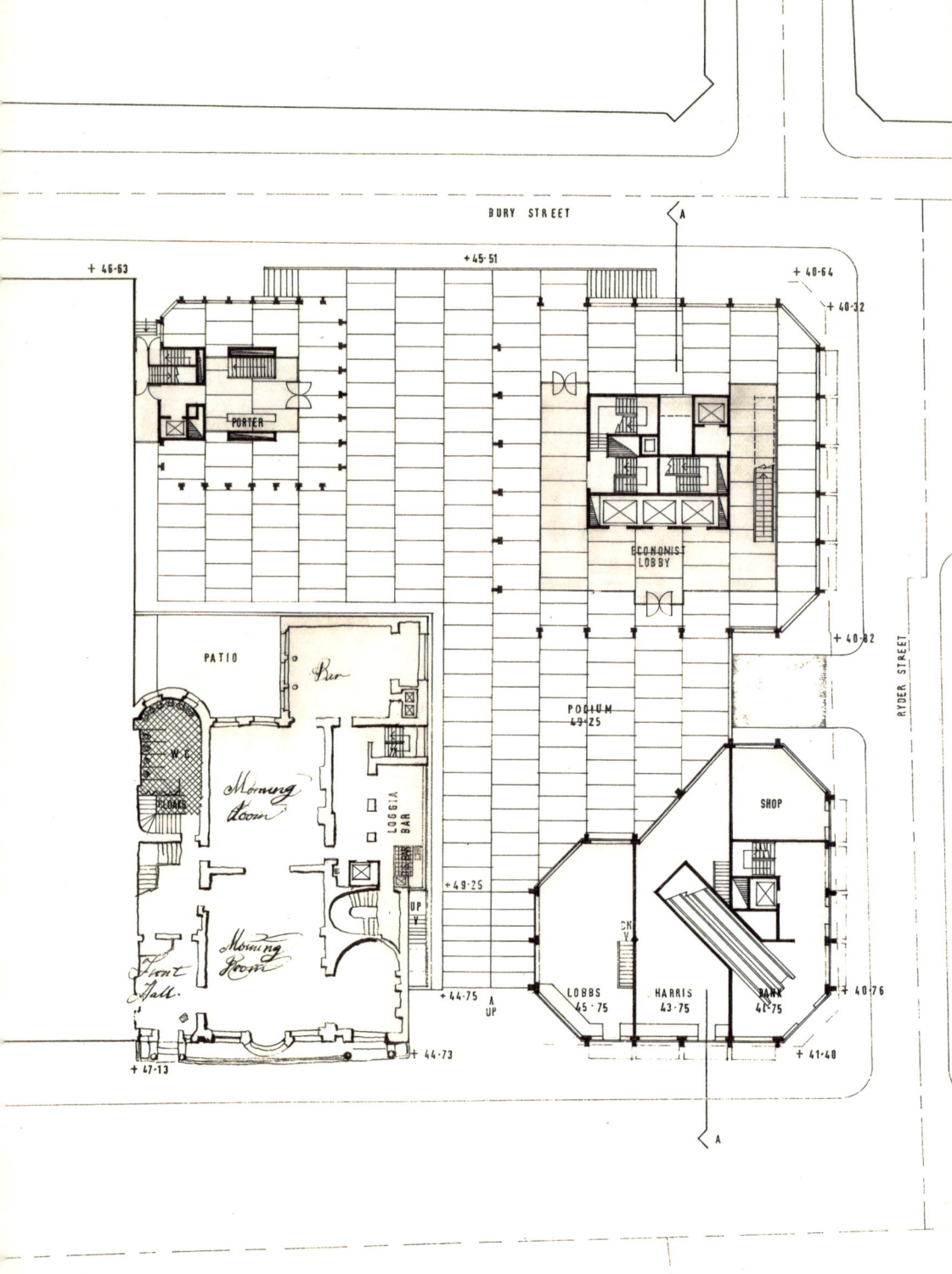

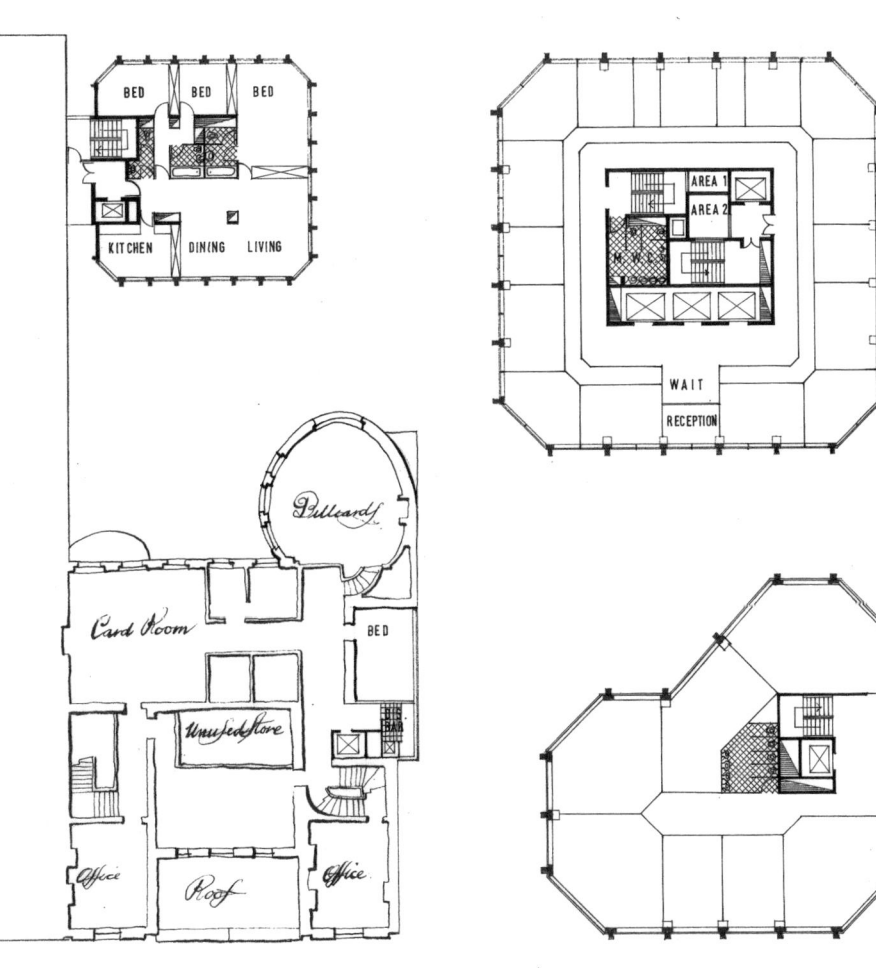

floor area. That it proved possible to purchase some 40 adjacent leases and sub-leases was in part due to the tacit support of the Crown Estates Commissioners, who owned the freeholds, as much as it gives an indication of Dallas-Smith's abilities as a project manager.

All the leaseholders ultimately gained from the development, not least *The Economist* itself. Its directors had supported the project from the outset, on the assumption that the building would pay for itself – which in the long term it did, many times over. Rents on the site tripled after completion and became so high that *The Economist* regularly had to ask itself whether it could afford to remain in the building.

Dallas-Smith began his search for an architect by approaching a number of architecture journalists, in particular the late Robert Furnaux-Jordan, at that time architecture correspondent of *The Observer.* On his advice Dallas-Smith interviewed around a dozen of the 21 invited participants to the Churchill Memorial College competition held in early 1959, who included the most creative practices of the time, among them the Smithsons. Dallas-Smith also consulted Leslie Martin, then professor of architecture at Cambridge. Martin privately suggested that the choice be narrowed down to Denys Lasdun or, if the clients were prepared to face possible difficulties, the Smithsons. In the event, Dallas-Smith retained two firms: the little-known George Trew & Dunn (Robin Dunn was a friend and neighbour) and the Smithsons, whose avant-garde reputation suited his mildly anti-establishment disposition.

Both teams of architects compiled a brief in collaboration with the staff of *The Economist* and at the end of a three-month period proposed an outline scheme. George Trew & Dunn produced a conventional, Lever House-like design, and it was immediately clear that the project by the Smithsons, who by then were favoured by the staff, was the more imaginative of the two. In May 1960 Leslie Martin offered his opinion to the board, and the Smithsons were given the commission.

Prior to the competition, McAlpine's in-house consultant architect, Maurice Bebb, had been independently appointed by the client as their consultant architect for the development.[19] He had already made preliminary studies which identified constraints on the building envelope. Planning legislation would allow a single-storey podium over the whole extent of the site. For the superstructure Bebb considered three options: a continuous perimeter block, a single tower set in the middle of the site, and a mixed solution where the frontage block on St James's Street continued the existing alignment, thus pushing the tower to the rear of the site.[20] A note on the drawing for this last option reads: 'A tower development may be set on a podium, with additional smaller blocks on the podium'.

The Smithsons adopted the third strategy, and it was this above all which persuaded the client in their favour. Their scheme divided the programme into three separate units, each accommodated in a separate building. Martins Bank and the retail businesses remaining on the site were rehoused in a block along St James's Street. The facade of this building re-established the alignment with the adjacent Boodle's club (the block which had previously stood on the site was two storeys higher), while the tall windows of the first-floor banking hall also echoed Boodle's *piano nobile*. *The Economist* itself was housed in a tower at the rear of the site, thus limiting the impact of its 14-storey height on St James's Street. A third block, which continued the existing alignment of Bury Street, accommodated the residential component of the brief – three floors of chambers for Boodle's (whose eighteenth-century premises were also refurbished as part of the development) and four flats above. The car park is housed beneath the podium, together with Boodle's new ladies' annexe, shops, various technical services and a now-disused restaurant for *The Economist*.

View north along Bury Street, London, 1988 © John Donat / RIBA Collections

The girth of the new buildings was to some extent predetermined by an obligation to maintain existing light levels inside the buildings facing on to the site. Constraints imposed by light angles further suggested the 45-degree truncation of the corners of the blocks (in his feasibility study Bebb had proposed that the single tower be twisted so that it stood at 45 degrees to the pavement line). This arrangement allowed maximum permeability of light through the site and a minimum loss of floor area in the new buildings. The decision to introduce these chamfered corners, not then fashionable as a form, is typical of the empirical priorities of postwar designers, who regarded daylight standards as critical.

Unlike the general massing of the scheme, which had been established during the short period of the competition, the internal plans evolved over the next two years. In *The Economist* tower the principal difficulty was that of containing the core within a neat, square curtilage. The service core was a recent American innovation, as yet untested in Britain, where the usual practice was to place the stairs of tall buildings against external walls, an arrangement which allowed natural ventilation. Similarly, the residential block was fitted with internal bathrooms, recently introduced in American hotels – though the plans for this block appear to have been low in the order of priorities, and were not completed until late in the design period.

The bank building presented the greatest difficulties. At first, its plan was indented at the rear in order to increase the area of the plaza, and to increase the sense of containment in front of *The Economist* entrance. Well into the design phase this dent was suppressed, a change that made it possible to clarify the vertical circulation to the upper office floors, which required separate access to the plaza. Escalators to the first-floor banking hall could now be positioned symmetrically on either side of the diagonal of the plan. The service areas were brought to the centre of the floors, according to the principles

already established for the tower. In addition, the dimensions of the revised northeast facade were such that it became possible to apply the same 10'6" grid to all three elevations (it was also applied to the tower). These changes were logical, and consistent with the overall design. Yet the diagonal orientation and the slashing of a corner in an otherwise square plan display a licence that at the time was unusual in Britan. Moreover, these features dispose of any suggestion that the three towers are merely variations on a theme borrowed from Mies van der Rohe or from SOM, and reflect, in a rather brutal way, the tension between an inherited Miesian sense of order and a desire to respond to local circumstance.

The decision to erect three separate buildings for the three distinct groups of tenants rather than a single tower greatly clarified the programme (even though the internal plans became more cramped as a result) and offered immediate advantages for the implementation of the project, and later its management. That it did not provide the maximum amount of floor space permissible on the site, and still less the maximum net-to-gross ratio of floor area in *The Economist* tower, gives a measure of the client's relative lack of concern for purely commercial considerations. As for the actual placement of the three buildings, it was perfectly logical, and the plaza was to a large extent a direct consequence of the *parti*.

Although the break in the street elevation between Boodle's club and the bank building represented a significant loss in frontage available for shops, the tower was, as a result, visible from the main street, and *The Economist* acquired a more prestigious address in St James's Street. The podium, accessible from the pavement via a shallow flight of stairs (the ramp was added later, to allow fire ladders access to the rear of the bank building), was conceived of as a public space comparable to the plazas which in the US had by then become a symbol of corporate munificence.

View south along Bury Street, London, 1968
© Nicholas Breach / RIBA Collections

Along Bury Street to the east, it was at first proposed that the two stairs leading up to the plaza be accommodated within the depth of the colonnades of both *The Economist* tower and the residential building. In this rather Italianate arrangement, which the Smithsons later incorporated in their design for the School of Architecture in Bath, the through-route would have engaged the actual structures of the buildings. In the final scheme the stairs were pushed outside the arcades, and were thus visible from afar, along Bury Street. When *The Economist* refurbished the building in 1990, they were replaced by a single flight of stairs on axis with the stairs in St James's Street to the west.[21] Sadly, this destroyed the careful grading of access to the plaza in relation to the scale of the adjoining streets.

The visibility of the plaza had from the start been a concern of the architects. Owing to the natural declivity of the site towards the south, cars were able to enter the car park from Ryder Street to the south, and the plaza could remain below eye level in relation to the busier pavements to the east and west of the site. Attempts were made to lower the podium further, and Peter Smithson still feels that the plaza would have been better had it been brought down another 30cm.

Boodle's blind party wall was another source of difficulties. How could it be anything but an oddity among its new neighbours, whose fenestration amply, if indiscriminately, acknowledged the public status of the plaza? How could it participate in the space of the plaza when, for its architects, the premodern fabric of cities had little if any formal interest beyond its function as the background of street life? The competition drawings convey the Smithsons' ambivalence towards this eighteenth-century building. Unlike the new buildings, which are drawn with a ruler and lettered with stencils, the freehand plans of Boodle's have a tongue-in-cheek quality and its rooms are labelled in an elegant round-hand, an ironic mode reminiscent of Saul Steinberg.

There was an early proposal to insert windows in the party wall, but this clashed with the Royal Fine Arts Commission's sense of propriety, which dictated that a terrace house must not be seen in the round. A later idea was to create in the upper southeast corner of the club a partly cantilevered oval billiard room which would project outwards over the plaza and articulate its spaces. In the end the architects accepted the presence of the party wall and simply continued the string courses of Boodle's St James's Street facade along the refaced side and rear brick walls. They may have found inspiration for this solution in the similar street elevation of Kahn's Yale University Art Gallery (1953), a building they knew and admired.

The party wall was interrupted midway by an existing light well. As this undoubtedly would have looked peculiar in its new surroundings, it was to be walled in and fitted with windows to provide additional rooms for the club. Not long before the building contract was negotiated, Tim Tinker, an assistant to the architects, proposed instead that it be enclosed within a new bay window. This ingenious addition with its 45-degree corners helped discreetly to bring Boodle's into the 'family' of towers, and alluded to the life beyond this expanse of brick.

The bay window was not well received by the critics, who interpreted it as a joke, and indeed it is not impossible that it was conceived in the same ironic spirit as the drawings of Boodle's. The lower opening casements sit uncomfortably on the ground, while the middle sash windows seem oddly attenuated, as if the bay window had emerged from the rabbit hole into which Alice disappeared.

The design of a podium for an urban setting demands a clear and confident interpretation which can overcome the impression that it merely represents space which was left over after the requirements of the brief were satisfied. Open to the street yet removed from it, plazas often seem to want

Overleaf
Domenico Veneziano,
The Annunciation,
c 1445–47
© The Fitzwilliam Museum, Cambridge

to be at once busy and secluded. On the one hand the Economist Building plaza was conceived of as a 'pool of quietude', a space which, like the courtyard of Aalto's Säynätsalo Town Hall (1951), would be raised above traffic noise and fumes.[22] Moreover, the Smithsons supplied incentives to contemplation – a long stone bench (which also masked a ventilation shaft to the car park) and a proposal for sculpture (Dallas-Smith visited Henry Moore with a view to finding a suitable piece for the podium).

On the other hand, the plaza was to serve as a way through to the entrance to the tower (what the architects later described as 'the pavilion and the route')[23] and as a short cut comparable to older passages in the district of St James's. In an attempt to relieve anxieties that the plaza might be underused, the Smithsons showed the client a film on their Berlin Hauptstadt competition entry, which proposed a parallel between the Berlin platforms, raised to the same level as the *S-Bahn*, and London's Liverpool Street Station, seductively shot at rush hour. It was envisaged that, as a consequence of the various activities housed in the towers, the platforms would be 'kept in full use'.[24] In the event, at the Economist Building a newsagent's kiosk set on the podium side of the bank building failed to survive for very long. The Hauptstadt proposal wanted to be at once empty and full. Unlike the Plan Voisin, in which isolation, whether on foot or at the wheel, was accepted as the norm, at Hauptstadt the sense of solitude was to be tempered with a promise of vitality. The Hauptstadt model was later adopted for the design of the platforms at the South Bank arts complex (1960–62). Here, as in the Berlin project and at St James's, the solitude implied or promoted by the circulation spaces was never successfully articulated by the conviviality envisaged at the 'pressure points'. In the case of the Economist Building's plaza, the density of the surroundings helped prevent the air of desolation which has always marred the South Bank complex.

Although something about the Economist Building wants to be open and expansive, like the Hauptstadt platforms, circumstances forced upon it a diminutive scale and the intimacy of the miniature. This inadvertent distortion was reinforced by the deliberate scaling-down of the modules of the facades: 10'6" for the bank building facing St James's Street, 10'6" with a central mullion for the Economist Building tower (based on the width of a two-person office), and 5'3" for the residential building on Bury Street. While the plaza tends to seem most deserted in the vicinity of Boodle's chambers, it is here, seen from behind the closely packed columns of the arcade, that it feels most intimate.

There is also an architectural density here, if not a human one, and it is something which seems to be implied by the architects' comparison of the podium and its towers to cups clustered on a table. This metaphor also hints at the seemingly spontaneous siting of the towers – though perhaps there were rather more constraints at the Economist Building than at Hauptstadt. The Smithsons were opposed to the megastructures which had become fashionable during the 1950s. Countering what might be described as an architecture of the airline dinner-pack with that of the tea set, they sought a more open-ended method of planning, one in which 'the circulation systems and the humanly occupied parts are [not] locked into an unalterable embrace'[25] – one in which function and structure, and building and city, can easily be accommodated with each other.

But a limiting framework for the exercise of such openness was needed in order to preserve the identity of a city. While most British architects opted for the picturesque, using art to combat ugliness, the Smithsons were more confident in the forces of modernity. Believing that architects themselves were at fault by interfering too much – whether for artistic or practical motives – with the organic workings of the city, they advocated a deliberate, Mies-inspired restraint, an overcoming

Overleaf
View of the plaza from Bury Street, 1964
Photograph
Michael Carapetian

of conscious intent (described by a journalist on *The Economist* as 'Buddhist').[26] They envisioned an urbanism in which functionally compatible buildings, like the components of a tea set, would acquire a kind of neutrality and family likeness, with the space between them becoming 'the collective of the spaces that each of the buildings carries with it'.[27] Peter Smithson recalls the genesis of this idea in a visit in 1947 to a housing estate in Sweden which consisted of a series of point blocks, their chamfered corners (a device which was later used in both Hauptstadt and the Economist Building) unifying the informal layout at the top of a hill in such a way that 'form and space cannot be pulled apart: they form a crown'.[28]

Such broadly symbolic preoccupations were accompanied by speculations on the nature of urban life. The Smithsons calculated that 'for some 40 per cent of the population of big cities "hotel life", by which is meant the maximum of privacy, anonymity, and simplicity of service, is suitable and pleasurable'.[29] Here again the Swedish point blocks served as a model, as did the Lake Shore Drive apartment blocks (1951). In 1959 they used a photograph of the latter, taken by Peter Smithson, to illustrate an article titled 'Scatter'.[30] Instead of the usual lake-front view, it shows Mies van der Rohe's towers relegated to a corner of the frame and partly concealed by a brick wall. They appear no less anonymous than the ordinary housing blocks by their side, and, like them, appear to have been conditioned more by property values and planning constraints than by visual or spatial concerns. Peter Smithson's photograph seems to suggest that if architecture is to make a genuine contribution to the modern city it must acknowledge, and work in conjunction with, the forces that contribute to its making. This position, developed by the Smithsons throughout the 1950s, was a highly original one, and some 40 years later it was still being worked out by Rem Koolhaas, Jean Nouvel and others.

The Smithsons further argued that the very notion of space, which they saw as a legacy of the baroque period, acted as an obstruction to responsive planning. To support their hypothesis they, like Le Corbusier, turned to the architecture of ancient Greece for evidence:

> in the case of the arrangement of buildings there was no system, no formalisation of relationship at all. There was instead that so-called spontaneous building which we are familiar with, for example, in the villages of modern India, or in the medieval European town. That is, decisions were made through some process, the mechanisms of which are now no longer available to us, which enabled the correct *gesture* to be made in the situation.[31]

Moreover, such a gesture was not merely appropriate, they maintained, but aimed to enhance experience:

> if a route ran along a certain way, it was to give importance to that route by the position of buildings in relationship to it. Similarly, if there was such an activity as going to the temple or going shopping, the organisation of the buildings was such that it gave an importance to that activity which, without the buildings, it would not otherwise have had. That is, it gives a sort of value to an activity which would be otherwise banal or at the worst would, if it were not given value, mean the well-springs of your existence dried up, because there was no system of relationship, no reason for going on doing that thing.[32]

Like the Pre-Raphaelites, the Smithsons sought to retrieve the directness and simplicity of a primitive awareness which had been buried under three centuries of neo-classical culture. The manipulation of space, which they regarded as an essentially cerebral imposition of art on life, was to make way for a visceral apprehension of buildings and experience rolled into one.

Overleaf
View into Martins Bank with the reflection of the Economist tower and the residential block to the left, and the party wall and new bay window of Boodle's Club to the right, 1964

Space itself, 'the invention of a later crowded age',[33] would again be taken for granted, becoming as natural and profuse as the air we breathe. Decades after the Plan Voisin, the Virgilian dream of a countryside at peace with itself would at last join the notion of the city. Yet why the apprehension of space, as opposed to buildings, should, once perceived, conflict with one's understanding of experience remains unclear.

In fact Peter Smithson emphasises the spatial qualities of the Economist Building plaza. Provided that the surroundings are made sufficiently recessive, as for instance in the painting of the Annunciation (c 1445–47) by Domenico Veneziano in the Fitzwilliam Museum, Cambridge, 'when something happens in the space, it becomes wonderfully full', and 'the gesture in calm space tells the story without having to draw the message'. At the Economist Building the very materials seem to suggest such self-effacement: the chunks (rather than leaves) of stone; the ample, origami-like extruded aluminium of the window frames, sills and gutters; and the vast brick flank of Boodle's, which helps to 'pull the temperature down'. The general arrangement of the facades is derived from Mies, but in the hands of Peter Smithson (who designed and drew most of the exterior details), the Miesian qualities of mass and gravity, if not suppressed, have at least been internalised. The same below-the-skin sensibility prevails in the herring-bone pattern of the paving which, as the joint lines zig-zag outwards from the axis of symmetry, guide the visitor 'subliminally' towards the building entrances on the plaza.[34]

The brutalists' predilection for using materials 'as found' is sometimes confused with a resistance to any form of expression, as exemplified in the work of an architect like Hannes Meyer. Like many artists of the 1950s the Smithsons valued materials, and all artefacts, including cities, insofar as they had *pattern:* electronic circuitry, lines in the palm of a hand, symbols of dead languages – all these were traces that hinted at a latent but more real world. The tiny shell encrustations of the roach-bed Portland stone at the Economist Building are the opposite of mute essence, and allude to what Henri Michaux, that great chronicler of subliminal experience, called 'the life in the folds'. The brutalists sought the magical within the ordinary,[35] which might in turn stimulate an increased awareness of, and sympathy with, the physical environment: 'a building today is only interesting if it is more than itself, if it charges the space around it with connective possibilities, especially if it does this by a quietness that until now our sensibilities could not recognise as architecture at all.'[36] In the article by Peter Smithson from which this quote is taken, there follows a long discussion of works by Mies which make it clear that what is being presented here is an instance of 'less is more'. However, by 'less' the Smithsons did not intend the reduction of a thing to its essence, and they rejected the formalism that such a practice engendered: 'On the way to IIT one sees derelict houses and workshops with all the vocabulary of IIT in embryo. These were buildings which were just made. With Mies, they become thought about. They become an idea, a stylistic operation.'[37] By contrast, 'the Economist Building is about manipulating the making. It is not about ideas'.[38] It merely represents the 'correct' degree of immersion in a situation.

This is why the label of masterpiece is not one which the Economist Building wears with ease. Unlike the Seagram Building (1957), it does not embody aspirations beyond the conditions that brought it into being – to reveal, as Mies described it, 'the significance of facts'. Nevertheless, the Smithsons recognised that in particular circumstances architecture can acquire the status of an idea. For example, the use of the Doric order in the Parthenon reflects a higher level of consciousness than in earlier temples such as the one at Bassae. Likewise, the Economist Building raised the awareness of space and technique that typified American office buildings of the 1950s, especially those by SOM.

View east from Park Place, London, 1964
Photograph Michael Carapetian

In this process the architect acts as midwife to, rather than the author of, a collective idea that responds to more than just the consumption of culture. As this idea makes it possible to convey the value of a building or of an aspect of it, it will enable the repetition and development of a particular thing – for example the Doric order – and will motivate further collective action. This thoughtful pragmatism is central to the Smithsons' approach. For the last two decades it has proved utterly alien to the abstractions and formalism which have prevailed in architecture. Today its emphasis on concrete experience and action seems refreshing and relevant.

*Originally published as
'"Architecture is not made with the Brain":
The Smithsons and the Economist Building Plaza',
Archis 7, 1995*

This essay is based on interviews with Peter Smithson, with the Smithsons' assistants George Kasabov and Tim Tinker, and with the client representative in charge of the project (and later managing director of *The Economist*), Peter Dallas-Smith. The title was suggested by Peter Smithson in a conversation with the author which took place in May 1994.

1. Brochure published by *The Economist,* 1964.
2. Tom Houston, in 'AA Visit: The Smithsons' "Economist" Buildings', *AA Journal,* February 1965, p 207.
3. N Keith Scott, 'The Economist Building: Review', *Architect & Building News,* 20 January 1965, vol 227, p 104.
4. Vincent Scully, 'New British Buildings', *Architectural Design,* May 1965, p 266.
5. Ian Nairn, 'The Establishment Strides Again!', *Architectural Forum,* April 1965, vol 122, no 1, p 13.
6. Unsigned, 'Economist Building', *Architect & Building News,* 20 January 1965, vol 227, p 112.
7. Peter Blake, in Ian Nairn, *op cit,* p 18.
8. Gordon Cullen, 'The Economist Buildings, St James's', *The Architectural Review,* February 1965, vol 137, no 816, p 115; and J M Richards, *The Listener,* 10 December 1964, p 933.
9. Kenneth Frampton, 'The Economist and the Hauptstadt', *Architectural Design,* February 1965, p 61.
10. Reyner Banham, 'Crowther's Acropolis', *New Statesman,* 15 January 1965, p 83.
11. See, for example, Alison and Peter Smithson, 'Today, we collect ads', ARK 18, November 1956, p 48.
12. Alison and Peter Smithson, 'Cluster City', *The Architectural Review,* November 1957, vol 122, no 730, p 334.
13. Louis Kahn, 'Towards a Plan for Midtown Philadelphia', *Perspecta* 2, 1953, p 11.
14. Alison and Peter Smithson, 'Scatter', *Architectural Design,* April 1959, p 149.
15. In French, *'rues de repos'*. See Le Corbusier, *Oeuvre complète,* vol 1 (Zurich: Girsberger, 1953), p 114; and Alison and Peter Smithson, 'Cluster City', *op cit,* 'Scatter', *op cit,* p 149.
16. Alison and Peter Smithson, 'Hauptstadt Berlin', *Architect & Building News,* 2 July 1958, vol 214, no 1, p 10.
17. For a history of *The Economist* see Ruth Dudley Edwards, *The Pursuit of Reason: The Economist 1843–1993* (London: Hamish Hamilton, 1993).
18. That is, the allowable building area was five times the area of the plot.
19. On Edwin McAlpine's advice, Maurice Bebb's services were retained throughout the contract, notably to ensure that the technical aspects of the project as well as its cost were kept under control. Bebb would have been perfectly able to carry out a commission such as the Economist development on his own, but he felt that the location of the site was too important not to make it the object of a competition. This was unusually generous on the part of an architect. As Peter Smithson put it, 'he changed our lives'.
20. Drawings of these are preserved in *The Economist* archives.
21. See Stephen Greenberg, 'The Economist Building: Going Club Class', *The Architects' Journal,* 28 November 1990, vol 192, no 22, p 53.
22. The description is Peter Smithson's (conversation with the author, 24 February 1994).

23 Alison and Peter Smithson, 'The Pavilion and the Route', *Architectural Design*, March 1965, p 143. The article was written in 1961.
24 Alison and Peter Smithson, 'Hauptstadt Berlin', *op cit*, p 8.
25 Alison and Peter Smithson, 'The Pavilion and the Route', *op cit*, p 143.
26 Tom Houston, *op cit*, p 207.
27 Alison and Peter Smithson, 'The Pavilion and the Route', *op cit*.
28 Conversation with the author, 19 May 1994.
29 Alison and Peter Smithson, 'Scatter', *op cit*, p 29.
30 *Ibid*.
31 Peter Smithson, 'Theories Concerning the Layout of Classical Greek Buildings', *AA Journal*, February 1959, vol LXXIV, no 829, p 207.
32 *Ibid*, p 208.
33 Alison and Peter Smithson, *Without Rhetoric* (Cambridge, MA: MIT Press, 1974), p 55.
34 Peter Smithson credits George Kasabov, one of the office assistants on the Economist Building, with the idea.
35 See Peter Smithson, 'Just a Few Chairs and a House: An Essay on the Eames Aesthetic', *Architectural Design*, September 1966, p 443.
36 Alison and Peter Smithson, *Without Rhetoric*, *op cit*, p 36.
37 Conversation with the author, 19 May 1994.
38 *Ibid*.

The Seed

Much uncertainty surrounds both the person and the works of Donato Bramante (1444–1514). How fitting, therefore, that his artistic education should have taken place at or near the Ducal Palace of Urbino, a building which witnessed the involvement of many of the greatest figures of the Renaissance, among them, Federico da Montefeltro, Piero della Francesca, Luciano Laurana and Francesco di Giorgio. With only few exceptions, none can be said for sure to have been responsible for the design of specific parts, prompting among scholars a never-ending game of musical chairs. In any case, according to one commentator the palace forms an artistic whole so great that the name of any individual master becomes irrelevant.[1] Instead it defines an ambience referred to as the 'spirit of Urbino', or even, in apparent disregard of the collective nature of its creation, the 'spirit of Piero'.

Bramante's own activity was first recorded in 1477, not in Urbino but in Bergamo. All that is known about his connection with the court of Urbino are brief accounts written 35 years after his death, in which mention is made of him having been a pupil of Piero della Francesca. From the latter, he would have learnt the art of perspective. This at least seems likely, given Piero's authoritative treatise on the subject, though he could equally have learnt it from Fra Carnevale, an Urbinate painter whose work he studied. It is on this basis that Bramante is said to have absorbed the 'civilisation of perspective' and the 'mathematical humanism' of Urbino.[2]

These are strange expressions. Can a civilisation really be founded on the discovery of perspective? Can humanism ever be said to be mathematical? Nevertheless, they eventually came to designate a distinctive conception of reality. Erwin Panofsky referred to the purely mathematical space of perspective, to a space that is infinite, unchanging and homogeneous[3] – to a space which Superstudio later parodied. What makes this space so distinctive is that the process of its geometrical construction binds air and bodies together in a quiver of projection lines.

Maarten van Heemskerck, interior of basilica of St Peter's, Rome © Staatliche Museen zu Berlin / De Agostini / Getty Images

By no means a merely theoretical thought, it is plain to see in so many paintings of the second half of the *Quattrocento*.

In Piero's *Flagellation*, for instance, the effect of perspective imparts to the space not only depth but also some of the movement implicit in the action. Conversely, it also lends to the human figures the stillness of the architecture, each one upright like a column, with the straps of the flagellant's whip perfectly plumb, like the fluting of adjacent shafts. Space is in itself an invitation to movement while movement is held in check by the tight construction of the space. The same could be said about the eight panels depicting the *Miracles of San Bernardino*, now in Perugia, a series with which the names of Bramante and of two of his artist friends, Perugino and Pinturicchio, have been associated. Dramatic and occasionally violent, the action is held in suspense by the architecture.

The 'seeing through' (which Panofsky reminds us is the etymological root of *perspectiva*) is manifest in these views. It can also be seen in the expression of Piero's portraits and more particularly in their eyes. Here, too, one finds a stillness, a depth, a quality of innocence equivalent in the realm of sensibility to the objective construction of the visual field. To the science of perspectival projection corresponds a distinct mentality, a carefully measured sense of perspective. To the specific universal space of the Renaissance corresponds an equally specific frame of mind.

The convergence of a constructed world and a virtuous mind became a fixture of Urbinate culture. It also found expression in the architecture of the ducal palace, in the breadth of its conception, in the stillness and the luminosity of its spaces and in the comeliness of its ornament. From Piero himself, according to a historian, would have originated a temperance in profusion, a specific feeling for space and for the relationship between structure and ornament.[4] Today, the palace commonly inspires among visitors an affection commensurate to the love which Federico inspired among his subjects.

Pietro Perugino, *The Miracles of San Bernardino: The Healing of a Young Girl*, 1473
©Galleria Nazionale dell'Umbria

Yet the duke's apartments form a most curious anomaly. Following the layout of the larger rooms around a spacious courtyard, this simple order was compromised and the western facade was oriented at an angle to face the valley, the incoming road and the view. The duke's apartments – 'the most beautiful and imaginative spatial conception of the *Quattrocento*'[5] and the expression of a comprehensive humanist programme – were then fitted in the opening wedge between courtyard and facade.

In sharp contrast with the ease shown elsewhere, the plan of the apartments is awkward, as if constrained by medieval practice. Sometimes a large room pushes outwards against the oblique facade, resulting in a splayed corner and irregularities in the vaulting above. On other occassions the small rooms – the two chapels on the ground floor and the *studiolo* on the first floor – appear to push inwards in search of the space they need. In these parts the intensification of the ornament struggles to conceal the irregularities in the plan. Whereas vaults throughout the palace are coved and plain, the loggias and, on the ground floor, the two chapels and the adjoining passage are each covered with a barrel vault decorated with coffers. This lends the crowded sequence of rooms a character that is at once primitive and antique, medieval and classical.

Throughout the Renaissance, writers from Dante onwards set the ancient world and the Christian world alongside one another. So did Federico in the alignment of the two sanctuaries, the pagan Tempietto delle Muse and the Christian Cappella del Perdono. About the Tempietto, little is known, its panels having been removed in the seventeenth century. Like the *studiolo* above it, it opens directly onto the loggia. While the vault of the latter recalls in a much reduced scale Alberti's portico at San Andrea in Mantua, the vault of the *tempietto* replicates in a still smaller scale that of the loggia. The reduction in scale of the ornament compensates for the reduction in size of the rooms, the rosette in the coffers of the vault now highlighted

Donato Bramante (attributed to), Cappella del Perdono, Palazzo Ducale, Urbino, 1472
©Alinari Archives, Florence

in gold against an ultramarine background. The wall decoration has not survived with the exception of eight panels painted by Raphael's father, Giovanni Santi, representing a muse and, on two instances, an ancient god.

The adjoining *cappella* is the only room in the palace that was clad in marble, a clear indication of the value in which it was held. Further proof is given by the existence of sketches by Leonardo da Vinci made on the occasion of a visit to Urbino in 1502 (three years after Bramante settled in Rome). They show the entrance portal, details of the ornament and a view of the interior. Leonardo was a friend of Bramante, making the attribution of the design to the latter tempting. A modern label by the entrance of the chapel proudly advertises his name but no hard evidence has survived to justify the attribution. More recently, the case has been made for the attribution of its design to Francesco di Giorgio.[6]

Deprived of natural light, the chapel must have been lit by candles (not, as now, floodlit by fluorescents). Its width is such that a person with arms outstretched can easily touch both sides. Unlike the *studiolo* above it, the vertical divisions of the walls bear little relation to human height. The wall cladding forms two horizontal registers, the lower with red and the upper with black decorative marble insets. Above the first, an exquisite frieze in bas-relief runs the whole perimeter of the room immediately above the altar top – a fact that must have determined its height. Awkwardly, it is not at eye level where its ancient motifs of winged animals would be most easily seen, but at shoulder height.

Another frieze of marble discs runs beneath the cornice, not overly concerned whether at the corners two discs shall meet or a single one shall be split in two halves – both solutions can be found. Above it, an architrave of black marble is carved with an inscription at once too high and too near to be read in comfort. On the vault, winged cherubs, each one unique, flutter inside compartments that were once gilded.

Piero della Francesca, *Brera Altarpiece*, 1472–74
©Pinacoteca di Brera, Milan

In its proportions if not in its detail, the *cappella* is like a small gothic church. An apse or, more accurately, a niche has been scooped above the altar. Inside a shelf once carried relics, while on either side two small onyx columns stand out with their unusual deep yellow colour, crowned with composite capitals. Upon them springs the ornamented arch of the niche.

Repeatedly, the arrangement has been compared to the background Piero created in the Brera Altarpiece. The painting was completed in 1474, the year he started work on his treatise on perspective, *De Perspectiva Pingendi*, and it predates by at least six years the completion of the chapel. It was attributed in the nineteenth century to Fra Carnevale (the painter under whom Bramante studied) on the misguided assumption that Piero did not paint on canvas. Jacob Burckhardt wrote of its background that it is 'clearly the work of an architect of genius', an observation which must have contributed to its association with the prestigious name of Bramante.[7]

There are indeed similarities, all of them noted by others, between the altarpiece and the chapel – the polychrome marble panels, the thin dark line of the architrave, the coffered vault and the half-dome of the apse – and they are considerably strengthened by the presence in Piero's painting of Federico kneeling in prayer. But there are significant differences, too. The proportions of the space in the altarpiece are broader and more classical in feeling. Instead of miniature columns framing the apse, Piero chose Corinthian pilasters rising (so it appears) the full height of the wall. In the *cappella*, the same arrangement may well have been envisaged, but the narrow width and the relatively tall height of the space must have argued against it. Most beautifully in the Brera Altarpiece, Piero fits inside the cavity of the half dome the delicate shape of a scallop shell – a feature which compares favourably with the dark vacancy of the half dome at Urbino.

Ten years after Piero, Bramante (or the artist in charge of the ornament) used the same motif in the choir and in the sacristy of Santa Maria presso Santa Satiro in Milan. But the ears of the shell are now at the base of the half dome, the ridges spreading upwards and forming a corrugated edge along the arc of the half dome. The motif, then relatively common in northern Italy, was more logical but less poetic. Towards the end of his life, Bramante appears to have repeated it in the choir of St Peter's, as shown in a drawing of the basilica under construction by Maarten van Heemskerck. He further repeated it in the choir of Santa Maria del Popolo. But the resilium of the shell is now firmly located at the apex of the dome, like in Piero's painting, with its ridges spreading downwards before disappearing behind the edge of the cornice.

The current historical tradition – one for which Arnaldo Bruschi is chiefly responsible – attributes a painterly origin to Bramante's work from which the architect would have gradually emancipated himself. Thus Bramante not merely 'designed' his buildings in the manner of Alberti, he painted and coloured them. Not merely intellectual, his early work affects us 'through the senses and the emotions, by means of colour, light, perspective and atmosphere'.[8] Was not the *cappella* more vivid in its polychromy than any Renaissance work that preceded it? And what of the 'false perspective' in the chancel of Santa Maria presso Santa Satiro? What of the decorative roundels painted all over the arches at Santa Maria della Grazie? Did Bramante not study, as Vasari tells us, with a painter, Fra Carnevale, rather than an architect? Did he not count among his friends Perugino, Pinturicchio and Signorelli, all of them painters associated with Piero's workshop? Besides, was not Bramante a gifted painter in his own right, as his *Christ at the Column* (now at the Brera) surely testifies?

Bramante's closeness to painters and his great reputation as an architect ensured that whenever architecture was represented in a painting, its design was spontaneously attributed to him. Thus the painting which today represents the sum of the architectural and urban ideas of the *Quattrocento*,

The Ideal City preserved in the ducal palace at Urbino, was in the eighteenth century attributed to Bramante. It was later attributed to Fra Carnevale, then to Piero, later still to Francesco di Giorgio and Luciano Laurana, and most recently to an 'unknown Umbrian painter'. So much for scholarship.

No wonder, then, that painting, architecture and perspective should have formed so durable an amalgam. Bruschi regarded the methods of Bramante the architect and Bramante the painter as interchangeable: 'essentially, architecture became "painting", a visual fact, a representation complete in itself'.[9] It was considered as appearance rather than physical reality. Thus the *cappella* would have been built to approximate the effect of Piero's altarpiece. But this hardly describes what the *cappella* actually feels like. Rather than an image, it feels very much 'there'.

More than any other room in the palace it is a place which encloses you and which you can touch, where the quality of the stonework can be felt with the hand. Rather than visual facts, the details of the *cappella*, being for most of the time in semi-darkness, would have been hard to see. 'Perspectival space', Panofsky wrote, 'transforms physiological space into mathematical space'.[10] Far from being a 'mathematical space', the *cappella* remains a physiological space. Standing at the entrance, one does not feel that one is looking through a window, as one does with a perspective. Standing inside it, no surface presents itself as a picture, unlike in the *studiolo* above. Its designer may have found inspiration in painting. But rather than designing the space to look like a perspective, the process would have been reversed, as if perspective, for instance that of the Brera Altarpiece, had been deconstructed to restore the space which it described.

The choir of Santa Maria presso Santa Satiro offers a demonstration of this process *ad absurdum*. For if a perspective is constructed on the basis of a single point of view, the 'false perspective' at Santa Maria presso Santa Satiro is indeed

Donato Bramante, choir of Santa Maria del Popolo, Rome, 1505–10
From Costantino Baroni, *Donato Bramante*, 1944

false in that it admits as many viewpoints as there are observers in the church. Hence the gross deformations and the unsettling, vicarious pleasure it offers of looking at the choir as if from the wings, into the mind of Bramante himself. The choir in Milan demonstrates the impossibility of reconstructing reality on the basis of a perspective. Perspective is a one-way street. In this sense, Bramante's choir in Milan is comparable to Cubist sculpture, for instance to Picasso's *Apple* (1909), an apple-size sculpture to which he gave the faceted appearance of a Cubist painting. It is seductive, delightful even, *because* it is absurd.

These reservations aside, the comparison between the *cappella* and the background on Piero's altarpiece remains attractive. The former's restricted width insures that it admits only a single viewpoint. Like the *studiolo*, the *cappella* is a space conceived for one man, Federico, who was able to celebrate a 'solitary mass'.[11] As such, it recalls the well-known drawings by Leonardo, Francesco di Giorgio and others depicting a man with arms and legs reaching out like spokes in a circle. Standing in the chapel one does feel, like Vitruvius who inspired these drawings, that 'in the human body the central point is naturally the navel'.[12]

One does feel, too, the aptness of Pico della Mirandola's phrase when he wrote: 'And if he [man] … gathers himself into the centre of his own unity, thus becoming a single spirit with God in the solitary darkness of the Father, he, who had been placed above all things, will become superior to all things.'[13] This phrase, by one of the foremost humanists of the late *Quattrocento*, powerfully suggests the mood inside the chapel. It offers a summary of Federico's humanist programme compressed in its miniature space.

The chapel evokes the ancient world but it is a world that was longed for and imagined more than it was actually known. Whoever was in charge of the design of the *cappella* combined grotesque figures in the dado-height frieze, roundels beneath

Donato Bramante, Santa Maria presso San Satiro, Milan, 1482–86
From Costantino Baroni, *Donato Bramante*, 1944

the 'correct' architrave and cherubs on the vault, none of them related in form, iconography or scale. Indeed, the dominant impression is of a design without scale, as if every detail had been determined by the technique and the application required by its particular craft.

Standing at the entrance of the *cappella* one has the intuition of a mysterious threshold between design and architecture. The space is small enough so that it can be contained in the mind (and remembered by Leonardo in a sketch) yet large enough, but only just, so that it can be entered and experienced. It is clearly a work of intellect, yet it appeals powerfully to human presence. It is as if the person of Federico, made conspicuous by his absence *a contrario* the Brera Altarpiece, gave expression to a generic humanity. Deep inside the palace, like a pip inside a fruit, the tiny *cappella* is at the core of Federico's humanist programme.

Its design fails to measure up to the promise of Piero's painting. It does not have the sophistication of Alberti's Tempietto of the Holy Sepulchre in Florence completed some ten years previously. But what it lacks in originality and consistency it makes up in craft and concentration. Standing inside it, one feels a primeval quality drawing from the most remote antiquity as well as the beginning of Christianity. Peering into it, one looks as if in miniature towards such 'universal' designs as the choir of Santa Maria del Popolo and the great vault of the *School of Athens* by Raphael, towards the pure, absolute essence of antiquity which has been claimed to be Bramante's stylistic ideal.

Alberti was the initiator, a *dilettante* for whom no subject or emotion failed to engage his all-sided nature. Then came Bramante, the finisher, the master who guided architecture towards an ideal of classical perfection. He became the model which later generations of classicists sought to emulate, and the only Renaissance architect whom Serlio and Palladio ranked alongside the ancients. With him architecture reached a plateau, offering no great expeditions inside a field that had been once

Detail, Santa Maria presso San Satiro, Milan, 1482–86
From Costantino Baroni, *Donato Bramante*, 1944

and for all circumscribed, and no great climbs on a terrain that had been made even and flat. It seemed to have attained the highest possible achievement, thus curtailing prospects for genuine invention.

Architecture became preoccupied instead with the establishment of types, with the establishment of norms and the application of rules. In this respect the buildings of the high Renaissance resemble that of the recent past. Similarly, Aldo Rossi, Giorgio Grassi and O M Ungers are finishers to initiators like Adolf Loos, Ludwig Hilberseimer and Le Corbusier. Their mode is one of abstinence from invention, their work, a pointed rebuff to an over-stimulated imagination. Today, we copy. But copy what? Or who? The moderns or the classics? Grassi? Hilberseimer? Durand? Bramante? Should we copy the copyists and observe the progressive dissolution of architectural meaning into abstraction?

Renaissance humanists had no such hesitations. They were avid copyists. They wanted to know what the ancients knew, to write as the ancients wrote, to think and soon to feel as the ancients thought and felt. Prior to the invention of printing, the prestige associated with copying and translating was great. In the fifteenth century quotation became the main concern of orators. The rhetorical style was clarified and classical perfection was attainable.

The same process characterised the imitation of ancient architecture and it contributed to the progressive refinement of Bramante's work. But refinement came at a price. As antiquity became the model for all thought and action, the conception of it became increasingly dogmatic. Quotation became valued at the expense of creation, and obedience to the authority of the ancients at the expense of freedom of thought. The history of architecture offers many such episodes, none more problematic than the bland neo-classicism of the period between the two world wars and its readiness to serve authoritarian regimes. Ironically, among these works is the small room designed in 1925 by Piero Portaluppi to accommodate Raphael's *Marriage of the Virgin* in the Pinacoteca di Brera, for which the architect imitated the Cappella del Perdono.

Not for the first time was classical architecture claimed as default architecture. Nor is it likely to be the last. In the call for papers for the present issue of *San Rocco*, the editors claim that Bramante set the foundation of universalism in western architecture. They commend his development of a more efficient grammar. They praise his indifference to style and the abstraction of his architecture. In this way Bramante could embrace an increasingly varied range of projects and absorb in his work contributions by others. 'Classicism', say the editors in a memorable phrase, 'is the conscious idea of a universal architecture'.[14]

The rediscovery of antiquity during the Renaissance was truly a revelation which affected Bramante and his contemporaries like a grace and led them to idolise the ancient world. This was not the work of particular individuals but, according to Burckhardt, the work of historical providence.[15] In this way the ancient world was instituted as a model and the grand manner of the Renaissance was born, one that was arguably independent from local identities and universal. In turn, this model could be copied with the means then made available in the arts, science and politics.

In our own time, the dominant belief is that art is founded on originality, on radicalism, on invention, and it places little or no value on imitation. But Bramante and his contemporaries saw no contradiction between the rise of individuality and the imitation of the ancients. On the contrary, since the publication of Burckhardt's great essay, both have remained central to any account of the Renaissance. The revelation of one's own individual capacity and the discovery of the ancient world and its presumed universal truth powerfully stimulated one another.

In a celebrated account of the Creation, Pico della Mirandola describes the freedom of the individual in a fully prescribed world. God had finished his work. Every place had been filled, and all things had been assigned to a particular order. The world being thus entirely determined, God still longed for there to be someone to ponder its meaning, to love its beauty and to marvel at its vastness. 'He therefore took man', Pico continues, 'a creature of indeterminate image, set him in the middle of the world and said to him:

> We have given you, Adam, no fixed seat or form of your own, no talent peculiar to you alone. This we have done so that whatever seat, whatever form, whatever talent you may judge desirable, these same you may have and possess according to your desire and judgement.[16]

Whereas all other beings are constrained by laws, man is constrained by none so that he may himself determine his nature according to his own free will. It is in his own power to either degenerate into the lower forms of life or to fly off and sit near the Divinity among seraphims and cherubs.

This conception of the Creation resonates with the invention of perspective. On one side of the picture plane is the world, rigidly determined by mathematical laws, where all things are assigned to a specific place and every place is filled. On the other side, at the end of the visual pyramid, is man, indeterminate and free to choose his place in the world. Looking through the picture plane, man can ponder the meaning of the world, love its beauty and marvel at its vastness, as one does when looking at a Renaissance painting.[17] Only then, when man marvels before the mystery of creation, can the imitation of the world become art. Similarly, only when the Renaissance architect marvels at the wealth of the ancients can the imitation of their work become art.

Between man and the world around him, between the viewer and the perspective view, between the Renaissance architect and the ancient world, there exists a necessary reciprocity. Without search, there can be no truth. Without freedom, there can be no authority. Without invention, there can be no model. Bramante demonstrated this relationship. Throughout his work, notably in the growing abstraction of his style in his later years, he gave expression to the aspiration to universality everywhere present in the Italian Renaissance. At the same time, he showed a desire to experiment without equal among his contemporaries, leaving an oeuvre which is unusually diverse, often incomplete and open to endless conjectures. His disputed first work, the Cappella del Perdono buried inside the palace of Urbino like the original seed of Renaissance humanism, is a case in point. The genius of Bramante resided in the search as much as in the works. Serlio and Palladio who praised him may have shown admirable consistency and, in the case of Palladio, supreme refinement. But Bramante alone was truly great, who stood before them and imagined a compelling and lasting model.

Originally published in San Rocco 11, 'Happy Birthday Bramante', 2015

1. Ludwig H Heydenreich, *Architecture in Italy 1400–1500* (New Haven, CT: Yale University Press, 1996), p 77.
2. Arnaldo Bruschi, *Bramante* (London: Thames and Hudson, 1973), p 16.
3. Erwin Panofsky, *Perspective as Symbolic Form*, 1924 (New York, NY: Zone Books, 1991), p 30.
4. Ludwig H Heydenreich, *op cit*, p 8.
5. *Ibid*, p 75.
6. Giacomo de Zoppi, 'La cappella del Perdono e il tempietto delle Muse nel Palazzo Ducale di Urbino: Analisi e proposta d'attribuzione a Francesco di Giorgio Martini', *Annali di Architettura*, no 16, 2004, p 10.
7. Jacob Burckhardt, *The Altarpiece in Renaissance Italy*, 1898 (London: Phaidon, 1988), p 73.
8. Arnaldo Bruschi, *op cit*, p 25.
9. *Ibid*, p 36.
10. Erwin Panofsky, *op cit*, p 31.
11. Giacomo de Zoppi, *op cit*, p 11.
12. Vitruvius, *The Ten Books on Architecture* (New York, NY: Dover, 1960), p 73.
13. Giovanni Pico della Mirandola, *Oration on the Dignity of Man* (Cambridge: Cambridge University Press, 2012), p 121.
14. *San Rocco* 10, 'Ecology', 2014, p 187.
15. Jacob Burckhardt, *The Civilisation of the Italian Renaissance*, 1860 (London: Phaidon, 1944), p 164.
16. Giovanni Pico della Mirandola, *op cit*, p 117.
17. This conception recalls Jean-Paul Sartre's famous phrase in *Existentialism is a Humanism*: 'In choosing what I want to be, I choose man.' It could be paraphrased as follows: 'When I choose where I want to be, I choose architecture.'

The New Art Gallery and its Geography

Few towns have been so completely shaped by work as Walsall. Streets and yards, buildings and vacant lots all bear the marks of relentless labour. For two centuries land here has been a source of raw materials and the place to work them. For this reason the town is a mess. Looking across the canal from the west, weather-beaten sheds and the cinder-like remains of factories lie between obsolete chimneys. Beyond, there stand in slow succession a 1960s office block, the New Art Gallery, the tower of the Edwardian town hall (disquietingly small), a dense cluster of multi-storey housing blocks and, some distance away, the parish church of St Matthew – all equally laconic and plain.

Previous
View towards the New Art Gallery from the west
©Hélène Binet

The only landmark in this uncommunicative, treeless landscape is the hill upon which St Matthew's stands. Moving towards it across the fractured field, now looking back from the steps descending from the church, a different view presents itself. At the bottom of the stairs, across the road, large brick planters keep cars out of the high street. To the left, the polycarbonate vault of a shopping arcade sets the tone for other commercial precincts in the town centre. Facing it to the right, the old Guildhall, built in the thick-set baroque favoured by Victorians, now hosts a pizzeria. Looking down the high street, its space, the market stalls and the crowd dominate the view while in the distance, seemingly on axis with the street, the New Art Gallery designed by Caruso St John appears to close the view.

Its scale is large, and the building can be clearly made out in the morning light. A tower rises asymmetrically above the main volume of the building, in the manner of the Palazzo Vecchio in Florence. As one walks from St Matthew's down into town, the silhouette of the building soon becomes lost in the crowd. It later reappears, head and one shoulder above the buildings which form the side of Digbeth Street and, later, Park Street, and vanishes again. But the gesture is not forgotten. It secures a connection between the gallery and the oldest public space of the town, its high street.

The two views could hardly be more opposed. From the west, a vision of entropy captures the pathology of many towns in Britain. It presents the image of a town where nothing adds up, without plan, impenetrable and inhospitable to life. Repeatedly subjected to development, little is left but the ruins of building, the cavities of mining and the waste. From the east, in contrast, the view is narrow, focused and crowded. If the whole of Walsall were to be laid to waste for profit, the integrity of the main street, one feels, would survive with its distinctive topography, with its high street tumbling down the hill, with the double bend leading into Digbeth, the level square at the 'Bridge' beneath which the River Tame has long been culverted, and the gentle rise of Park Street beyond, which fans out in front of Woolworths, a few metres short of the New Art Gallery. Unaffected by the industrial revolution, impervious to the quick succession of shopping developments, resistant to attempts at gentrification by paving and by design, the endurance of this space is mysterious and affecting. It is the definitive monument to the resilience of a people who continue 'going down the town', to borrow a local expression.

The early plan of Walsall has been compared to a human figure, its head resting on the hillside of St Matthew's, its arms branching out at the Bridge and its feet lying at the end of Park Street. For centuries this body was laid in open fields and meadows if not, still earlier, in the forest of Cannock. Today it is spread in a half-industrialised, half-urbanised landscape, but the simile retains its force. The gallery stands at the feet of this figure, on a site aptly known as Town End, where Park Street forks out into lesser roads leading into the Black Country. Here it articulates the transition between the public character of the high street and the emptiness of the waste, St Matthew's on the hill and stand-alone factories in the plain, between figurative expression and terse objectivity, between morning vista and late-afternoon panorama.

View down the main street towards the New Art Gallery from the east
© Mike Hayward / Alamy

Geological Survey of England, 1855 (Walsall is in the centre right of the map, in the mauve section) © British Library

This position can seem fortuitous, revealing no more than a banal contrast between a town centre and its periphery. But there exist in Walsall underlying, geological reasons which confer the character of necessity on this confrontation, and therefore on the gallery and its site. The centre of Walsall sits on some of the oldest ground in the country, on an outpost of the Pennine ridges in the Welsh borderlands. Formed some 400 million years ago, the grey mudstone and shale slope gently together with the high street, while a short distance to the west, the inclined strata of this ancient island slip beneath the coal measures to the bottom of a large carboniferous basin.

Directly above these geological seams the New Art Gallery stands like a beacon on the shore, surrounded on three sides by this great lake of coal and melancholy. From its terrace the entire coalfield of South Staffordshire can be embraced, 10km across and 37km long. Here men have mined coal, clay and ironstone. Here they built railways and factories, they erected whole towns which stand on a ground repeatedly disturbed and now so tired that it has long been prone to subsidence. Intense activity broke out at the dawn of the nineteenth century then redoubled around 1850 in a prodigious display of resourcefulness and collective willpower. The Black Country and the towns which grew along its perimeter, notably Birmingham, Wolverhampton and Walsall, were the great manufacturing centres of the nation and Britain was known as the workshop of the world.

An Industrial Landscape

In no other place was there such an abundance of coal lying so close to the surface. As a result, mining on a large scale started early in the Black Country and a pattern was set for the extraction of coal, characterised by small, primitive and wasteful undertakings. A first generation of operators took the pickings where they were easily accessible. Others worked over the uncharted field again and again, until mines were seldom more than 300m apart. With no consistent drainage policy

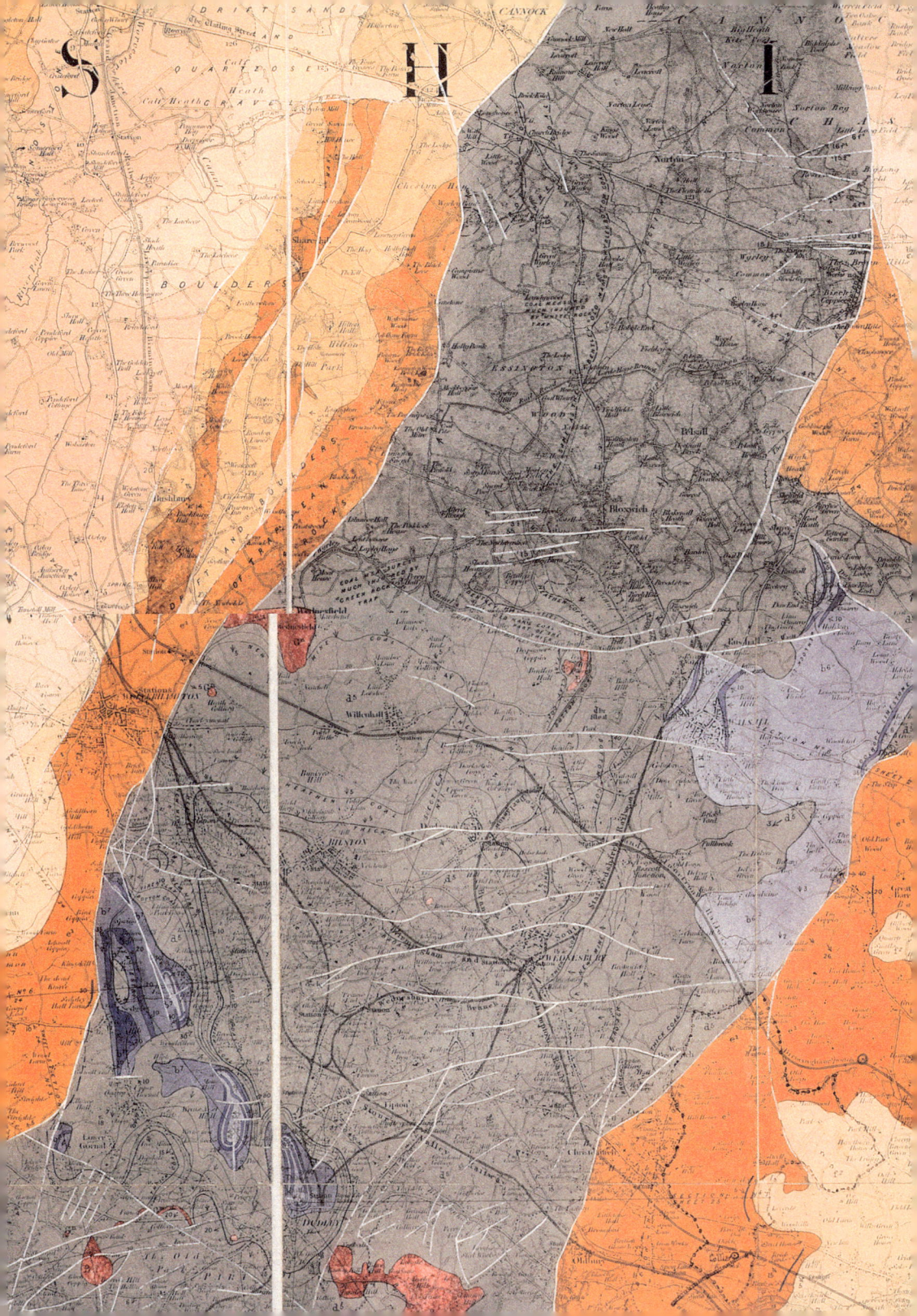

these became waterlogged. Soon, the 400 collieries in the exposed coalfield were no longer viable or simply exhausted. By 1920 all had closed, and mining activity moved to a few large, deep winnings in the borders of the field.

It is often assumed that Walsall, being on the edge of the Black Country, was chiefly occupied if not in mining, then in iron smelting. But in a town with up to 80,000 inhabitants in the 1880s, the entire borough contained just six furnaces. Instead, development which, in the words used in the first and only guide book to Walsall (published in 1889), was 'truly marvellous', favoured industries like smitheries and bit-making. These grew from the requirements of horse-drawn transport and it is in bit-making, in particular, that the extraordinary industrial diversity of Walsall, dubbed 'the town with a thousand trades', can be most clearly appreciated.

By the end of the nineteenth century products made in Walsall were exported to every part of the world, while raw materials were imported to the town from just as many locations. In brush-making, for example, in the piles of materials awaiting to be turned by a single firm into '5,000 kinds of brooms and brushes of various sizes and shapes, from the large unwieldy gun brush for cleaning cannon to the tiniest camel-hair pencil for the artist's use', there could be found 'bristles of all colours and qualities from Germany, Russia, Siberia, China, India and America; fibres from Mexico, Ceylon, and South Africa; weeds from Italy and South America, beautifully dressed horse and camel hair, and carefully prepared whale bone'. Nothing was too remote for import or too special for manufacture.

In 'the race of intelligent progress', intelligence was concentrated in the work place. Gradually the need for independent centres of knowledge became felt. In 1831, when the town was just 15,000 strong, a first library was opened and served principally middle-class subscribers. Ten years later it was renamed the Walsall Literary and Philosophical Institution, suggesting a growing ambition that was legitimised by the visits of, inter alia, Oscar Wilde and Prince Kropotkin. In addition to lectures, the institution included, until its closure in 1875, the first museum in the town and a laboratory whose purpose is unlikely to have been conservation.

In the 1880s Sunday morning adult schools were founded. One of them, the Artisans' Art Class, was located 400m away from the site of the New Art Gallery, in a backyard off Bridgeman Street. Its premises were hemmed in between narrow cottages, a Methodist chapel, a harness furniture manufacturer, an inn and a chain manufactory. After this humble beginning, the Art Class was amalgamated with the Science Institution, and the Science and Art Institute was created. In 1988 it was rehoused in Bradford Place in a purpose-build red brick neo-gothic edifice, between a railway shed and a stone yard, and, abutting at the rear, the largest currying works in the town 'and in the world'.

No less than 1,600 students enrolled in its first session, in classes which included many branches of science, the fine arts, literature and music, as well as leather tanning, metallurgy, carpentry and joinery, steam and the steam engine, and shorthand. In the race for intelligent progress there was no time for the fine distinctions, now taken for granted and carefully maintained, between education, aesthetic appreciation and recreation. The building still exists. It currently hosts a school for painters and decorators with, in its great hall, a surreal display of old-fashioned shop signs and cubicles for painting practice.

A hundred years have passed and the town's goods do not attract as many visitors as they did in the past. But its art still might. In 1972 Walsall was fortunate in being offered works assembled by Kathleen Garman and Sally Ryan, all of which are now housed in the New Art Gallery. The presence of Jacob Epstein, partner of Garman, the teacher of Ryan and the greatest sculptor working in Britain in the first half of the twentieth century, can be felt throughout the collection.

View towards the New Art Gallery from the south © Hélène Binet

Pieces include portraits of the collectors' relatives, which give to the collection an intimate, almost biographical character – a sense of familiarity and accessibility further emphasised by the diversity of media on display (drawings, watercolours, etchings, oils and sculptures) and by the thematic arrangement of the works.

Developing Town Wharf

Walsall ranks among the poorest local-authority districts in Britain, faring badly in education where aspirations are low, and it has more derelict land than most districts in the country. One of the worst affected areas is Town End. A hundred years ago it was densely built up with houses, workshops, factories, wharves and mining facilities, but today the area is defined only by industrial sheds in the Town Wharf Business Park to the north, and a wasteland to the south awaiting an imminent 16,000m2 retail development. Walsall has become a typical post-industrial town, even though close to half its working population is employed, still, in manufacturing industries.

For more than a century the caverns of disused limestone quarries had been supported by monolithic pillars and made much of the ground in Town End unsafe for construction. In the late 1980s ash from power stations mixed with cement was pumped into them, thus clearing the way for redevelopment. The area was close to the town centre and to the motorway. The canal provided an amenity upon whose value everyone could agree and it enabled Town End to metamorphose into Town Wharf. In the early 1990s the municipality commissioned a feasibility study for the area. Perspective drawings rehearsed familiar scenes, most of them Mediterranean in character, in keeping with the urban design which has prevailed since the war. A sketch plan showed two new stores closing the end of Park Street where they formed a public space complete with a 'focal feature' – clock, sundial, statue or fountain. A passage led between them into a new square beyond – the space in which the New Art Gallery now stands.

This study, in which the provision of a new gallery for the Garman Ryan Collection in Town End was first envisaged, formed the basis for a successful application for government funding. Land was purchased, the bus station was moved, services were installed and the canal dredged. Once the area between Park Street and the canal had been prepared, a developer was appointed, and the two stores, leased to Woolworths and BHS, were built at the end of Park Street between 1994 and 1996. Profits from the successful commercial operation were capped and the proceeds to the municipality secured the purchase of land for the new gallery. In addition, the developer, Chartwell, financed the construction of a pub on the new square and sponsored an international architectural competition for the gallery, launched in July 1995.

The site was not promising. It was cut off from Park Street and the main public space of the town. The canal had not been dredged and most buildings alongside it were derelict. The elevations of the Woolworths and BHS stores were supplied in the brief and gave no hint of local architecture patronage. From the top of a pile of rubble standing on the site, St Matthew's was clearly visible beyond the vacant lots where the stores were still to be built. This suggested to Caruso St John that a direct visual connection between the new gallery and the parish church might be established. In this town where everything that was good – industry, wealth, learning and urbanity – appeared to be vanishing, the new building was going to be tall and civic in character.

Illustrated with pictures of local children, the competition brief conveyed the commitment of Peter Jenkinson, the Director of Museums and Galleries in Walsall, to education. It also made clear his desire to achieve a high public profile for the gallery. Thus the tone of the project was set right at the beginning, before architects and client had even met: it embraced the architects' implicit protest at the town's neglect and the client's belief in the value of education and openness.

View from the canal onto the west façade of the New Art Gallery © View Pictures / Getty Images

Between Warehouse and Arthouse

The three A1 boards submitted by the architects for the first stage of the competition have been lost. Only a card model of the site and a few photographs of another, showing a tentative section through the building, survive. This last indicates five storeys of equal height, connected by stairs which, rather than being regularly stacked, one above the other, rose in different places within the floors. Pieces of corrugated cardboard were inserted, suggesting intimate, house-like spaces embedded in the more generalised space of a warehouse-like structure. The arrangement drew from Kettle's Yard in Cambridge, which remained a point of reference throughout the design. Adolf Loos's *Raumplan* in the Villa Müller in Prague was another immediate source – even though it was the plan of another building, an arts and crafts house from Sweden, which featured on one of the presentation boards.

The sectional model was faced with sacking, masking the interior behind a semi-transparent curtain wall. A section in mere outline included the names of the most important spaces – café, exhibition, Garman Ryan collection, terrace, restaurant, etc – and hinted at a possible vertical sequence. The squat proportions of the volume, the mesh-like screen of its elevations, the serial arrangement of floors suggesting autonomy and variety: all drew from the same source, OMA's celebrated ZKM project for the city of Karlsruhe.

The site model, complete with access ramp to the railway station, reflects the extent of the architects' knowledge of the town, obtained during a first visit to Walsall. It also betrays their lack of enthusiasm for the commercial architecture (much of it from the 1970s) along the sides of the high street, which has been neatly omitted. Conversely, it conveys the importance ascribed to the ground as a public, connecting element which prefigures Richard Wentworth's design adopted for the square a year later (bar the stripes). At this early stage, the position of roads on the site had not been decided. Like other buildings in the vicinity, the lock keeper's cottage by the side of the canal was derelict. The architects did not like the shape proposed by British Waterways for the new basin, designed to accommodate the turning circles of barges and to align with the sides of the new stores. On all sides they were faced with prospects which were either undecided or dismal.

Only the canal appeared permanent, and it seemed natural therefore to position the new tower on its axis. In the second stage of the competition the architects gambled on the redrawing of the basin. They aligned its long sides with the axis of the canal and gave it dimensions which reflect those of the gallery facade that was to abut it. Alongside it to the north, the pub fronted the new square with a gable end. Thus both the axis of the canal and that of Park Street were closed, the first by the full stop of the gallery, the second by the comma of the pub.

Moreover, the placing of these two buildings helped to establish a relation of equivalence between the basin and the square. In this way the problem of the articulation between the canal and Park Street was solved through its replay on the site itself. The two axes were allowed to slide past one another and were brought into relation by a series of diagonal, informal stitches: from basin to square, from pub to gallery, from gallery entrance to Park Street, and from wasteland to town centre. Axial or local symmetries are replaced, according to Peter St John, with 'organic frontalities', the entrance of the gallery, for example, dominating the entire square even though it faces no specific element within it.

Beyond the area of the model, two buildings remained impressed in the architects' mind: the parish church of St Matthew, which suggested the tower, and the factory rising at the end of Station Road to the south. Their images were projected in the design and became 'figures' or 'gestures', two notions often referred to by both Caruso and St John. From the church, a generic sense of relationship to the surroundings was retained. As you turn the corner by BHS and Woolworths,

Adam Caruso and Peter St John, sketch model, 1995 © Caruso St John Architects

the New Art Gallery looms improbably close to them, reminding St John of how Chartres cathedral suddenly appears at the end of the small surrounding streets. Coming from the opposite side, from the canal, it appears to push against the back of the stores to make space for the basin and to assert its presence on the high street. From the town centre, chandeliers hung inside the tower of the building can be clearly made out from a distance in the tall 'church-like' space of the restaurant, like bells.

The factory, described by the architects as 'very sheer, very clean … very confident and right', contributed architectural rather than urban qualities. It shares with the gallery the precision, the lack of affectation in the details which one expects in the workplaces of the Midlands. Its conspicuous water tower, positioned asymmetrically above the main volume of the building, painted black with 'BOAK' painted in tall white letters on its four sides, triggered the process of modelling which has made the profile of the gallery at least equally distinctive and memorable. Like the influence and counter influence of the canal and the high street on the site plan, the impressions left by the factory and by the church played against one another. They were gradually absorbed in the design and helped to emphasise the shifts of mood which occur throughout the building, between factual and expressive qualities, between warehouse and art house.

First Impressions

Already in the first stage of the competition, the large cut-out of the entrance undermined the volume of the building where it is tallest and most prominent. In the second stage, in September and October 1995, it was made bigger still. Two single-storey volumes projecting out at the base of the building locked the volume of the gallery to the shape of the site. The first, a café, reached westwards almost to the edge of the basin. The other, the bookshop, was adjacent to the entrance and wrapped around the eastern corner of the ground floor. Subsequently,

Previous
View of the main entrance, the square and the pub looking west
© Hélène Binet

a display window for art replaced the shop (which was too small), and the shop was combined with the café.

Once past the entrance, the entire lobby is visible at a glance. Being approached diagonally, its vast dimensions are given additional emphasis. The eye is first drawn to the main stairs. Other spaces are soon noticed, dispersed across a broad panoramic arc: the discovery gallery which forms the lower level of a three-storey 'children's house', the library on the mezzanine, the lifts, the bookshop and, last and tucked to the side, an information desk dwarfed by so much space and so vast an acreage of concrete.

The client brief stressed that 'first impressions matter'. Here they do in a manner which outreaches the previsions of the architects. The space of the lobby is sombre in tone and cavernous in a way the plan submitted for the competition, then almost wholly open to the square on the north side, did not anticipate. Its 7m height is spectacular, and its concrete structure is so plainly exposed that one feels the weight of the building resting on the precast beams overhead. As often in the tradition of civic architecture, first impressions entail both a display of largesse and a rite of passage.

The broad flights reach to the mezzanine between timber-lined walls on either side. After the first landing, the stairs diminish in width, turn back on themselves and exit to the first floor in a pirouette, as if to confirm that the civic display had been staged for effect. This, after all, is a multi-storey building serviced by lifts, precluding from the outset a sense of hierarchy between floors.

A Proper Gesture

The glazed lifts face out towards the canal and bring one directly to the roof terrace. Picking here the spire of St Matthew's, there the tower of the town hall above the high parapet, a low timber-lined passage leads to the main space of the restaurant, described by the architects as the 'grand finale'. Five large openings file round the corner of the room, held down to the floor by a timber dado. They are so large that everything behind the glass, for example the 1960s tower block planted at the end of Park Street, dubbed by St John a 'little piece of New York', appears close enough to touch. Looking east, the eye skims along the high street, all the way to St Matthew's. Looking up, the eye rises into the concrete shell of the tower.

In the early sectional model the room within the tower was given the same height as all other floors in the building. The sides of the terrace also rose to the same height, creating a room without a roof, like a space by the artist James Turrell. But this contributed awkward proportions to the east elevation: the body of the building seemed hunched and its head sunk inside it. The architects then lowered the enclosure of the terrace to the height of a parapet. The silhouette of the gallery became more irregular and varied. On the east side the tower, stamped with a cyclopean eye, rises above the mass of the building and makes a proper gesture, which the architects liken in jest to the Modulor Man of Le Corbusier and to the Statue of Liberty facing out into the Atlantic.

In the early stages of the design the height and size of rooms, like the height of the tiles on the outside, decreased as one ascended in the building. After the competition the most significant change demanded by Peter Jenkinson was to reverse the order between temporary exhibitions and permanent collections. Now starting on the first floor, the Garman Ryan collection became more easily accessible and formed the centre of gravity of the building. Moreover, its layout, consisting of small rooms arranged on two storeys, forms a structural 'net' which carries the entire weight of the building to the perimeter walls (a further legacy of OMA's ZKM project and its Vierendeel-truss structure) and leaves the entrance hall on the ground floor column-free and undivided.

The temporary-exhibition spaces were relocated on the penultimate floor. Its clerestory windows form on the outside a nearly continuous frieze which becomes fluorescent after dark.

Overleaf
View of the Garman Ryan collection
©Hisao Suzuki
/ *el Croquis*

The long stairs were introduced. They provide a separate route to the side of the Garman Ryan collection, and repeat on the upper floors. Narrow and very tall, they are monumental but one remains surprisingly unaware of their presence, like the stairs concealed within the wall thickness of medieval castles.

More deliberately medieval in character, the concrete beams contribute a powerful effect on the temporary exhibition floor, likened by Caruso to the state rooms in the Papal Palace at Avignon. On the Garman Ryan floors, medieval allusions continue in the central two-storey hall, and in the long adjacent gallery. Unlike the neo-classical *enfilade* which became fashionable in new galleries in the last 20 years, openings are made in the corners of the rooms, circulation leading outward to the perimeter of the building and to the light.

The architects wanted a 'tower' to make the building visible in the town, and a 'house' to give a domestic character to its spaces. What they achieved is more particular. They created a big tower which feels small like a house, and a house whose spaces feel big like those inside a tower. This play between the very small and the very large distinguishes many public buildings, for instance cathedrals which combine fine details and big scale. Indeed, the New Art Gallery appears to prefigure a medieval revival, set against modernism and corporate capitalism. It echoes the nearby Art and Science Institute, itself a plain example of the gothic revival defined a century earlier in opposition to neo-classicism and industrialisation.

The characteristic window scatter was adopted early by the architects during the second stage of the competition. It merely hints at the range of spaces within, and it maintains the veil-like effect of the initial proposal. But the scale of the windows relative to the overall volume of the gallery was too abrupt and required mediation. Hence tiles were introduced, giving the building a texture within which the random pattern formed by the windows could be effectively absorbed. At first it was

View of the café inside the tower
© Hisao Suzuki / el Croquis

A Moralised Landscape

View of the canal from the Garman Ryan collection © Hélène Binet

envisaged that they be made in pigmented concrete, silk-screened in places with images of Epstein's sculptures in a 'fit of homage' to Herzog & de Meuron. The specification was later upgraded to terracotta, a material that was often used on Victorian buildings and seemed appropriate in Walsall. Moreover, the density of the material contributes a strong tactile sense and its thinness produces an impression of lightness. The effect, described by the architects as feather-like, is both archaic and delicate.

The progress of the design was accompanied by a gradual awakening to the particularities of the view. At first the sum of Walsall in the architects' mind had been two or three monuments, a street, a canal, and little in between save ugliness and dereliction. Born blind as it were, in the second stage of the competition, the building acquired windows that were peppered across the surface of its volume. Yet it was only when construction was well under way that the architects took stock of the view. The fragmented panorama of the town, now visible from the shell of the building, became in their eyes like a Cézanne or a cubist painting. Constantly changing in grain and orientation, the mostly small industrial buildings composed, to the west and to the south, a field within which a few tall multi-storey factories rose like castles.

The view is at its most affecting in the spaces of the Garman Ryan collection facing toward the canal. In the room ascribed to landscapes, there is, to the right of the window, a marvellous oil sketch by Constable in which, above the darkest of grounds, clouds stretch, warp and distort to expose the bluest of skies. To the left of the window a small impressionist painting shows two fishermen and a dog on the grass bank of a canal, neatly juxtaposed with the real view outside.

Late in the nineteenth century Patrick Geddes founded the Outlook Tower in Edinburgh, where it still stands in the Royal Mile. Visitors entered an exhibition which explained how the local geography and the local communities formed

a unified and coherent landscape. At the end of their visit they reached the roof terrace where the view became an object lesson in the evolution of the city and its region. The New Art Gallery achieves a comparable effect, the views being remembered long after the memory of the Constable and the Lépine started to fade. Beautifully framed behind glass, the seemingly demoralised landscape of Walsall recovers its humanity: it is, so to speak, moralised.

The architects refer to the 'loose body' of the building, within which space has been carved and is 'kicking'. Likewise they refer to the 'loose space' of the square, where specific connections are made across the townscape. Among nearby buildings, most of them greatly mismatched in scale and 'swimming at different rates', the pub which faces visitors as they walk into the square remains a rare stable element. Yet even here the stabilising axial quality has been toned down by its architects, Jonathan Sergison and Stephen Bates. The gable wall, previously described merely in outline by Caruso St John, has disappeared. Instead the shallow asymmetric profile of the roof deflects the eye skywards and sideways to the canal. At the same time its dark prismatic form (suggested by the coal heap that once stood in its place) ensures that the pub retains a central position on the site.

The entire square, indeed the entire site of the gallery and the towpath running along one side of the canal, are covered with a continuous asphalt surface. The design, by Richard Wentworth, alternates broad, strongly contrasted black and yellow stripes. Laid parallel and at right angles to the main direction of pedestrian movement, they appear to distort according to the variations in level of the ground. The effect is striking and weird. Stepping on the asphalt between the two department stores, one is made keenly aware of the ground and the space appears uncommonly vast and open.

Metaphors come thick and fast to Wentworth, for whom the square is in turn a pedestrian crossing, a 1950s tie, a carpet, bands left after mowing the lawn and heraldry. A further comparison, made by the artist with Princess Diana's funeral, with the particular moment when the hearse inched onto the empty M1 motorway, is strangely apposite. From the inception of the project, Peter Jenkinson and Tim Howard, then responsible for education and culture on the local council, argued that Walsall is not a 'fish and chips town' and that its inhabitants should be entitled to the best quality. This is arguably what they got: a square which is dignified like the M1 briefly was.

Nothing but excellence, it seems, could wake Walsall from the relative torpor in which it has sunk after one magnificent century. Dereliction on a vast scale, on land so close to the town centre, stirs deep emotions and prompts a longing for care and beauty. While the high street remains the necessary spine, contributing a sense of unity to the town centre, the workaday Walsall starts in Town End on the site where the gallery now stands. For Caruso and St John it is a Cézanne; for Wentworth it signifies the end of the British Empire, a 'sort of Russia, nothing'.

Intelligent Progress

To find the right emotional pitch on such a site became a major concern. The construction of the New Art Gallery is precise and robust. Its form is powerful and unequivocal. Its siting is incomparably bold. Yet surprisingly St John describes the building as a ruin steeped in melancholy. The west facade is broadly square and appears complete, but as one approaches the gallery along the canal, aspects of it seem inexplicable. Set back far behind the plane of the facade, the stainless-steel cladding at the top of the building does not seem to belong to a tower. Rather, it appears to be the back of some protrusion, possibly plant, with a window punched into it at a height that seems too low for elegance and convenience. To the right of the lift cage a metal screen fills the gap at the corner of the building with an apparent lack of conviction.

Unlike the more deliberate east side, this facade betrays not a composition but seemingly unrelated decisions. Could the building have been modified over the years? Could its windows have been fitted at different times? The metal screen was indeed an afterthought prompted by a late request by the client. It protects the roof terrace against the prevailing wind and it is fitted with two viewing windows. Behind it a timber platform was installed for children who would otherwise have had no access to the view. The overall composition is weak but it has a different merit, St John argues, namely the freedom to which, 'when looking with kind eyes', ordinary buildings testify after having been modified over long periods of time.

Informed by Alison and Peter Smithson's notion of conglomerate order, this facade is among the most singular inventions of the architects. Unlike the contextual approach which still prevails, and which is exemplified by the elevations of the Sainsbury Wing of London's National Gallery, it requires no mimetic acknowledgement of the surroundings. It demands, instead, empathy and constant adjustments in the course of design. Sometimes intentions are formalised, for example on the east facade where strong expressive gestures are made. Sometimes they are muted and a more pragmatic approach dominates, for instance on the west facade and the roof terrace. When to be expressive and when to be factual is decided not by rule but by a sensitive conformation with circumstances.

However, not even the most sensitive connections between the form of a building and the local townscape will secure a sense of belonging. The ingenious transition made by the gallery between the high street and the canal, the association with the parish church, the 'BOAK' factory and other buildings, help to lock the building into a place, but they do not make it of this place. Ultimately buildings are rooted in the institutions which they accommodate – something which Jenkinson and Caruso St John understand. No less care went into placing the building on its site than in situating its experience within the life of the town. Regional galleries are proud as well as vulnerable. The new building does not merely accommodate the New Art Gallery. By the robustness of its structure it protects it. By the prestige of its architecture, it enhances it. By the rare dignity with which it invests a municipal initiative, it enshrines it. It is a further contribution to 'the race of intelligent progress', to a set of living institutions rooted in the working life of the town and once nourished – and with what prodigality! – by its soil.

Originally published in The New Art Gallery Walsall (London: Batsford, 2002)

Thanks to Peter Jenkinson, Tim Howard, Hardial Bhogal, Kath Phillips and Bryan Pell, all from the Walsall Metropolitan Borough Council; David Owen, from the New Art Gallery Walsall; Adam Caruso and Peter St John; Colin Jackson, from Ove Arup & Partners; Richard Wentworth; Catherine Yass; Ann French, from the Walsall Local History Centre; Deborah Smith, from Smith & Fowle; Jonathan Sergison; David Gregory, from Chartwell Land; and David Edgar, from Business Links Walsall.

London After the Green Belt

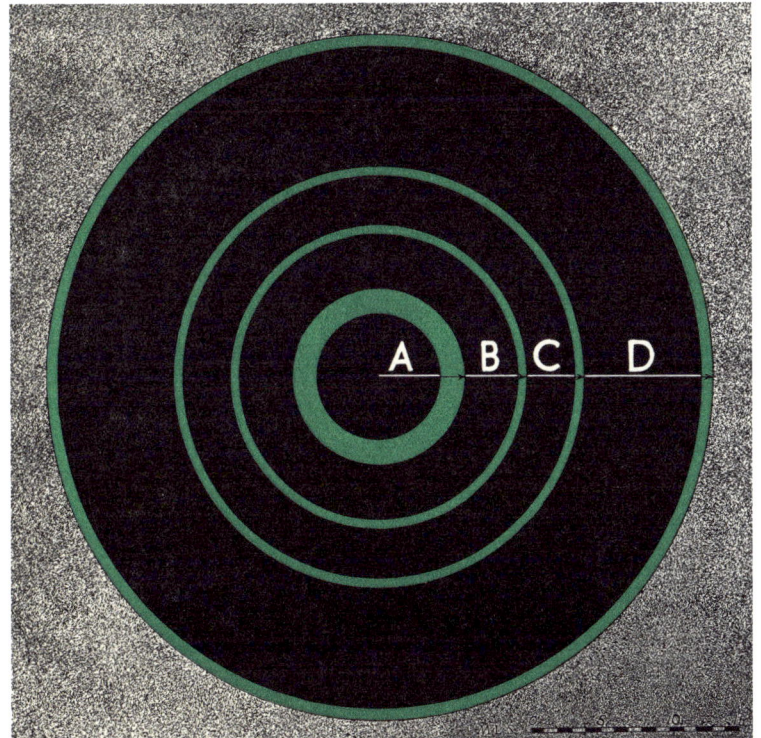

Raymond Unwin, 'Diagram of Open Space', First Report of the Greater London Regional Planning Committee, December 1929 ©British Library

Unlike many other cities in Europe, London lacks the common attributes of a large city. Its centre, for example, shows few outward signs of density – no closely packed urban blocks, no streets gasping for a view of the sky – and its identity lies not in squares, streets and yards but in a network of often interconnecting parks and gardens. These and the many other open spaces are often difficult to categorise. Where the land is not paved or covered in tarmac and where species are not groomed and domesticated nature grows wherever it can and in whatever ways it desires.

Steen Eiler Rasmussen claimed that Londoners felt a more primitive relationship to nature than other Europeans. 'They walk', he wrote in 1934, 'in the high grass when they escape from the streets. They not only see but feel the forms of the land when they wearily plod up the hill.'¹ For Rasmussen, Hampstead Heath was a touchstone for the way in which nature should be preserved, having been pieced together and managed not for the sake of plants but for people. Only on the Heath, Rasmussen argued, could Londoners find what he called 'human nature'.

However ambivalent, this expression touches on a fundamental characteristic of London's open spaces – namely that here humans and other species share a greater intimacy with nature than in any other large European city. This fact is neatly underscored by RSR Fitter in his pioneering 1945 study, *London's Natural History.* Rather than discussing the flora and fauna according to the order established by biological classifications and taxonomies, Fitter's book presented the natural history of London through the context of its human history, from Roman times to the modern period. In it, Fitter described how animals and plants were displaced, changed, moved and removed, introduced, dispersed, conserved, lost or forgotten by humans. Significantly, he also showed how non-human species adapted to circumstances induced by humans: buildings, gardens and parks, quarries, water supply, refuse disposal, smoke, sport, food production and even war.

The handsome plates in the book offer a wartime portrait of London that remains surprisingly current – a city as a melting pot not only of races but of species. Fitter also described what was so common as to be overlooked – for instance, the spiders and mice that live in most London houses – and through them drew attention to the presence of nature in the very heart of the city. But the greatest surprises in the book relate to sites overlooked by humans, from a disused sandpit colonized by sand-martins to the ruins of a bombed church invaded by rosebay willow-herb and Canadian fleabane.

In this sense, long before Bruno Latour published *We Have Never Been Modern* in 1991, Fitter was offering an account of a city (then the largest in the world) in which the non-human and the human – nature and the social sphere – were created together and were mutually dependent. Though not understood as such at the time, Fitter's field was actually that of urban ecology, a subject that was only properly recognised as a discipline in the 1970s, when a number of cities, notably in West Germany, started to develop nature-conservation programmes. Among the first of these was West Berlin, which in 1979 carried out a comprehensive mapping of all of the city's bio-topes. In a kind of reversal of Robinson Crusoe, who builds a fence to enclose what could be saved of civilisation, the city responded to its island condition within East Germany by looking to encompass nature within the confines of its own urban boundary.

The architect O M Ungers had formulated the concept of a green archipelago for West Berlin just one year earlier, a fact that is unlikely to be mere coincidence. In his proposal, built enclaves – in effect quasi-islands – were dispersed across a 'green lagoon', forming an extensive zone of nature that accommodated parks, gardens and allotments, sports and recreational facilities, mobile homes and amusement parks as well as agriculture. Taken as a whole, these elements constituted a 'natural grid', offering 'a new type of town in which the main interest is the employment of leisure time'.[2] In this archipelago, islands and lagoon, city and country, culture and nature were reunited.

An English programme of nature conservation similar to West Berlin's was initiated just a few years later, in 1982, by David Goode, the senior ecologist in the Greater London Council (GLC). With the help of aerial photographs, over 1,500 sites covering some 20 per cent of the London area were surveyed and graded according to their site-specific or city-wide ecologies. Focusing largely on quarries, railway sidings, reservoirs, etc, the audited sites were of the kind originally analysed by Fitter, and collectively constituted the foundation

Right and overleaf
Photographic plates from RSR Fitter, *London's Natural History*, 1945

of a new sensibility relating to urban open spaces. By the early 1990s, Goode's team, renamed the London Ecology Unit after the abolition of the GLC, published a nature-conservation handbook for most of the capital's boroughs. Each included maps, and in addition to parks (which are often relatively sterile from the point of view of ecology) identified those areas that both hosted wildlife and facilitated its movement across the city.

The work of the London Ecology Unit was remarkable in its scope and detail, and continued right up to the publication of Mayor Ken Livingstone's *Biodiversity Strategy* in 2002. At that point, for lack of political support, the unit was disbanded, although its findings were absorbed into the Geographic Information Systems data available to planners working for the successor Greater London Authority (GLA), and they remain significant in so far as ecology continues to provide, both practically and intellectually, the environmental norm in matters of nature and pollution.

For Goode, 'the most important single document' that helped to foreground urban ecology and make conservation

a matter of public policy was W G ('Bunny') Teagle's *The Endless Village* (1978), a small publication that established a bridge between natural history and nature conservation in cities.[3] The area under study in *The Endless Village* was not London but an urbanised region of the West Midlands, and the publication drew attention to the way in which expanding industry had competed for land with woodlands, marshes and quarries right from the outset of the industrial revolution. By the 1970s, however, much of this industry was derelict, resulting in a semi-wild landscape, where only poor fragments of the original pattern could be seen, 'as in a damaged mosaic pavement revealed by excavation'.[4] These pre-industrial *tesserae* took the form of heath bogs, marshes and woods.

The originality of *The Endless Village* lay in its comparison of built and natural settings. Teagle argued that natural history was no less worthy of protection than architectural history – than a Jacobean mansion, say, or a Telford bridge. He also noted that derelict industrial settings were of considerable natural interest, providing rich wildlife habitats. These urban wastelands had a picturesque beauty of their own, their scars healed by natural growth. A few black-and-white photographs illustrate Teagle's point. What seem at first to be ragged scrub and shapeless pools are revealed, on a second glance, to have a uniqueness derived from unintentional human intervention. Through these exemplars, Teagle appeared to appreciate as great a sense of mystery and poetry in the combined history of nature and human industry as there was in either of these histories individually.

Today the type of urban wasteland studied by Teagle conjures up images that seem almost banal, of the *terrains vagues* that provided the backdrops to films by Wim Wenders and Andrei Tarkovsky, of power cables leapfrogging a characterless grassland, or of literary explorers like Iain Sinclair scouring a landscape without qualities. But the questions posed by these environments continue to be relevant because they form the basis for an understanding of open spaces, their relationship to the city and ultimately the conception of the city itself. The example of London, with its 'human nature', has much to offer in this respect, all the more so because in recent years a concerted effort has been made to supplement nature conservation in open spaces with a new approach to the human presence within them.

In 2002, just as a statutory biodiversity strategy for London was being adopted, there was a growing sense that the enthusiasm for nature conservation had led to the neglect of humans. Tellingly, at the very moment when the London Ecology Unit was being disbanded, the Architecture and Urbanism Unit was created under the leadership of Richard Rogers. In the context of a city as populous as London, urban ecology seemed not human enough. The maps in the borough conservation handbooks described species and habitats in open spaces, but despite the relatively recent inauguration of a mayor well-known for his love of newts and other indigenous amphibians, these appeared to have neither a form nor a purpose that could be readily conveyed to the public.

The concept that bound together the constellation of sites surveyed by the London Ecology Unit was that of 'areas of deficiency'. Adopted from the world of planning, this term had been routinely employed to ensure the even distribution of playing fields, public parks and allotments. What the London Ecology Unit did was to apply it in terms of access to nature. The aim was for every locality in London to be within a maximum distance of 1km from a place of nature conservation. If this was not possible it was deemed to be an area of deficiency, needing to be made good by improving access – for example, with a bridge over a railway or with the upgrading of a site that previously held little value for wildlife. The objective human need for access to nature was not so easily demonstrated, nor was the distance beyond which the provision became deficient, but the conclusions of the unit nonetheless became statutory.

Collated together, the open spaces in the inventory amounted to a significant area of London, but they did not cohere into a pattern that could be recognised and planned for. This lacuna was made good with the Architecture and Urbanism Unit's invention of the East London Green Grid, described by Rogers as 'peopled landscapes'.[5] The idea slowly gained ground, and in 2006 was formalized with the publication of the *East London Green Grid Primer*. Its departure from the work of the London Ecology Unit is not immediately apparent. From it, the *Primer* adopted the concept of deficiency in access to nature, the notion of a grid further suggesting the promise of a guaranteed even distribution. Where it did differ, however, was that this was underpinned by a design. More than a constellation of discrete sites, the Green Grid brought the totality of open spaces in East London into a single unified figure. Sites that until then had been meaningful only within the limited range of their locality – the quarries, reservoirs, bomb sites and neglected gardens first surveyed by Fitter – became part of a London-wide network.

They became part of a plan that reached, from west to east, from the Lea Valley and its reservoirs to the Ingrebourne Valley and Rainham Marshes (inside the bend of the river) and, south of the Thames, from Greenwich Park along the South East London Green Chain to the River Darent. For the ecologist it created links between otherwise isolated habitats.

For the hydrologist it helped regulate the flows of water through the landscape. And for the architect it suggested by its connections an invitation to walk and to cycle, and brought closer together – or back together – people and landscape.

In the heydays of ecology in the 1980s and 1990s, nature conservation was seen to have value in itself. If it accommodated humans at all, it was on the plane made familiar by David Attenborough – that of education and wonderment. Having successfully made the case for wildlife and biodiversity, ecologists then struggled to articulate the human uses of nature. The London Ecology Unit argued that in the context of local sites, in particular, the experience of nature should be made integral to everyday life. However, this did not go far enough for the main instigator of the East London Green Grid, Mark Brearley, who envisaged a much wider range of uses for London's open spaces. So did Peter Beard, the lead designer for Rainham Marshes, by far the largest open space in the East London Green Grid, indeed in the whole of London, and one that is for this reason alone exemplary.

Brearley and Beard had met at the AA School in 1989, when the then chairman Alvin Boyarsky invited first Beard, then Brearley and Liza Fior, to run a studio in the school's First Year. They set projects in the north of England – for instance in Redcar, in areas where animals, people and machines shared a hybrid landscape – and they promoted direct observation, mapping and recording of the history of particular sites. In doing so they stood out against the esoteric mood at the AA at the time, carrying forward instead the phenomenological architectural approach that prevailed at the school of architecture at Cambridge, where both Brearley and Beard had studied.

At Cambridge, Peter Salter had taught Brearley the fundamental value of first-hand experience which he conveyed through anecdotal stories drawn from direct observation. In contrast to the symbolism that dominated architectural discussion, he described landscapes and buildings in a highly visceral way – an approach that immediately appealed to a new generation of young architects keen to extricate themselves from postmodernism and find a way back to a more grounded reality. Brearley recalls buying a copy of the Spanish magazine *Quaderns* that opened with an article by Josep Lluís Mateo titled 'Reality and Project'.[6] As postmodernism became spent, the emerging sense of reality was deliberately and almost wilfully ordinary, so much so that the dirt and junk produced by contemporary society was offered as the basis for a new theoretical project. A photograph in *Quaderns* by Walker Evans illustrated the point. Titled *Garbage*, the close-up shot showed a roadside gutter in which the pull-rings of tin cans competed with dirt for a lack of attention. Also in the same issue Hans Kollhoff (who had participated in the Green Archipelago project with Ungers) discussed the wastelands of Berlin with Wim Wenders. The most attractive parts of the city, Wenders argued, were the wild areas crossed by dirt paths and frequented by mice and rabbits: the value of a city was in direct proportion to the possibility of gaps in the planning system.

Stimulated by this emerging sensibility, Brearley's early work entailed observation and documentation. Starting in the early 1990s, he worked his way from North London, where he lived, progressively eastwards, first to the Lea Valley, then along the River Thames and beyond. The river economy was more active at that time than it is today. Goods facilities, marshalling yards, depots, factories and vehicle parks remained in use, though many were in the process of being dismantled. To Brearley, these places were consistent with the realism promoted in *Quaderns*, and the same trend, it seemed, had taken root in London. For example, Tony Fretton, who had joined the staff of the AA in the same year as Brearley, was similarly drawn to edgy, grimy urban places, and Peter St John, with whom Brearley later taught at the University of North

London, likewise developed an interest in the neglected places that hosted ordinary experience.

For Brearley, however, this sensibility was less a vehicle for an architectural aesthetic, and more a means to open up a large geographical area for study. The method also differed. In the first instance it demanded a great deal of walking and recording. Each place was carefully documented, contacts were made with local people, photographs (more documentary than aesthetic) were taken, and maps that had been traced at the British Library (the Ordnance Survey charged fees that were scarcely affordable to a young architect) were spliced and written over during walks. In addition, new maps were drawn, seeking a coherent understanding of precisely the geographical area that was to correspond to the East London Green Grid.

There was also a propositional side to this documentation. While at Cambridge, Brearley had come under the influence of the New Left, notably Raphael Samuel, Colin Ward (whose columns in the *New Statesman* he collected) and Raymond Williams. He singles out as particularly important the essay 'Culture is Ordinary', in which Williams argues that there is no culture in a special sense, no 'cultivated' people; instead, culture engages everyone in an active debate through which common meanings 'write themselves into the land' (a belief that resonated with the teaching of Beard, Brearley and Fior at the AA).[7]

At the same time Brearley also became involved with pressure groups, notably with Newham Friends of the Earth and the Socialist Environment and Resources Association, at precisely that moment in the early 1990s when issues of social equity and an emerging concern with sustainability came together in a green–red moment. This in turn led him to the more vulnerable sites of the city, to sites of industry and to green spaces, both of which were coming under increasing pressure from development. Representation to councils and to government were also initiated. By 1994, when Brearley and Julian Lewis came together to found the architecture practice East, this work had become more propositional in nature. Their first large-scale project, River Places, was a bold plan for a pleasure garden on both sides of the lower Thames at Rainham and Dartford. It is a tribute to their commitment that 17 years on they remain closely involved with these places, notably with Rainham and the adjoining marshes.

In 2000 the city was the main topic of discussion among architects. But the feeling at East was that these discussions had little or no impact on the actual course of events. Faced with this apparent reality, a member of the practice, Marianne Christiansen, obtained a small research grant from the RIBA to build a website drawing attention to London's future. Two years later East produced not a website but a witty pamphlet, *Picnics in the Green Belt*. In hindsight it can be regarded as a seminal document, and a declaration of intent for the East London Green Grid. Rhetorical in tone, it refers to the Green Belt as a 'great conceptual space without density' – so conceptual that it could neither be reached nor used.

First mooted at the beginning of the twentieth century, fought for by Raymond Unwin, passed into law in 1938, the Green Belt – a 8km-deep ring around London – was intended to limit the growth of the capital while meeting the needs for recreation which the centre of the city could no longer satisfy. It recognised, in its author Patrick Abercrombie's words, 'the value of keeping open large tracts of land for the visual solace of man'.[8] All open spaces were to be surveyed and every available inch of them safeguarded. Six years later, Abercrombie's Greater London Plan of 1944 acknowledged that 'little has, so far, been done to knit the whole together into a continuous system by footpaths, park strips, riverside walks, bridle-ways and green lanes', and proposed the creation of a park system providing for various types of use.[9] The Greater London Plan thus anticipated the survey of the London Ecology Unit and key aspects of the Green Grid.

The immediate context for *Picnics in the Green Belt* was Rogers' 1999 polemical report, *Towards an Urban Renaissance*, which drew attention to the fact that London was running out of space. No one, however, seemed ready to discuss the potential represented by the countryside and the Green Belt. In response, *Picnics* called for the re-examination of the Green Belt and its human potential. It argued that the compact city described by Rogers had to find a complement in 'spaces of slackness, wildness and escape' – spaces like Rainham Marshes, which Brearley had been exploring in the 1990s. Moreover, the Green Belt was an integral part of the city: the distinction between city and countryside needed to be relaxed and a dialogue between them initiated – a task that Fitter in *London's Natural History* had pioneered in his own way. In a tongue-in-cheek reference to Rogers' programme, the pamphlet concluded, 'The countryside can assist an *urban renaissance*; and the city can assist a *rural baroque*.'

For East, achieving this would require the 485,000 hectares of the Green Belt to be re-evaluated with due regard for

specifics. Every type of use was to be considered: recreation, agriculture, residential, industry and leisure. But use provision was not all. Indebted to Colin Ward's anarchist arcadia, *Picnics* was an exhortation to exercise 'Green Belt rights': public rights-of-way, rights to roam, rights to common land, rights to permitted development. As a consequence, the Green Belt was envisaged as an enormous common where the activities of both individuals and collectives could be spontaneous, experimental and daring. It was to be London's back garden, a welcoming place embracing each and everyone's fantasy, a vast territorial *bricolage*.

Picnics in the Green Belt was printed but never distributed. However, the momentum it generated was maintained by Brearley when he left East in 2001 to join the GLA's newly created Architecture and Urbanism Unit. The conscious ambition behind the move was to find the means to push forward an agenda that up until then had been pursued only in ad-hoc ways. The new mayor's radical urban planning initiatives and the influence enjoyed by Rogers within the GLA seemed to offer an ideal context. Rogers had launched the

mayor's '100 Public Spaces Project' – an initiative that emulated Barcelona's commitment to the creation of public spaces during the 1990s. With the support of Jamie Dean, who from the beginning coordinated the Green Grid project, Brearley introduced a green component that progressively gained acceptance within the Architecture and Urbanism Unit.

The provision of green space in London had long been popular with the public. Moreover, precedents for its implementation could easily be found – for example, the concept of the South East London Green Chain dated from the 1970s, while the potential of the Lea Valley had been recognised by Abercrombie as early as the 1930s. Indeed, the idea of a regional park for London goes back even earlier, to Unwin's Green Girdle of 1929 – a ring formed by the Chilterns and the North Downs connected to the centre of London by the radiating spokes of its valleys. More recently, plans for the development of the Thames Gateway – so called because it was envisaged to serve as a future gateway to London from mainland Europe – had been under consideration since the mid 1980s. Twenty years later, with central government losing patience with the GLA, the Architecture and Urbanism Unit took up the earlier idea of a 'Thames Gateway Green Grid' (coined by an anonymous civil servant), and renamed it the East London Green Grid. Immediately budgets were unlocked and a process of exploration and mapping began. The resulting data was pulled together into a single 100MB Adobe Illustrator file that became the basis for the maps included in the *Green Grid Primer* and for all subsequent work on the Green Grid. East London was divided into six distinct areas, each assigned a consultant (usually an architect) providing support in discussions with local stakeholders.[10] The Architecture and Urbanism Unit (renamed Design for London in 2008, and led first by Peter Bishop and two years later by Brearley) thereby established a framework that sought to balance top-down and bottom-up initiatives in the planning of London's open spaces.[11]

The architectural career of Peter Beard, the lead consultant on Rainham Marshes, followed a parallel trajectory to Brearley's. In 1992 he assisted Peter Salter on a project in Japan, and five years later worked alongside Florian Beigel on two competitions for large landscape masterplans near Leipzig and in Berlin. His interest in place – which broadly connected with Brearley's – was also allied to a specific interest in landscape developed in part through his acquaintance with landscape architect James Corner, who invited him to teach at the University of Pennsylvania in the mid-1990s, and through his readings of Ian McHarg, Denis Cosgrove and others.

As the largest protected open space in London, Rainham Marshes was a crucial test case for the East London Green Grid – 4km in length, 2.5km at its widest point, it is more than twice as big as Hampstead Heath. The area was largely manmade – a result of seventeenth-century land reclamation designed to provide more grazing for sheep and exploit river access to London's markets. By the mid-nineteenth century, the railway had reached this part of the Thames, in turn prompting the spread of industry along the River Ingrebourne and through the more developed parts of Tilbury and Southend. In 1906 the War Office bought a large part of the marshes and began to use it as a rifle range. Despite this, the sheep went on grazing. In the same year, a dredging business was established to the south of the site at Coldharbour Point, and a decade later an iron-foundry was established alongside the eighteenth-century Ferry House, generating enough pollution to deter day-trippers from the city. In the 1960s the Port of London Authority leased the central part of the site from the Ministry of Defence and filled it with dredged soil from the Thames, causing the level of the land to rise by five metres – as high above the high-water mark as the forest of yew trees that had occupied the marshes before the arrival of the Romans.

For decades, if not centuries, then, much of Rainham Marshes was overlaid with a thick crust of spoil material. As a consequence, it is a wilderness of sorts though not one typically associated with wildlife. And yet, somehow, grazing flocks, stray bullets, dredging and land fill all added to the intertidal mud of the Thames to create an ideal site for migrating birds. Bob Flindall, Regeneration Officer for Havering Council, recalls visiting the lagoons as a boy in the 1960s. The silt beds, then younger, shimmered in the light and were full of wildfowl. Few but the most intrepid people ventured into the marshes: the more faint-hearted faced a battery of deterrents – the red flags by which the military indicated its presence, the dubious types working in the nearby breakers' yards and the general air of desolation.

Since the marshes were owned by the Ministry of Defence they were not subject to Green Belt planning restrictions, and were therefore considered ripe for development in the boom years of the 1980s. Various schemes were put forward – including a proposal by the Music Corporation of America for a vast theme park – but except for a new triple carriageway along the west of the site, and the new Channel Tunnel rail link to the north, the marshes remained intact. As the last remaining expanse of wetland in the lower Thames, Rainham Marshes was designated a Site of Special Scientific Interest in the 1980s and a Site of Metropolitan Importance for nature conservation in 2000. Development proposals continued, but ironically these now drew attention to the ecological value of the site. Seizing the moment, in 2002 the Royal Society for the Protection of Birds (RSPB), which had been looking for a site close to London, bought the eastern part of the marshes from the Ministry of Defence.

The landscape value represented by the Thames had been recognised for some time. Abercrombie described it as a great national possession, rising in a few places to a pitch of scenic grandeur. These places – Richmond and Cliveden – were upriver, west of London, but Abercrombie's Greater London Plan had also proposed two large parks north and south of the river, just below Barking and on Erith Marshes. 'A wild park', he wrote, 'would spring up almost unaided', and it would be something quite new among London's open spaces.[12] This was effectively the same prospect that Beard and his office, Landroom, faced 70 years later, when they were commissioned by the RSPB to explore how to make the Rainham Marshes site available to a wide public without undoing the qualities that marked it out in the first place.

The initial study was carried out in collaboration with the landscape architect Peter Latz, who had been responsible for the park at Duisburg-Nord. Beard had met Latz in 1996 on the occasion of a lecture at the AA, and later invited him to review proposals for the Duisburg site made by his Cambridge students. Then six years in the making, the park at Duisburg-Nord integrated disused furnaces, cranes and bunkers and was widely regarded as a model for dealing with post-industrial wastelands. What was *a priori* the most artificial landscape imaginable was reclaimed as nature, causing nature to appear

as futuristic in places, while culture seemed regressive. It was also a place where the verb to 'wild' – initially applied to extreme forms of violence in American urban parks – came to describe softer, acceptable forms of marginal behaviour.

Similarly, for Landroom, wild nature does not start where the city ends but is integral to its dynamic. Biodiversity and ecology are inextricably bound up with the economic and social conditions of human life. J B Jackson, an American advocate of 'vernacular' or common landscape, and an early influence on both Beard and Brearley, subscribed to this view. A landscape, he argued, is not subject to natural laws: it is a synthetic, man-made space superimposed onto the land to serve a community – a point sometimes lost on environmentalists, for whom human presence in nature reserves is often a reluctant concession. As a consequence, landscaped parks tend to encourage passive enjoyment. At Rainham, however, Beard sought to rediscover a more socially active conception of landscape, consistent with Jackson's views on the American urban park.

The original feasibility study for Rainham Marshes, 'Wildspace for a World City', was carried out between 2003 and 2005. It proposed keeping the site more or less as it was, restoring the ecological balance between wildlife and livestock (which had been neglected), preserving the rifle ranges and bringing salt-water wildfowl back into silt lagoons. With the conservation of the marshes and the implementation of a complete network of paths, this first phase of development is now largely complete. Development plans had envisaged a second phase leading to the increase in the number of visitors to one million per year, although this ambition presented a dilemma. On the one hand, the considerable size of the marshes and their position within the Thames Gateway suggested a themed park, a Kew Gardens of the east. On the other, similarly ambitious millennium projects were then struggling with faulty business plans and some, like the Earth Centre at Doncaster, had been forced to close. This suggested that a better strategy would be to offer minimal, incremental changes to the land. Like Hampstead Heath, Rainham Marshes consists of land parcels pieced together over several decades. What makes them natural is not just the presence of wildlife, but also – and especially – their 'as found' quality, complete with what Rasmussen called 'human nature'. This same quality, which we find still at Hampstead Heath, is the most essential source of their wildness, complexity and appeal. Looking at the work already completed, we see considerable discretion in Landroom's designs for the many pieces across the site – boardwalks, bridges, benches, fencing, gates, fingerposts, yardmarkers or paths topped with limestone fines to allow plants to encroach along the verges. Some pieces come directly from farming catalogues, the concrete used for the bridges refers in part to the existing military and flood-defence structures, and the corten steel of the signs brings to mind the nearby scrapyards. The stone benches scattered across the site have a shelf-life of thousands of years. Each consists of a massive Portland stone slab, rounded at the edges and dropped on a bed of reclaimed concrete railway sleepers. Tom Emerson (once a teaching assistant of Beard at the AA and co-founder of 6a architects) nicknamed them 'soap bars'; Beard himself invokes something less soluble: churches designed by Hawksmoor, built 'with stones laid upon the mud and dust' – to use the words of Iain Sinclair.[13] On the RSPB site to the east, Landroom designed classrooms using standard shipping containers sandblasted to the deep-ochre red colour of rust. On the Havering site to the northwest, they created new wetlands, accessible by boardwalks linked to the path network. To the west, along the main path from Rainham's trackway to the Thames, earth embankments shelter cyclists, walkers and workers on the local industrial estates from the traffic and noise on Ferry Lane. Those areas excavated were then flooded, helping to manage the flow of water in the marshes, and were planted with reeds.

In developing these designs, Beard looked at the work of Swiss landscape architect Georges Descombes, whose Voie Suisse along the edge of Lake Uri created a path some 35 km long that was so discreet and ephemeral as to become over time almost invisible. Like Beard, Descombes concentrated

his efforts on the most ordinary aspects that are commonly brushed aside. Rather than highlighting particular things and views and interpreting them, his aim was to create situations by which a visitor might be drawn to the things themselves – an attitude he summarised as 'I tidy things up. I reveal things, I underline certain traces which show the actual constitution of the path.'[14] Though on a different scale, the work at Rainham and on the Green Grid has much in common with Descombes' approach.

In the great expanse of the marshes there is little that draws the eye and adds even the smallest touch of the picturesque. The sense of remoteness so close to London, the wildness, the unbroken horizon, the enormous scale of the river (over 1km wide at this point) all add to an exhilarating experience of vacancy. The full extent of this landscape becomes clear when you reach the slight outcrop to the north of Aveley Bay and discover a view likened by Beard to a seventeenth-century Dutch painting. In the far distance, the passing trains, the pylons, the A13 and the breakers' yards all reinforce the feeling of emptiness, and yet they also confirm

that one is still surrounded by the city. But it is as one walks around the marsh, especially to the east, that the emptiness of the site is at its most affecting. Here the remains from the military are the only follies in the decidedly unpicturesque scenery – part hidden and discreet, they communicate a faint threat of violence and a sense of arrested time. The true monuments, though, are the cows – as monumental as *The Young Bull*, Paulus Potter's celebrated life size painting of 1647. They contribute the only bucolic note in the mournful landscape. Walking around here, one is reminded of the lake of Nemi near Rome, painted time and again by Claude Lorrain and others. The eastern marsh has the emptiness and the stillness of a crater, though it lacks the mountains, the rushing water, the sunset and the perspective of Nemi. Instead, there is a kind of universal viewpoint and an even light illuminating the entire scene. But this painterliness, or the lack of it, is in many ways peripheral. Beard prefers instead to allude to a quality of happenstance, indicating, like the word itself, the combined effect of events and circumstance. From this standpoint, there is no ultimate designer, the more so in a landscape project involving multiple owners and organisations, policy changes and a considerable time-scale. This is the basis for an aesthetic of 'slack nature' rooted in place and local memory, one that is supple, historical and empirical, like the Green Grid itself.

In March 2012 the East London Green Grid was extended to become the All London Green Grid. After more than 60 years, Abercrombie's recommendation that London's parks be brought together in a coherent whole was to be fulfilled. Of course, by the 1940s much of London had already been built and it was too late to obtain a perfectly articulated system. But 'it is surprising', Abercrombie wrote, 'how nearly it is possible to penetrate from the outer areas towards the centre'.[15] In practice, however, the interconnection of the Green Grid remains difficult to achieve. The village of Rainham, for instance, was cut off from the marshes and the river by the railway. The marshes were further separated from the Ingrebourne Valley by industry, and this same valley was segregated from the village first by wharves and then by a giant Tesco supermarket. Landroom have since provided a path along Ferry Lane. More recently East extended this path through the old iron-foundry site to the river, where they plan to rebuild the Three Crowns public house.

In addition East prepared a detailed masterplan for the public spaces in Rainham. They described this space with a sketch model made of felt (indicating open spaces) and threaded beads (suggesting buildings) – the one forming the background to the texture of the other. The sewing metaphor seems apposite with regard to the patience required in negotiating local interests, the plan in effect being realised only metre by metre. For every connection in the Green Grid through-ways must be found and tunnels and bridges must be built. Connecting things remains its essence, a multitude of local improvements together producing a recognisable pattern and greater resonance.

Both of the predecessors to the Green Grid – Unwin's Green Girdle and Abercrombie's Green Belt – in addition to a catchy name, were made visible and memorable by a pattern that ensured the durability of the idea. This clarity of image is all the more necessary for the Green Grid, which is made up of an ad-hoc compilation of projects loosely connected with one another. From the seemingly random patchwork mapped by the London Ecology Unit, the tentative figure of the East London Green Grid has gradually emerged. The most visible strands are broad swathes of land – the flood plains, woods and forests that belong in the main to the Green Belt. More often, thin, cranked, jagged lines infiltrate development like cracks in the pavement. They are guided here by a stream, there by disused infrastructure, seeking to connect miscellaneous amenities. Everywhere else a more or less evenly distributed scattering of open spaces forms a constant background to the pattern.

The resulting map offers an alternative to the traditional figure–ground plan in which figure describes all that is solid, and ground all that is air. Instead, the Green Grid encompasses all open space, everything else – namely development – being left blank. The principle is similar to that adopted by OMA in the 1987 competition for the new town of Melun-Sénart, where bands of open space indicate areas that are to be protected from development. But the Green Grid is not limited to a programme of conservation; rather, it participates in the dynamic succession of abandonment, conservation and development, of neglect, maintenance and project. Its outstanding quality resides in the extent to which it is embedded in the increasingly intensive and diverse life-process of the city, and in its capacity to embrace what Bruno Latour calls 'nature-culture'.

As if in a miniature of the Green Grid, Fitter showed in *London's Natural History* how animals and plants, notably weeds, infiltrate fractures in the city and settle in unlikely places. Plants are commonly divided between those that are wild and others that benefit humans. But weeds occur instead in places where the distinction between nature and culture, wildness and cultivation has broken down. They can rarely be traced to a habitat in which they are truly wild. They do best in the company of humans, in open sites where the soil has been disturbed, including fields, gardens, roadsides and wastelands. They thrive in *terrains vagues*, like drop-outs and travellers opting out from conventional society, and present to the modern eye the promise of romance and authenticity. The editor of Edward Salisbury's standard book, *Weeds and Aliens* (1961), claimed poetically that 'weeds, as a class, have much in common with criminals'.

Charlock, shepherd's purse and chickweed, creeping cinquefoil, scentless mayweed and groundsel, sow-thistle, dandelion, field bindweed, red dead nettle, greater plantain, white goosefoot and fat-hen, garden orache, broad dock, black bindweed, sun spurge and annual meadow grass were carefully inventoried by Fitter. Likewise, new species of open spaces are gradually being recognised and nurtured, the Green Grid and Rainham Marshes testifying to the colonisation of land only recently deemed to be waste.

The affinity between weeds and urban open spaces is acknowledged in Richard Mabey's writings, notably in *The Unofficial Countryside* (1973), a eulogy to places that are neither urban nor rural yet wild, and followed some 30 years later with *Weeds* (2010). It is acknowledged, too, in the 'Robinsonism' of Patrick Keiller, in his films *London* and *Robinson in Space*, and in the peripatetic digressions of Iain Sinclair in *London Orbital* – a growing body of work that combines walking, storytelling and history. The affinity was foretold in Fitter's *London's Natural History*, a landmark study in the convergence between nature and wastelands, between natural history and human history. Sites that were once *terrains vagues* lost their nondescript vagueness, became definite and manifold, and claimed a legitimate place in geography and in history. The Green Grid is a map of such sites and a first step towards their systematic reclamation on behalf of the city. It bears witness to a fast-changing relationship between nature and culture. It presumes a more human ecology – one in which humans are not merely tolerated but are a vital and necessary part – and it augurs, in both a literal and a figurative sense, a more natural city.

Overleaf
Rainham Marshes, grazing cow in the RSPB part of the site, July 2012
© Irénée Scalbert

Originally published in AA Files 66, 2013

This essay is based on interviews held in June and July 2012 with Mark Brearley, Peter Beard, David Goode, Julian Lewis, Bob Flindall, Peter Massini (GLA) and Jenny Scholfield (Environmental Agency).

1. Steen Eiler Rasmussen, *London, the Unique City*, 1937 (Cambridge, MA: MIT Press, 1982), p 337.
2. O M Ungers, Rem Koolhaas, Hans Kollhoff *et al*, 'Cities Within the City: Proposals by the Sommerakademie for Berlin', *Lotus International*, no 19, June 1978.
3. Interview with the author, June 2012.
4. W G Teagle, *The Endless Village* (London: Nature Conservancy Council, West Midlands Region, 1978), p 37.
5. *East London Green Grid Primer* (London: GLA, 2006), p 3.
6. 'New Narrations', *Quaderns*, no 177, April–June 1988.
7. Raymond Williams, 'Culture is Ordinary', 1958, in *Resources of Hope: Culture, Democracy, Socialism* (London: Verso, 1989).
8. Patrick Abercrombie, *Greater London Plan 1944* (London: HM Stationery Office, 1945), p 3.
9. *Ibid*, p 11.
10. The original area consultants were East, Landroom, Adams & Sutherland, Witherford Watson Mann, J & L Gibbons and 5th Studio.
11. In March 2013, for reasons that have not been made public, Design for London was dissolved and Mark Brearley left the GLA.
12. Patrick Abercrombie, *op cit*, p 105.
13. Iain Sinclair, *Flesh Eggs and Scalp Metal* (London: Paladin, 1989), p 57.
14. Georges Descombes, 'Entretien avec François-Yves Morin', *Voie Suisse, L'Itinéraire Genevois: De Morschach à Brunnen* (Fribourg: Office du Livre 1991), p 47.
15. Patrick Abercrombie, *op cit*, p 103.

If a direct contact with things taught me how to think, an association with magazine editors taught me how to write. Two editors in particular must be mentioned: Elizabeth Allain-Dupré, the late editor of *Le Moniteur-Architecture-AMC*, who published my first essays in translation, notably 'Mind into Matter', included in the present collection, and Mary Crettier, the first editor of AA *Files* (then Mary Wall), who showed me how to use the English language precisely. Other editors from whose kindness I have benefited include Geert Bekaert at *Archis* and Pamela Johnston, Mark Rappolt, David Terrien and Thomas Weaver at AA Publications.

As chairman of the AA School, Alvin Boyarsky gave me employment and the support needed to write. So did Mohsen Mostafavi in the same capacity and, more recently, as dean of the GSD at Harvard, and Merritt Bucholz as director of the school of architecture at the University of Limerick. My greatest debt is to architects, most notably to Peter St John, Adam Caruso, Tony Fretton, Sophie Le Bourva, John Winter, Farshid Moussavi, Alejandro Zaera-Polo, Tom Emerson, Stephanie Macdonald and Pier Paolo Tamburelli, with whom I have had more conversations than I can remember. They also designed buildings discussed in this book and prompted, for the most part unknowingly, my interest in the historical subjects explored within it.

Robert Harbison gave encouragement for the idea of a collection and read some of the essays that have been selected. Mary Crettier edited several pieces in the book and Françoise Fromonot commented on specific aspects of it. Acting as general editor, Thomas Weaver gave a strong sense of direction to the project and offered his invariably sound judgment. Mathias Clottu designed the book with characteristic enthusiasm and refinement. My wife, Nathalie, and my son, Francis, contributed the calm and the gaiety which made writing considerably more pleasant. I am especially grateful to them.

Irénée Scalbert

A Real Living Contact with the Things Themselves
Essays on Architecture
by Irénée Scalbert

Edited by Thomas Weaver
Design and production by Mathias Clottu
Proofreading by Ian McDonald
Printed by Druckerei zu Altenburg GmbH

© 2018 Irénée Scalbert and Park Books AG, Zurich
© for the texts: the author
© for the images: see captions

ISBN 978-3-03860-111-1

Park Books
Niederdorfstrasse 54
8001 Zurich
Switzerland
www.park-books.com

Park Books is being supported by the Federal Office of Culture with a general subsidy for the years 2016–2020.

All rights reserved; no part of this work may be reproduced or edited using electronic systems, copied or distributed in any form whatsoever without previous written consent from the publisher.

Frontispice
Thomas Jones,
A Wall in Naples,
c 1782
© The National Gallery, London